Bryn Mawr Gree

Greek Prose Composition

Susan A. Stephens

PREFACE

In preparing this text for the teaching of Greek prose composition, it has been my intention to combine more grammatical detail than is currently available in elementary textbooks (or in those prose composition texts written in the main at the beginning of the century for the English schoolboy) with a broad selection of illustrative prose passages. Learning to write idiomatic Greek is not imagined, therefore, to be an end in itself, but a means of reading more fluently and of increasing understanding of the subtleties of the Greek language. I have assumed that the students who use this text will be advanced undergraduates or graduate students who will be able to write the proper forms for Attic Greek and who are already familiar with its basic grammar.

Each chapter is constructed to provide the salient details about a common syntactical construction found in standard Attic prose. The constructions are illustrated by means of short passages from familiar Greek authors, and a series of English sentences and continuous passages based on the vocabulary found in the readings and the points of syntax under discussion (or from previous chapters) are provided for translation into Greek. I have not provided a "key" of Greek translations for these passages, because even within the limits of the syntax that is under discussion, there will be more than one acceptable means of rendering a sentence or passage into Greek, and students should be encouraged to explore the variety of possible expressions rather than be tracked subconsciously into imagining that English and Greek have one-to-one correspondences. In general, examples from poetry are omitted, though there are occasional discussions of markedly different usage. References for fuller grammatical explanations are given regularly to sections of Smyth's *Greek Grammar* (**Smyth**), Goodwin and Gulick's *Greek Grammar* (**GG**), and, where appropriate, to Goodwin's *Syntax of the Moods and Tenses of the Greek Verb* (**MT**). And although there are no citations to either of the more comprehensive German grammars, graduate students should become familiar with them.

I have tried to provide more readings and exercises for each chapter than an instructor will necessarily wish to use, in order to allow room for individual taste. In general, each chapter contains at least three readings--one each from Plato, an historian, and an orator--many of which will already be familiar. However, not all syntax is so easily accommodated, with the result that in some cases more than three readings are necessary to provide adequate illustration. Chapters are organized into major syntactical categories, for example, questions, conditions, temporal clauses. Not all chapters are of equal difficulty or complexity; for example, Chapters Nine to Eleven may be easily combined into one lesson, while Chapters Fourteen or Eighteen will require several. The more complex chapters contain a larger number of readings. The whole has been designed to fit into a quarter or semester course.

The preparation of this text has taken many years. I wish to express my thanks to the following for their invaluable comments, criticisms, and encouragments during that period: Cynthia Damon, Mark Edwards, Michael Haslam, Eric Handley, Dirk Obbink, the late Lionel Pearson, Jay Reed, Joseph Solodow, and the many Stanford graduate students who have worked through previous versions.

S. A. Stephens
September, 1996

FOR FURTHER REFERENCE:

Chandler, H.W. *A Practical Introduction to Greek Accentuation* (Oxford, 1881, reprinted).

Comrie, Bernard *Aspect: An Introduction to the Study of the Verbal Aspect and Related Problems* (Cambridge, 1976).

--- *Tense* (Cambridge, 1985).

Denniston, J.D. *Greek Prose Style* (Oxford, 1952).

--- *The Greek Particles*[2] (Oxford, 1954, reprinted 1966).

Dover, K.J. *Greek Word Order* (Cambridge, 1960).

Gildersleeve, B. *Syntax of Classical Greek*, 2 vols. (New York, 1900).

Goodwin, W.W. *Syntax of the Moods and Tenses of the Greek Verb* (New York, 1965, reprinted) = **MT**.

---, *Greek Grammar*, revised by C.B. Gulick (New York, 1958) = **GG.**

Kühner, R. and F. Blass, *Ausführliche Grammatik der griechischen Sprache: Erster Teil* 1-2 (Hanover and Leipzig, 1890, reprinted Darmstadt, 1966).

Kühner, R. and B. Gerth, *Ausführliche Grammatik der griechischen Sprache: Zweiter Teil* 1-2 (Hanover and Leipzig, 1898-1904, reprinted Darmstadt, 1966).

Postgate, J.P. *A Short Guide to the Accentuation of Ancient Greek* (London, 1924).

Schwyzer, Eduard. *Griechische Grammatik auf der Grundlage von Karl Brugmanns Griechische Grammatik* 3 vols. (Berlin, 1938, reprinted 1968).

Smyth, H. W. *Greek Grammar* (Harvard University Press, 1920) = **Smyth.**

Wackernagel, J.W. *Vorlesungen über Syntax mit besonderer Berücksichtigung von Griechisch, Lateinisch und Deutsch..* Second edition, 2 vols (Basel, 1920-1928, reprinted 1950).

GREEK PROSE COMPOSITION

TABLE OF CONTENTS

INDICES:

CHAPTER ONE—WORD ORDER[1]

1. The Greek language permits great variety in word order, and Greek writers show much ingenuity in arranging their words in the way that best meets the requirements of logic and rhetoric. A skillful writer presents his words in the order in which he wants them brought to the attention of his hearer (or reader), with suitable emphasis on the words that he considers the most important. For words that may float freely in a sentence—nouns, verbs, adverbs, adjectives—it is difficult to identify any one order as "normal," though it is possible to observe that the emphatic positions seem to occur at the beginning and at the end of phrases or sentences. It is possible to observe further that the order of subject (S), object (direct or indirect) (O) and verb (V) or the order subject (S), verb (V) and object (O) occurs much more frequently in prose writers than other possible arrangements (e.g., VSO, VOS).

Consider the following passage from Diodorus of Sicily, who lived in the first century B.C. and wrote a history of the world in 40 books. Diodorus is discussing Xerxes' rise to power over Persia and his preparations for the invasion of Greece.

1.1 Diodorus 11.2.1-3. ὁ δὲ Ξέρξης τριετῆ . . . χρόνον

παρασκευασάμενος κατεσκεύασε ναῦς μακρὰς πλείους τῶν

χιλίων καὶ διακοσίων. συνεβάλετο δὲ αὐτῷ καὶ ὁ πατὴρ Δαρεῖος

πρὸ τῆς τελευτῆς παρασκευὰς πεποιημένος μεγάλων δυνάμεων·

καὶ γὰρ ἐκεῖνος ἡττημένος ὑπὸ Ἀθηναίων ἐν Μαραθῶνι, Δάτιδος

ἡγουμένου, χαλεπῶς διέκειτο πρὸς τοὺς νενικηκότας Ἀθηναίους.

ἀλλὰ Δαρεῖος μὲν μέλλων ἤδη διαβαίνειν ἐπὶ τοὺς Ἕλληνας

ἐμεσολαβήθη τελευτήσας, ὁ δὲ Ξέρξης (διά τε τὴν τοῦ πατρὸς

---

[1] For further discussion see J. D. Denniston, *Greek Prose Style* and K. J. Dover, *Greek Word Order*.

ἐπιβολὴν καὶ τὴν τοῦ Μαρδονίου συμβουλίαν), καθότι προείρηται,
διέγνω πολεμεῖν τοῖς Ἕλλησιν. ὡς δ' αὐτῷ πάντα τὰ πρὸς τὴν
στρατείαν ἡτοίμαστο, τοῖς μὲν ναυάρχοις παρήγγειλεν ἀθροίζειν
τὰς ναῦς εἰς Κύμην καὶ Φώκαιαν, αὐτὸς δ' ἐξ ἀπασῶν τῶν
σατραπειῶν συναγαγὼν τὰς πεζὰς καὶ ἱππικὰς δυνάμεις
προῆγεν ἐκ τῶν Σούσων. ὡς δ' ἧκεν εἰς Σάρδεις, κήρυκας
ἐξέπεμψεν εἰς τὴν Ἑλλάδα, προστάξας εἰς πάσας τὰς πόλεις
ἰέναι καὶ τοὺς Ἕλληνας αἰτεῖν ὕδωρ καὶ γῆν.

The organization of the main sentences in this passage may be
schematized as follows:

ὁ δὲ Ξέρξης. . . κατεσκεύασε ναῦς μακρὰς (SVO)

συνεβάλετο δὲ αὐτῷ καὶ ὁ πατὴρ Δαρεῖος (VOS)

καὶ γὰρ ἐκεῖνος. . . χαλεπῶς διέκειτο πρὸς τοὺς νενικηκότας
 Ἀθηναίους (SVO)

ἀλλὰ Δαρεῖος μὲν . . . ἐμεσολαβήθη (SV)

ὁ δὲ Ξέρξης . . . διέγνω πολεμεῖν τοῖς Ἕλλησιν (SVO)

τοῖς μὲν ναυάρχοις παρήγγειλεν (OV)

αὐτὸς δ' . . . προῆγεν (SV)

κήρυκας ἐξέπεμψεν (OV)

Consider next this selection from a speech attributed to Isocrates.
It consists of series of aphoristic statements on the value of
learning and how to acquire it.   Although the passage is
relatively straightforward syntactically, notice the way that the
author achieves an effect quite different from Diodorus by using
symmetry, balance, and similarity of sounds, particularly at the
ends of phrases (homoioteleuton), to emphasize his meaning.

1.2 Isocrates, **To Demonicus** §§18-19. ἐὰν ᾖς φιλομαθής, ἔσει

πολυμαθής. ἃ μὲν ἐπίστασαι, ταῦτα διαφύλαττε ταῖς μελέταις, ἃ δὲ μὴ μεμάθηκας, προσλάμβανε ταῖς ἐπιστήμαις· ὁμοίως γὰρ αἰσχρὸν ἀκούσαντα χρήσιμον λόγον μὴ μαθεῖν καὶ διδόμενόν τι ἀγαθὸν παρὰ τῶν φίλων μὴ λαβεῖν. κατανάλισκε τὴν ἐν τῷ βίῳ σχολὴν εἰς τὴν τῶν λόγων φιληκοΐαν· οὕτω γὰρ τὰ τοῖς ἄλλοις χαλεπῶς εὑρημένα συμβήσεταί σοι ῥᾳδίως μανθάνειν. ἡγοῦ τῶν ἀκουσμάτων πολλὰ πολλῶν εἶναι χρημάτων κρείττω· τὰ μὲν γὰρ ταχέως ἀπολείπει, τὰ δὲ πάντα τὸν χρόνον παραμένει· σοφία γὰρ μόνον τῶν κτημάτων ἀθάνατον.

2. In both of these passages notice the way in which relatively long sentences have been constructed from smaller units arranged along the same principles—subject, verb or participle, object(s) and attendant modifiers. The following sentence from Diodorus, for example, is divisible into three discrete grammatical parts—participial phrase, genitive absolute, finite verb—that have been combined with a clear sense of balance and proportion:

καὶ γὰρ ἐκεῖνος ἡττημένος ὑπὸ ᾿Αθηναίων ἐν Μαραθῶνι,

Δάτιδος ἡγουμένου,

χαλεπῶς διέκειτο πρὸς τοὺς νενικηκότας ᾿Αθηναίους.

Contrast this sentence from Isocrates: it is initially divisible into two parts as the punctuation makes clear. The first half of the sentence consists of four units—two relative clauses + two main clauses linked by μέν. . .δέ; the second half of consists of two participial phrases linked by καί, thus:

(a) ἃ μὲν ἐπίστασαι,

  ταῦτα διαφύλαττε ταῖς μελέταις,

ἃ δὲ μὴ μεμάθηκας,

  προσλάμβανε ταῖς ἐπιστήμαις·

(b) ὁμοίως γὰρ αἰσχρὸν ἀκούσαντα χρήσιμον λόγον μὴ μαθεῖν

  καὶ διδόμενόν τι ἀγαθὸν παρὰ τῶν φίλων μὴ λαβεῖν.

Greek prose tends to be built up from such relatively short sense units called κῶλα (= "limbs" or "members") to form longer and, occasionally, very elaborate sentences. Units may be organized by simple coordination, called parataxis (e.g., A καὶ B καὶ C καὶ D), or no coordination at all. Ancient rhetoricians called this loosely connected style λέξις εἰρομένη. But such simple and unrelieved prose gave way to the more complex "periodic" style favored by Attic writers of the fifth and fourth centuries B.C. in which the sentences are built up by subordination, called hypotaxis, and can show great variety in their syntax. This was called λέξις κατεσ-τραμμένη. Isocrates provides an excellent example of this style.

Even a relatively unelaborated style like that of Diodorus does not consist of strings of SVO or SOV linked only by "and". Virtually every clause and sentence is connected to its predecessor(s) by a series of particles that knit together the whole. μέν and δέ (= "on the one hand," "on the other") show contrast; καί = "and"; δέ alone indicates the start of a new sentence or clause, and is sometimes mildly adversative; ἀλλά and μέντοι ("but" or "however") are adversative; γάρ ("for") introduces an explanation of what has preceded; οὖν ("therefore") introduces a conclusion. This is the logic that holds a paragraph together. It is reinforced by participial phrases (frequent in the Diodorus passage), by relative clauses, subordinate clauses introduced by conjunctions, or by adverbial phrases.

Skilled writers, however, will sometimes combine short, paratactic sections with more elaborately organized sentences. Notice, for example, how Lysias uses the effect of parataxis in the opening of 1.4 below to characterize a simple man relating his complaint: ἐμοίχευεν 'Ερατοσθένης τὴν γυναῖκα τὴν ἐμὴν καὶ ἐκείνην τε διέφθειρε καὶ τοὺς παῖδας τοὺς ἐμοὺς ᾔσχυνε καὶ ἐμὲ αὐτὸν ὕβρισεν εἰς τὴν οἰκίαν τὴν ἐμὴν εἰσιών.

3. In addition to words that may move freely within a sentence or phrase, there are many words which have some restrictions:

(a) Conjunctions (e.g., ἐπεί, ὅτι, ὡς, ὅτε, εἰ) and interrogatives (e.g., τίς, ποῦ) normally begin sentences or phrases.

(b) Particles categorized as postpositive (e.g., μέν, δέ, γάρ, ἄρα, ἄν), as their name implies, cannot stand at the beginning of a sentence; they often occur **after** the first word of the sentence or phrase, or immediately following the word they emphasize. A few particles are prepositive (e.g., ἦ, ἆρα introducing a question) and may only stand at the beginning of a phrase.

(c) Enclitics are closely connected to the word they follow and an accent is thrown back back onto that word, e.g., **1.1**: διά τε τὴν τοῦ πατρὸς ἐπιβολὴν, where τε is enclitic. For a discussion of the accent of enclitics see **Smyth** §§ 181-187.

(d) Prepositions regularly stand immediately before the word or phrase that depends on them. A few disyllabic prepositions, however, usually follow their objects (e.g., ἕνεκα, χάριν, and sometimes ἄνευ). περί in prose and several others in poetry will sometimes precede, sometimes follow their objects. In the latter case their accents fall on the initial syllable (πέρι).

4. A third group that shows some restriction is the article + noun group. This will be taken up in the next chapter.

EXERCISES:

1. Consider the following two passages. In what ways do they resemble the first two passages? In what ways do they differ? What are the words—verbs, nouns, adjectives, adverbial or prepositional phrases—that the writers choose to emphasize? How does the word order reveal this? Would any alteration of the order of words or clauses spoil the effect? How many words in these passages are restricted to certain positions in the sentence? What happens if they are absent or wrongly placed?

1.3 Plato, **Apology** §38c1-d1. The **Apology** is supposed to have been Socrates' defense against the charges of impiety and corrupting the young leveled against him by several prominent Athenians in 399 B.C. At this point Socrates argues that it is foolish for the Athenians to execute him when he is so old (70), because nature will soon rid them of him.

οὐ πολλοῦ γ᾽ ἕνεκα χρόνου, ὦ ἄνδρες ᾽Αθηναῖοι, ὄνομα ἕξετε καὶ

αἰτίαν ὑπὸ τῶν βουλομένων τὴν πόλιν λοιδορεῖν ὡς Σωκράτη

ἀπεκτόνατε, ἄνδρα σοφόνᾠφήσουσι γὰρ δὴ σοφὸν εἶναι, εἰ καὶ μή εἰμι, οἱ βουλόμενοι ὑμῖν ὀνειδίζεινᾠεἰ γοῦν περιεμείνατε ὀλίγον χρόνον, ἀπὸ τοῦ αὐτομάτου ἂν ὑμῖν τοῦτο ἐγένετο· ὁρᾶτε γὰρ δὴ τὴν ἡλικίαν ὅτι πόρρω ἤδη ἐστὶ τοῦ βίου θανάτου δὲ ἐγγύς. λέγω δὲ τοῦτο οὐ πρὸς πάντας ὑμᾶς, ἀλλὰ πρὸς τοὺς ἐμοῦ καταψηφισαμένους θάνατον.

1.4 Lysias, The Murder of Eratosthenes §§4-5. The speaker suspected that his wife was committing adultery with an Athenian named Eratosthenes. Gathering a few of his friends he set a trap for the lovers and, when he caught them together, he killed the man. This is his legal defense against a charge of murder. Note that he admits to having killed Eratosthenes (ἔπραξα ταῦτα, line 4), but claims that he was entirely justified in so doing. Here he is establishing that he is the injured party and could have had nothing to gain financially or otherwise by killing Eratosthenes.

ἡγοῦμαι δέ, ὦ ἄνδρες, τοῦτό με δεῖν ἐπιδεῖξαι, ὡς ἐμοίχευεν Ἐρατοσθένης τὴν γυναῖκα τὴν ἐμὴν καὶ ἐκείνην τε διέφθειρε καὶ τοὺς παῖδας τοὺς ἐμοὺς ᾔσχυνε καὶ ἐμὲ αὐτὸν ὕβρισεν εἰς τὴν οἰκίαν τὴν ἐμὴν εἰσιών, καὶ οὔτε ἔχθρα ἐμοὶ καὶ ἐκείνῳ οὐδεμία ἦν πλὴν ταύτης, οὔτε χρημάτων ἕνεκα ἔπραξα ταῦτα, ἵνα πλούσιος ἐκ πένητος γένωμαι, οὔτε ἄλλου κέρδους οὐδενὸς πλὴν τῆς κατὰ τοὺς νόμους τιμωρίας. ἐγὼ τοίνυν ἐξ ἀρχῆς ὑμῖν ἅπαντα ἐπιδείξω τὰ ἐμαυτοῦ πράγματα, οὐδὲν παραλείπων, ἀλλὰ λέγων τἀληθῆ· ταύτην γὰρ ἐμαυτῷ μόνην ἡγοῦμαι σωτηρίαν, ἐὰν ὑμῖν εἰπεῖν ἅπαντα δυνηθῶ τὰ πεπραγμένα.

2. There are several changes in word order in the following paragraph. For each change indicate (a) whether or not it is acceptable in Greek prose; (b) then, if it is, what emphasis or meaning the new order would have; or, if it is not, explain why it is wrong.

ὁ Ξέρξης δὲ παρασκευασάμενος τριετῆ χρόνον κατεσκεύασε μακρὰς ναῦς πλείους τῶν χιλίων καὶ διακοσίων. αὐτῷ δὲ καὶ ὁ πατὴρ Δαρεῖος συνεβάλετο παρασκευὰς πεποιημένος μεγάλων δυνάμεων πρὸ τῆς τελευτῆς· ἐκεῖνος γὰρ ἡττημένος ὑπὸ ἐν Μαραθῶνι Ἀθηναίων, Δάτιδος πρὸς τοὺς νενικηκότας Ἀθηναίους ἡγουμένου, χαλεπῶς διέκειτο. ἀλλὰ Δαρεῖος μὲν τελευτήσας μέλλων ἤδη διαβαίνειν ἐπὶ τοὺς Ἕλληνας ἐμεσολαβήθη, ὁ δὲ Ξέρξης (διά τε τήν τοῦ πατρὸς ἐπιβολὴν καὶ τὴν τοῦ Μαρδονίου συμβουλίαν), τοῖς Ἕλλησιν διέγνω πολεμεῖν, καθότι προείρηται. ὡς δ' αὐτῷ τὰ πρὸς τὴν στρατείαν πάντα ἡτοίμαστο, παρήγγειλεν μὲν τοῖς ναυάρχοις ἀθροίζειν τὰς εἰς Κύμην καὶ Φώκαιαν ναῦς, προῆγεν δ' αὐτός, ἐκ τῶν ἁπασῶν σατραπειῶν συναγαγὼν τὰς πεζὰς καὶ ἱππικὰς δυνάμεις, ἐκ τῶν Σούσων. ὡς δ' εἰς Σάρδεις ἧκεν, κήρυκας εἰς τὴν Ἑλλάδα ἐξέπεμψεν, προστάξας εἰς πάσας τὰς πόλεις ἰέναι καὶ τοὺς Ἕλληνας αἰτεῖν ὕδωρ καὶ γῆν.

CHAPTER TWO—THE DEFINITE ARTICLE[1]

1. The definite article was in origin a demonstrative pronoun. In classical Attic and later its pronominal use is primarily in the following constructions:

(a) The article, when used with μέν and δέ and confined to the opening of the sentence or phrase, means "the one. . .the other" or "some. . .others." In **2.1** the article is followed by a partitive genitive: τοὺς μὲν αὐτῶν ἀπέκτεινε, τοὺς δ' ἐξέβαλεν = "some of them he killed, others he exiled."

(b) ὁ (ἡ, τό, οἱ) μὲν or ὁ (ἡ, τό, οἱ) δέ in the nominative may also stand by itself as in **2.1**: ὁ δὲ πείθεται = "and he is convinced" or ὁ δὲ ὡς ἀπῆλθε = "and he, when he left." This use **always** changes the subject.

2. The definite article, when prefixed to adjectives, participles, or adverbial or other expressions, will make the unit behave like a noun:

(a) ὁ ἀγαθός = "the good man"; it is not necessary for ἄνθρωπος or ἀνήρ to be expressed. This is very common with neuter adjectives which form abstracts, e.g., τὸ δίκαιον = "justice," τὸ καλόν = "beauty."

(b) Similarly, the article + a participle acts as an indefinite substantive, see Chapter Four, 3 (a), as does the article + infinitive, see Chapter Five, 2 (b).

(c) Phrases consisting simply of article + adverb (e.g. οἱ νῦν, = "people of the present day") or adverbial or prepositional

---

[1]For further discussion on the demonstrative use of the article see **Smyth** §§1106-1117, especially 1117; for ὁ, ἡ, τό as an article, see **Smyth** §1118-1189, **GG** §§933-983.

phrase (e.g., οἱ ἐν τῇ Θετταλίᾳ = "the people in Thessaly") are common.

(d) The neuter article (τό, τά) is often used with a following genitive, e.g., τὰ τῶν Θετταλῶν = "Thessalian matters," τὰ τῶν φίλων = "the property of friends." These expressions can almost never be translated literally.

(e) A masculine or feminine article + a name in the genitive case indicates origin, e.g., Περικλῆς ὁ Ξανθίππου = "Pericles, the son of Xanthippos."

3. The definite article when attached to a noun in Greek, as in English, functions to particularize. It may be used with the name of a person, place, or institution, or with any noun, abstract or concrete. As a general practice in writing Greek, if the English has an article, write one in Greek. However, you should be aware of the following considerations.

(a) Greek regularly has ὁ Σοφοκλῆς, ὁ Πλάτων, αἱ Ἀθῆναι, ἡ Σπάρτη, ἡ Αἴγυπτος, ἡ φιλοσοφία, ἡ ἀρετή, ἡ δικαιοσύνη, all instances where English would not use "the." But also οἱ θεοί, ἡ θάλαττα, ὁ Νεῖλος, οἱ Ἀθηναῖοι, ἡ ἐκκλησία, οἱ νόμοι, all examples of where English does use the definite article. Also, some article + noun phrases may be translated both with and without the article in English, e.g., ἡ ἀλήθεια = "truth," but also "the truth," ὁ πόλεμος = "war," but also "the war," that is, "this war." In reading, of course, context will decide.

(b) When a writer first introduces persons, it is usually without the article, unless they are already familiar in some way, but once introduced they may take the article (but will not necessarily do so consistently). In the first sentence of 2.1 Darius and Parysatis are introduced without the definite article, as are their two sons, Artaxerxes and Cyrus. Later Cyrus is referred to as ὁ Κῦρος, τὸν Κῦρον, and τῷ Κύρῳ, but also as Κῦρον.

(c) Quite often Greek uses the definite article where English prefers a possessive pronoun (e.g., "my," "your," "his," or "her,"), as in 2.1: ἡ μήτηρ = "his mother," τὸν ἀδελφόν = "his brother," unless it results in ambiguity. Contrast 1.4, however, where τὴν γυναῖκα τὴν ἐμήν, τοὺς παῖδας τοὺς ἐμούς, and τὴν οἰκίαν τὴν ἐμήν are emphatically positioned and expressed. See below 5 (c).

(d) Further, there are occasions when Greek does not need to use the definite article, though it would be almost obligatory in English, e.g, **2.1**: τελευτήν = "the end," Πίσιδας = "the Pisidians," Καστωλοῦ πεδίον = "the plain of the Castolus." You will easily find other examples.

4. When the definite article is combined with a substantive and its modifier(s), the article may occupy five different positions; three are **attributive**, two **predicative**.

(a) The **attributive position** includes (1) οἱ ἀγαθοί ἄνθρωποι, (2) οἱ ἄνθρωποι οἱ ἀγαθοί, and (3) ἄνθρωποι οἱ ἀγαθοί. Notice that in each example the article directly precedes the modifier, whatever its position relative to the substantive, and turns it into a characteristic or attribute of the substantive. In emphasis, (1) is most common, (2) somewhat more rhetorical or emphatic in effect, and (3) gives an effect of afterthought, hence marks an easier style.

In addition to adjectives, possessive pronouns, possessive genitives, participles, adverbial and prepositional phrases may be used attributively: e.g., **1.1**: τὴν τοῦ Μαρδονίου συμβουλίας, **1.4**: τῆς κατὰ τοὺς νόμους τιμωρίας, **2.2**: τοῦ ἄνω τόπου. English idiom will not tolerate this kind of expression, e.g., "the in accordance with the laws redress," but Greek can mark the modifying word or phrase as belonging to the noun by the word order, either by preceding it (as above) with the definite article, or enclosing it within the article-noun unit.

(b) The **predicative** position inclues (1) ἀγαθοί οἱ ἄνθρωποι and (2) οἱ ἄνθρωποι ἀγαθοί. Note that here the article directly precedes the noun and the modifier stands outside of the article + noun unit. This construction has the effect of turning the word or phrase into a predicate, i.e., "men are good." The nominative use of the construction is very familiar, but it is important to realize that it also functions in oblique cases.

(c) When no article is present, an attributive adjective normally precedes the noun, e.g, μακρὰς ναῦς κατεσκεύασε = "he fitted out long ships." When the adjective follows its noun, it is often in the predicative position, e.g., ναῦς μακρὰς κατεσκεύασε = "he fitted out ships **to be long**."

5. A number of categories of expression in Greek are restricted either to attributive or predicative position, or change meaning depending on their position:

(a) Possessive adjectives like ἐμός or ἡμέτερος occupy the **attributive** position as do the possessive genitives of reflexive and demonstrative pronouns, and forms of αὐτός when it = "same," e.g. ὁ αὐτὸς σοφιστής = "the same sophist."

(b) Demonstrative adjectives, οὗτος, ὅδε, and ἐκεῖνος, as well as ἄμφω, ἀμφότερος, ἑκάτερος, and ἕκαστος take the **predicative** position, e.g. **2.2**: ἑκάστης τῆς τέχνης, τοῦτο τὸ μάθημα.

(c) Possessive genitives of personal and relative pronouns (e.g., μου, ἡμῶν, αὐτοῦ) and partitive genitives take a **predicative** position. So too do forms of αὐτός when it = "self," "very," e.g., αὐτὸς ὁ σοφιστής = "the sophist himself."

Note the positions of possessives, relatives, and demonstratives in the following and their emphases:

τὴν γυναῖκα	"my wife" (used when possessor is obvious)
τὴν γυναῖκά μου	"my wife" (most common, no special emphasis)
τὴν ἐμὴν γυναῖκα	"**my** wife" (more emphatic than μου)
τὴν γυναῖκα τὴν ἐμήν	"my **wife** or **my** wife" (very emphatic)
τὴν γυναῖκα αὐτοῦ	"his wife" (no special emphasis)
τὴν τούτου γυναῖκα	"**his** wife"
ταύτην τὴν γυναῖκα	"this wife" or "this woman"

(d) Πᾶς (σύμπας, ἅπας, and ὅλος) usually take the predicative position, but may take the attributive position with a slight change in emphasis:

(1) In the **predicative** position, πᾶς means "all", with the members of the group taken as individuals, e.g., πᾶσαι αἱ πόλεις = "all the cities" (taken one by one).

(2) In the **attributive** position, πᾶς refers to the whole in its entirety: ἡ πᾶσα πόλις = "the entire city," "οἱ πάντες 'Αθηναῖοι" = "all the Athenians" (as a group). πᾶς is used without the article when the noun is used without an article, e.g., πᾶσα πόλις = the city taken in a general sense. This use is often translated "every" in the singular (see **Smyth** §1174 and **GG** §977).

READINGS:

2.1 Xenophon, **Anabasis** 1.1.1-4. Xenophon lived from about 430-355 B.C. He wrote a number of historical works including this account of his experience as a Greek soldier in the army of the Persian king, Cyrus. This passage comes from the opening of the **Anabasis** in which Xenophon provides his audience with the necessary background information on the members of the Persian court.

Δαρείου καὶ Παρυσάτιδος γίγνονται παῖδες δύο, πρεσβύτερος μὲν

'Αρταξέρξης, νεώτερος δὲ Κῦρος. ἐπεὶ δὲ ἠσθένει Δαρεῖος καὶ

ὑπώπτευε τελευτὴν τοῦ βίου, ἐβούλετο τὼ παῖδε ἀμφοτέρω

παρεῖναι. ὁ μὲν οὖν πρεσβύτερος παρὼν ἐτύγχανε· Κῦρον δὲ

μεταπέμπεται ἀπὸ τῆς ἀρχῆς ἧς αὐτὸν σατράπην ἐποίησε, καὶ

στρατηγὸν δὲ αὐτὸν ἀπέδειξε πάντων ὅσοι εἰς Καστωλοῦ πεδίον

ἀθροίζονται. ἀναβαίνει οὖν ὁ Κῦρος λαβὼν Τισσαφέρνην ὡς φίλον

καὶ τῶν 'Ελλήνων ἔχων ὁπλίτας τριακοσίους, ἄρχοντα δὲ αὐτῶν

Ξενίαν Παρράσιον. ἐπεὶ δὲ ἐτελεύτησε Δαρεῖος καὶ κατέστη εἰς τὴν

βασιλείαν 'Αρταξέρξης, Τισσαφέρνης διαβάλλει τὸν Κῦρον πρὸς τὸν

ἀδελφὸν ὡς ἐπιβουλεύοι αὐτῷ. ὁ δὲ πείθεται καὶ συλλαμβάνει

Κῦρον ὡς ἀποκτενῶν· ἡ δὲ μήτηρ ἐξαιτησαμένη αὐτὸν ἀποπέμπει

πάλιν ἐπὶ τὴν ἀρχήν. ὁ δ' ὡς ἀπῆλθε κινδυνεύσας καὶ ἀτιμασθείς,

βουλεύεται ὅπως μήποτε ἔτι ἔσται ἐπὶ τῷ ἀδελφῷ, ἀλλ', ἢν δύν-

ηται, βασιλεύσει ἀντ' ἐκείνου. Παρύσατις μὲν δὴ ἡ μήτηρ ὑπῆρχε τῷ
Κύρῳ, φιλοῦσα αὐτὸν μᾶλλον ἢ τὸν βασιλεύοντα 'Αρταξέρξην.

2.2 Plato, Phaedrus §§274c5-275b1. This is a famous anecdote
about the Egyptian god of wisdom, Theuth, inventing writing.

ΣΩ. ἤκουσα τοίνυν περὶ Ναύκρατιν τῆς Αἰγύπτου γενέσθαι τῶν
ἐκεῖ παλαιῶν τινα θεῶν, οὗ καὶ τὸ ὄρνεον ἱερὸν ὃ δὴ καλοῦσιν Ἶβιν·
αὐτῷ δὲ ὄνομα τῷ δαίμονι εἶναι Θεύθ. τοῦτον δὴ πρῶτον ἀριθμόν τε
καὶ λογισμὸν εὑρεῖν καὶ γεωμετρίαν καὶ ἀστρονομίαν, ἔτι δὲ
πεττείας τε καὶ κυβείας, καὶ δὴ καὶ γράμματα. βασιλέως δ' αὖ
τότε ὄντος Αἰγύπτου ὅλης Θαμοῦ περὶ τὴν μεγάλην πόλιν τοῦ ἄνω
τόπου (= Upper Egypt) ἣν οἱ Ἕλληνες Αἰγυπτίας Θήβας καλοῦσι,
καὶ τὸν θεὸν "Αμμωνα, παρὰ τοῦτον ἐλθὼν ὁ Θεὺθ τὰς τέχνας
ἐπέδειξεν, καὶ ἔφη δεῖν διαδοθῆναι τοῖς ἄλλοις Αἰγυπτίοις· ὁ δὲ
ἤρετο ἥντινα ἑκάστη ἔχοι ὠφελίαν, διεξιόντος δέ, ὅτι καλῶς ἢ μὴ
καλῶς δοκοῖ λέγειν, τὸ μὲν ἔψεγεν, τὸ δ' ἐπῄνει. πολλὰ μὲν δὴ
περὶ ἑκάστης τῆς τέχνης ἐπ' ἀμφότερα Θαμοῦν τῷ Θεὺθ λέγεται
ἀποφήνασθαι, ἃ λόγος πολὺς ἂν εἴη διελθεῖν· ἐπειδὴ δὲ ἐπὶ τοῖς
γράμμασιν ἦν, "τοῦτο δέ, ὦ βασιλεῦ, τὸ μάθημα," ἔφη ὁ Θεύθ,
"σοφωτέρους Αἰγυπτίους καὶ μνημονικωτέρους παρέξει· μνήμης τε
γὰρ καὶ σοφίας φάρμακον ηὑρέθη." ὁ δ' εἶπεν· "ὦ τεχνικώτατε
Θεύθ, ἄλλος μὲν τεκεῖν δυνατὸς τὰ τέχνης, ἄλλος δὲ κρῖναι τίν'
ἔχει μοῖραν βλάβης τε καὶ ὠφελίας τοῖς μέλλουσι χρῆσθαι· καὶ νῦν
σύ, πατὴρ ὢν γραμμάτων, δι' εὔνοιαν τοὐναντίον εἶπες ἢ δύναται.
τοῦτο γὰρ τῶν μαθόντων λήθην μὲν ἐν ψυχαῖς παρέξει μνήμης
ἀμελετησίᾳ, ἅτε διὰ πίστιν γραφῆς ἔξωθεν ὑπ' ἀλλοτρίων τύπων,
οὐκ ἔνδοθεν αὐτοὺς ὑφ' αὑτῶν ἀναμιμνῃσκομένους· οὔκουν μνήμης
ἀλλὰ ὑπομνήσεως φάρμακον ηὗρες. σοφίας δὲ τοῖς μαθηταῖς δόξαν,
οὐκ ἀλήθειαν πορίζεις· πολυήκοοι γάρ σοι γενόμενοι ἄνευ διδαχῆς

πολυγνώμονες εἶναι δόξουσιν, ἀγνώμονες ὡς ἐπὶ τὸ πλῆθος ὄντες, καὶ χαλεποὶ συνεῖναι, δοξόσοφοι γεγονότες ἀντὶ σοφῶν.

2.3 Isocrates, Panegyricus §§28-29. This is a description of the benefits conferred upon Athens by the goddess Demeter.

Πρῶτον μὲν οὖν, οὗ πρῶτον ἡ φύσις ἡμῶν ἐδεήθη, διὰ τῆς πόλεως τῆς ἡμετέρας ἐπορίσθη· καὶ γὰρ εἰ μυθώδης ὁ λόγος γέγονεν, ὅμως αὐτῷ καὶ νῦν ῥηθῆναι προσήκει. Δήμητρος γὰρ ἀφικομένης εἰς τὴν χώραν ὅτ᾽ ἐπλανήθη τῆς Κόρης ἁρπασθείσης, καὶ πρὸς τοὺς προγόνους ἡμῶν εὐμενῶς διατεθείσης ἐκ τῶν εὐεργεσιῶν ἃς οὐχ οἷόν τ᾽ ἄλλοις ἢ τοῖς μεμυημένοις ἀκούειν, καὶ δούσης δωρεὰς διττὰς αἵπερ μέγισται τυγχάνουσιν οὖσαι, τούς τε καρπούς, οἳ τοῦ μὴ θηριωδῶς ζῆν ἡμᾶς αἴτιοι γεγόνασι, καὶ τὴν τελετήν, ἧς οἱ μετασχόντες περί τε τῆς τοῦ βίου τελευτῆς καὶ τοῦ σύμπαντος αἰῶνος ἡδίους τὰς ἐλπίδας ἔχουσιν, οὕτως ἡ πόλις ἡμῶν οὐ μόνον θεοφιλῶς ἀλλὰ καὶ φιλανθρώπως ἔσχεν, ὥστε κυρία γενομένη τοσούτων ἀγαθῶν οὐκ ἐφθόνησε τοῖς ἄλλοις, ἀλλ᾽ ὧν ἔλαβεν ἅπασι μετέδωκεν. καὶ τὰ μὲν ἔτι καὶ νῦν καθ᾽ ἕκαστον τὸν ἐνιαυτὸν δείκνυμεν, τῶν δὲ συλλήβδην τάς τε χρείας καὶ τὰς ἐργασίας καὶ τὰς ὠφελίας τὰς ἀπ᾽ αὐτῶν γιγνομένας ἐδίδαξεν.

EXERCISES:

Write in Greek:

A Sentences:

1. Cyrus, the son of Darius and Parysatis, plotted against his brother the king.
2. The plot against Artaxerxes, the king, did not escape his notice.
3. But he decided to attack the Greeks in Ionia rather than his brother's forces in Thrace.

4. Some of his brother's men were unwilling to fight against the king.

5. So Cyrus sent messengers to his brother to ask for peace.

6. Many of these stories are unsuitable for children. And they are shameful even for their fathers to hear.

7. What is learned with difficulty is much better than what is learned with ease; it will remain with us for many years.

8. The Egyptians were wiser than the rest of mankind because they did not use writing to aid their memories.

9. It was the Athenians, not the Corinthians, who defeated the father of Xerxes.

10. Xerxes and Darius disagreed about Mardonius' advice; the one wished to make preparations for three years, the other to go to war against Greece in that same year.

B Sentences:

1. I will tell you the whole story from the beginning. This man, Eratosthenes, was responsible for a great injury to me and my children.   For he entered my house without fear of me or any of my servants, seduced my wife and destroyed her reputation. But I had never done him any harm.   Therefore, I am asking this court to grant me redress in accordance with our laws.

2. All of Xerxes' admirals gathered in Phocaia. Now, Xerxes had many admirals, but few ships. So he was advised to build more than three hundred ships before attacking Greece. Then Xerxes sent all his heralds to the cities of the Greeks to demand surrender. The Greeks, however, had already built a large number of ships and had assembled several thousand foot soldiers. These men were ready to defend their homeland. When the armies met at Marathon, the Athenians won the battle; after the victory, they determined always to be mindful of that day.

3. The messengers from Egypt tell this story: Theuth and Thamous had a long conversation about writing. Thamous did not want the Egyptians to learn letters which Theuth had invented.   But the Egyptians themselves, who have a reputation for wisdom wished to have this remedy for forgetfulness.   Nevertheless, Thamous refused them this skill, because the man who invents something is not the best judge of its benefit or harm and because those who use

writing will have the reputation for learning, but will not possess wisdom itself.

CHAPTER THREE—THE VERB[1]

The Greek verb system is formally subdivided into three categories—voice, mood and tense.

1. **Voice** expresses a view about the verbal activity, indicated in Greek by three forms, active, middle or passive. Active and passive voices behave as they do in English.

In the **active** voice, the subject or actor is in the nominative, the object of the verbal activity (if stated) in the accusative or whatever other case the verb requires (see **1.1**: κατεσκεύασε ναῦς μακράς; **1.4**: ἔπραξα ταῦτα; **2.1**: ὑπῆρχε τῷ Κύρῳ).

Verbs that take a direct object are called **transitive**, verbs that take an indirect object or that cannot take an object at all are called **intransitive**. This distinction is a matter of use, not necessarily the nature of the verb. Many verbs like σιωπάω (= "I am silent") or τρέχω (= "I run") do not normally take objects, but may occasionally do so. English usage is not a useful predictor in determining whether or not a verb is transitive in Greek; many common verbs like hear (ἀκούω), obey (ὑπακούω), or threaten (ἀπειλέω), which would seem to take a direct object based on English, in fact can take cases other than the accusative. If verbs have both a first and second aorist or a first and second perfect in use, commonly the first forms are transitive, the second, intransitive (e.g., ἔστησα and ἔστην from ἵστημι). For a list of such verbs, see **Smyth** §819.

---

[1]For further discussion see **Smyth** §§1703-1760, 1850-1858, 1875-1958, **MT** §§19-84, and **GG** §§447-474, §1240-1345.

In the **passive** voice, the recipient of the verbal activity is in the nominative; the doer of the action, if expressed, will follow ὑπό in the genitive case (see **1.1**: ἡττημένος ὑπὸ ᾿Αθηναίων) or occasionally another preposition, such as ἐκ.

In the **middle** voice, the subject (in the nominative) is directly or indirectly involved in or interested in the action of the verb. Uses include a direct reflexive sense (see **1.1**: παρασκευασάμενος = "having prepared himself"), indirect sense (αἱροῦμαι = "I take for myself", i.e., "I choose"), reciprocity (ἐμάχοντο = "they were fighting one another"), causation (ἐπαιδεύετο τὸν παῖδα = "he had his son educated"). Some verbs have a future that is middle in form, but active in meaning (e.g., λαμβάνω, λήψομαι); or the middle may have come to have an active meaning in all forms (called "deponent").

Many Greek verbs have all three voices in common use: for example, γράφω ὑπομνήματα = "I write notes," γράφομαι ὑπομνήματα = "I write notes for myself", or "I cause someone to write notes down for me" and ὑπομνήματα ἐγράφη ὑπ᾿ ἐμοῦ = "notes were written by me." λόγον ἐποίησε = "he wrote (constructed) a speech," λόγον ἐποιήσατο = "he delivered a speech (made a speech for himself)", and λόγος ἐποιήθη ὑπ᾿ αὐτοῦ = "a speech was written (or delivered) by him." With both of these verbs, however, the middle form may have a different meaning from the active, while the passive serves as the passive for both, depending on context. But not all verbs employ all three voices regularly. Some may lack middle or passive forms; forms common in Homer or archaic poetry may no longer be used in Attic Greek, or the verb may be deponent. The behavior of individual verbs can only be learned from observation; in your reading you should familiarize yourself with the voices of verbs in actual use. For further discussion see **Smyth** §§1703-1758 and **GG** §§1230-1248.

2. Greek distinguishes four finite (i.e., taking a nominative subject) **moods**, or modes of expressing activity—indicative, subjunctive, optative, and imperative—as well as the infinitive, which is a non-finite mood taking an accusative subject, and the participle, which is a verbal adjective.

Indicative is used to express or deny facts or what the speaker or writer regards as fact. It regularly occurs in independent statements and in direct questions.

Subjunctive originally seems to have expressed futurity (as very often it does in Homer in independent assertions); by the fifth century its chief independent uses are the hortatory and deliberative subjunctives. Its main use, however, is in dependent constructions—final clauses, expressions of fear, if-clauses, temporal clauses—which refer or look to the future. The subjunctive is discussed in Chapters Seven, Nine through Eleven, Fourteen, Sixteen and Seventeen.

Optative is used independently to express wish ("if only she would come") or potentiality ("this might be so"), and in a variety of dependent constructions parallel in use to the subjunctive, as well as in indirect speech. Wishes are taken up in Chapter Twelve, potential expressions in Chapter Thirteen, indirect speech in Chapter Eighteen.

Imperative is used for commands and prohibitions. It normally occurs in independent statements. The imperative is discussed in Chapter Seven.

Infinitive, as its name implies, is not limited by person, number, or mood; it does have voice and tense, however. It functions as a verbal noun. Uses of the infinitive are discussed in Chapter Five.

Participle may take an object, like a verb, but agrees in gender, number and case with the noun it modifies. Uses of the participle are discussed in Chapter Four.

3. The tense of the Greek verb normally expresses two relations: **time**, that is, when the action takes place—past, present or future—and **aspect**. Aspect describes the way the writer or speaker conceives of the event, e.g., in process, as complete. Verbs may also express **relative** time—that is, time with respect to other verbs in the narrative. Relative time is especially significant for infinitives and participles. Finite verbs distinguish three different **aspects:**

(a) an event may be viewed as **single and instantaneous**, that is, not divided into constituent parts (she **read** the book, he **died**). Hence, its name in Greek, ἀόριστος, which means "indeterminate" or "un-delimited."

(b) In contrast the event may be viewed as a **continuous or recurring** process, often as an event during which other events can happen (she **is reading** as I enter the room, they **were serving** as archons during that year, they **are dying**). The difference between these two is not duration or length of activity, but the viewpoint of the narrator; the same event can easily be described as a single, complete action and as in process depending on the requirements of context (he **died** three days ago and he **was dying** three days ago).

(c) An event may be perceived as a **current situation** or state that is the **result of completed past activity** (the door **is closed** because someone closed it in the past and it has not been reopened).

4. Greek has seven **tenses** in the indicative mood: present, imperfect, aorist, perfect, pluperfect, future perfect, and future. The subjunctive and imperative moods have only three tenses: present, aorist and perfect. The optative mood, participles and infinitives have four tenses: present, aorist, perfect and future.

(a) **Present indicative** describes continuing or repeated action, action that is in process rather than concluded. Present indicates such activity as going on at the time of the writing (or speaking), which by its nature must be incomplete. The Greek present is the equivalent of English "he does" and "he is doing" (see **3.2**: λέγεις, καθεύδεις).

Present tense may also be used in extended narrative, usually as a substitute for the aorist, but also for the imperfect, to make the dramatic events more immediate. This is called the **historical present**. In all respects but its form it functions like a past tense (see **4.1**: ἀποσφάττει, πέμπει).

Present subjunctive and **optative** describe process or continuing activity. (See Chapters Ten to Twelve.)

(b) **Imperfect indicative** describes an action in process or going on in the past. It is also used for repeated or customary action (the equivalent of "he used to do" or "he repeatedly did"). The imperfect contrasts with the aorist (see **1.4**: ἐμοίχευεν, **3.3**: διέτριβον).

(c) **Aorist indicative** describes a single action or event as something completed. (See **3.3** ἔδοξε, ἐπύθοντο.) The difference between imperfect and aorist results from the perspective of the writer not from the verb itself. For example, ἐβασίλευσε δέκα ἔτη means "he had a reign of ten years" (now seen as completed), while ἐβασίλευε δέκα ἔτη would mean "he was reigning during a ten year period" (now stressing the process). However, it must be noted that many verbs occur more often in one tense than the other, which suggests that meaning could influence the writer's choice of aspect. These usages must be noted in reading; they **cannot** be inferred from the English translations assigned to Greek verbs.

Aorist subjunctive and **optative** describe an action in its completed aspect (see Chapters Ten through Twelve).

(d) **Perfect** represents the present result of a past action.[1] It is present in time, since present result is an essential part of its meaning (see **3.2**: ἐπιδεδήμηκεν, ἐγρήγορας).

---

[1] The so-called "dative of agent" is used with the perfect and pluperfect passive (rather than ὑπό + genitive, which is the normal means of expressing agent with a passive verb) because these tenses describe a condition or state that exists for an individual. Hence the dative is analogous to a dative of interest (see **Smyth** §1488-89).

Pluperfect shifts this perspective into the past; it is therefore a past tense (see **1.1** ἡτοίμαστο, **3.3**: ἐδεδώκεσαν).

Future perfect tense shifts it into the future; hence it is a future tense.

(e) **Future indicative** expresses intention as well as futurity. Its use is not as clear-cut as other tenses; in Homer, for example, futurity could be expressed by the subjunctive. Also intention may be expressed by μέλλω + the infinitive. Greek does not normally distinguish aspect in the future, though it does in the subjunctive and optative, which behave like future tenses in subordinate clauses (see **1.3**: ἕξετε, **3.2**: μέλλει φαίνεσθαι, μέλλων φράζειν).

Future optative is restricted in use to indirect speech in secondary sequence where it may substitute for a future indicative.

(f) There are **four tenses of participles and infinitives**: present, aorist, perfect, and future. Their usage is discussed in Chapters Four and Five.

5. Verbs are further divided into **primary** tenses, which denote **present or future** time and **secondary** tenses (also called historical), which denote **past** time. Primary tenses include PRESENT, FUTURE, PERFECT and FUTURE PERFECT. Secondary, IMPERFECT, AORIST, PLUPERFECT and HISTORICAL PRESENT. This division is based on time, not aspect. It determines what kind of verb will appear in subordinate constructions.

(a) For final clauses, temporal clauses, and indefinite relative clauses the **subjunctive** mood follows leading verbs in **primary tenses**, the **optative** mood, or occasionally the subjunctive, follows **secondary tenses**.

(b) For indirect speech, the **tenses and moods of the direct speech are retained** after **primary tenses**, but may be changed, if they are subjunctive or a primary tense of the indicative, to the **optative** after **secondary** tenses, unless the infinitive construction is used.

Greek and Latin differ in this respect; in Latin the sequence is based on **tense** (present or perfect subjunctive after primary tenses, imperfect or pluperfect subjunctive after secondary tenses); Greek, however, shows a **sequence of mood**.

READINGS:

3.1 Lysias, **The Murder of Eratosthenes** §4 (repeated from 1.4).

ἡγοῦμαι δέ, ὦ ἄνδρες, τοῦτό με δεῖν ἐπιδεῖξαι, ὡς ἐμοίχευεν

'Ερατοσθένης τὴν γυναῖκα τὴν ἐμὴν καὶ ἐκείνην τε διέφθειρε καὶ

τοὺς παῖδας τοὺς ἐμοὺς ᾔσχυνε καὶ ἐμὲ αὐτὸν ὕβρισεν εἰς τὴν

οἰκίαν τὴν ἐμὴν εἰσιών, καὶ οὔτε ἔχθρα ἐμοὶ καὶ ἐκείνῳ οὐδεμία

ἦν πλὴν ταύτης, οὔτε χρημάτων ἕνεκα ἔπραξα ταῦτα, ἵνα

πλούσιος ἐκ πένητος γένωμαι, οὔτε ἄλλου κέρδους οὐδενὸς πλὴν τῆς

κατὰ τοὺς νόμους τιμωρίας. ἐγὼ τοίνυν ἐξ ἀρχῆς ὑμῖν ἅπαντα

ἐπιδείξω τὰ ἐμαυτοῦ πράγματα, οὐδὲν παραλείπων, ἀλλὰ

λέγων τἀληθῆ· ταύτην γὰρ ἐμαυτῷ μόνην ἡγοῦμαι σωτηρίαν,

ἐὰν ὑμῖν εἰπεῖν ἅπαντα δυνηθῶ τὰ πεπραγμένα.

3.2 Plato, **Protagoras** §§309c9-310c4. In the Platonic dialogues, Socrates is often said to have been in love with Alcibiades. Here, in the opening of this speech, Socrates jokingly claims that the philosopher, Protagoras, who is visiting Athens, has eclipsed Alcibiades in his eyes. He then goes on to describe how his friend, Hippocrates, came early that very morning to tell him that Protagoras was in town.

'Εταῖρος.   καὶ οὕτω καλός τις ὁ ξένος ἔδοξέν σοι εἶναι, ὥστε τοῦ

Κλεινίου ὑέος (= Alcibiades) καλλίων σοι φανῆναι;

Σωκράτης. πῶς δ' οὐ **μέλλει**, ὦ μακάριε, τὸ σοφώτατον κάλλιον **φαίνεσθαι**;

ΕΤ. ἀλλ' ἦ σοφῷ τινι ἡμῖν, ὦ Σώκρατες, **ἐντυχὼν πάρει**;

ΣΩ. σοφωτάτῳ μὲν οὖν δήπου τῶν γε νῦν, εἴ σοι δοκεῖ σοφώτατος **εἶναι** Πρωταγόρας.

ΕΤ. ὦ τί **λέγεις**; Πρωταγόρας **ἐπιδεδήμηκεν**;

ΣΩ. τρίτην γε ἤδη ἡμέραν.

ΕΤ. καὶ ἄρτι ἄρα ἐκείνῳ **συγγεγονὼς ἥκεις**;

ΣΩ. πάνυ γε, πολλὰ καὶ **εἰπὼν** καὶ **ἀκούσας**.

ΕΤ. τί οὖν οὐ **διηγήσω** ἡμῖν τὴν συνουσίαν, εἰ μή σέ τι **κωλύει**, **καθεζόμενος** ἐνταυθί, **ἐξαναστήσας** τὸν παῖδα τουτονί;

ΣΩ. πάνυ μὲν οὖν· καὶ χάριν γε **εἴσομαι**,[1] ἐὰν ἀκούητε.

ΕΤ. καὶ μὴν καὶ ἡμεῖς σοί, ἐὰν λέγῃς.

ΣΩ. διπλῆ ἂν εἴη ἡ χάρις. ἀλλ' οὖν **ἀκούετε**.

τῆς γὰρ **παρελθούσης** νυκτὸς ταυτησί, ἔτι βαθέος ὄρθρου, Ἱπποκράτης, ὁ Ἀπολλοδώρου ὑὸς Φάσωνος δὲ ἀδελφός, τὴν θύραν τῇ βακτηρίᾳ πάνυ σφόδρα **ἔκρουε**, καὶ ἐπειδὴ αὐτῷ **ἀνέῳξέ** τις, εὐθὺς εἴσω **ᾔει** **ἐπειγόμενος**, καὶ τῇ φωνῇ μέγα **λέγων**, "ὦ Σώκρατες," **ἔφη**, "**ἐγρήγορας** ἢ **καθεύδεις**"; καὶ ἐγὼ τὴν φωνὴν **γνοὺς** αὐτοῦ, "Ἱπποκράτης," **ἔφην**, "οὗτος· μή τι νεώτερον **ἀγγέλλεις**"; "οὐδέν γ'," **ἦ δ' ὅς**, "εἰ μὴ ἀγαθά γε." "εὖ ἂν λέγοις," ἦν δ' ἐγώ· "**ἔστι** δὲ τί, καὶ τοῦ ἕνεκα τηνικάδε **ἀφίκου**"; "Πρωταγόρας," **ἔφη**, "**ἥκει**," **στὰς** παρ' ἐμοί. "πρῴην," **ἔφην** ἐγώ· "σὺ δὲ ἄρτι **πέπυσαι**"; "νὴ τοὺς θεούς," **ἔφη**, "ἑσπέρας γε." καὶ ἅμα **ἐπιψηλαφήσας** τοῦ σκίμποδος **ἐκαθέζετο** παρὰ τοὺς πόδας μου, καὶ **εἶπεν**· "ἑσπέρας δῆτα, μάλα γε ὀψὲ **ἀφικόμενος** ἐξ Οἰνόης. ὁ γάρ τοι παῖς με ὁ Σάτυρος **ἀπέδρα**· καὶ δῆτα **μέλλων** σοι **φράζειν** ὅτι διωξοίμην αὐτόν, ὑπό τινος ἄλλου **ἐπελαθόμην**."

[1]χάριν εἰδέναι τινί is a common prose idiom = "to be grateful to someone."

3.3 Diodorus 11.4.1-2, 6-7 (with omissions). This passage decribes the preparations of the Greeks before the battle of Thermopylae.

τοῖς δὲ συνέδροις τῶν Ἑλλήνων, ἐπειδὴ πλησίον εἶναι προσαπηγγέλθησαν αἱ τῶν Περσῶν δυνάμεις, ἔδοξε ταχέως ἀποστέλλειν τὴν μὲν ναυτικὴν δύναμιν ἐπ' Ἀρτεμίσιον τῆς Εὐβοίας, εὔθετον ὁρῶσι τὸν τόπον τοῦτον πρὸς τὴν ἀπάντησιν τῶν πολεμίων, εἰς δὲ τὰς Θερμοπύλας τοὺς ἱκανοὺς ὁπλίτας, προκαταληψομένους τὰς ἐν τοῖς στενοῖς παρόδους καὶ κωλύσοντας προάγειν ἐπὶ τὴν Ἑλλάδα τοὺς βαρβάρους. . . . ἡγεῖτο δὲ τοῦ μὲν στόλου παντὸς Εὐρυβιάδης ὁ Λακεδαιμόνιος, τῶν δὲ εἰς Θερμοπύλας ἐκπεμφθέντων Λεωνίδης ὁ τῶν Σπαρτιατῶν βασιλεύς, μέγα φρονῶν ἐπ' ἀνδρείᾳ καὶ στρατηγίᾳ. . . . ὁ μὲν οὖν Λεωνίδης μετὰ τετρακισχιλίων προῆγεν ἐπὶ τὰς Θερμοπύλας, Λοκροὶ δὲ οἱ πλησίον τῶν παρόδων κατοικοῦντες ἐδεδώκεσαν μὲν γῆν καὶ ὕδωρ τοῖς Πέρσαις, κατεπηγγελμένοι δ' ἦσαν προκαταλήψεσθαι τὰς παρόδους· ὡς δ' ἐπύθοντο τὸν Λεωνίδην ἥκειν εἰς Θερμοπύλας, μετενόησαν καὶ μετέθεντο πρὸς τοὺς Ἕλληνας. ἧκον δὲ εἰς τὰς Θερμοπύλας καὶ Λοκροὶ χίλιοι καὶ Μηλιέων τοσοῦτοι καὶ Φωκέων οὐ πολὺ λειπόμενοι τῶν χιλίων, ὁμοίως δὲ καὶ Θηβαίων ἀπὸ τῆς ἑτέρας μερίδος ὡς τετρακόσιοι· διεφέροντο γὰρ οἱ τὰς Θήβας κατοικοῦντες πρὸς ἀλλήλους περὶ τῆς πρὸς τοὺς Πέρσας συμμαχίας. οἱ μὲν οὖν μετὰ Λεωνίδου συνταχθέντες Ἕλληνες τοσοῦτοι τὸν ἀριθμὸν ὄντες διέτριβον περὶ τὰς Θερμοπύλας, ἀναμένοντες τὴν τῶν Περσῶν παρουσίαν.

EXERCISES:

Write in Greek:

A Sentences:

1. Xerxes has already made preparations for war.
2. Mardonius will advise him to go to war against the Greeks.
3. Eratosthenes did not shame me for the sake of money.
4. I am being insulted only because I am poor.
5. Darius continuously urged his son to fit out the ships for war.
6. I will demonstrate to you how many insults I received at the hands of Eratosthenes.
7. He entered my house and was seducing my wife.
8. But he is unable to tell the truth about these matters.
9. He was sending his heralds to all of the cities of Greece when the admirals arrived with the ships.
10. The Athenians were the victors at Marathon.
11. He saw that his life was drawing near to death.
12. The Athenians will kill Socrates.
13. Socrates said this to those wishing to reproach the Athenians.
14. Those who wish to condemn me should wait. I will die soon.
15. The many will say that Socrates is a wise man.

B Sentences:

1. More than four thousand Athenians heard the heralds whom Xerxes had sent to demand earth and water, but they refused to surrender. The Phocaians, however, when they learned that all of the Locrians had already promised the Persians that they would take the passes in Thermopylae, decided that they too would give earth and water to the herald sent by Xerxes. At the time that the Persians were ready to cross over into Greece, the Greeks themselves decided to send Leonidas, who had a reputation for courage, to Thermopylae to stop the Persians from advancing.

2. Xerxes and Darios disagreed about the advice of Mardonios; the former wished to make preparations for three years, the latter, perceiving that he was going to die, and because he had been defeated by the Greeks at Marathon, wished to make war in that

same year.   Later, after preparations had been made, Xerxes gathered his whole fleet at Cyme and intended to cross over into Greece at the head of his cavalry.

3. When Protagoras arrived in Athens, Socrates was still asleep, but he woke up immediately and went out to visit him. His friend Hippocrates, however, did not learn that Protagoras was in town for several days, because he had gone off to pursue a runaway slave. For this reason Hippocrates was very grateful to Socrates for telling him about his conversation with Protagoras.

CHAPTER FOUR—PARTICIPLES[1]

1. Participles are adjectives in form, agreeing in gender, number, and case with the nouns they modify. Like other adjectives they can be used attributively with an article or predicatively without. They also behave like verbs in that they may take an object. Greek has present, aorist, perfect, and future participles, in active, middle, and passive voice, all of which are regularly used. In contrast, Latin has a more limited number of participles and a more restricted use, so you should be cautious about imitating the practice of one language when writing the other.

2. The tenses of participles behave differently from indicative verbs. For participles that are not in indirect statement, the time of their activity is relative to the main verb on which they depend and, with the exception of the future participle, aspect is the determining feature in choice of tense.

Present participles express continuous or repeated action or process, usually contemporaneous with the main verb, even when that action has taken place in the past. Present participles represent both the present and the imperfect of indicative verbs. See **4.2**: πολλοί μοι προσιόντες. . .καὶ τῶν ἐν τῷ δικαστηρίῳ νῦν ὄντων ὑμῶν καὶ τῶν ἄλλων πολιτῶν ἠξίουν. (= "many. . .of those of you who are now in the courtroom and of the other citizens, were coming up to me and demanding. . ."). Note that προσιόντες refers to an event in the past, contemporaneous with ἠξίουν, or the equivalent of an imperfect indicative, while ὄντων refers to the present circumstances of the speaker and his audience.

Aorist expresses action completed prior to or at the time of the main verb. See **4.1**: παροινήσας οὖν καὶ ὀργισθεὶς τῶν οἰκετῶν τινι τῶν ἡμετέρων ἀποσφάττει αὐτόν (= "then drunk and enraged at one of our servants, he cut his throat.")   In this example, the man was already drunk (παροινήσας) and enraged

---

[1] For further discussion see **Smyth** §§2039-2148 and **GG** §§1560-1595

(ὀργισθεὶς) at the time he killed the servant. (Here ἀποσφάττει is an historical present.)

Perfect expresses a past event with present consequence. Perfect participles may represent the pluperfect as well as future perfect indicative. See **4.1**: τοῦ δεδεμένου ὠλιγώρει (= " he was neglectful of the man who **had been** bound...").

Future expresses future events, intention or purpose. See **4.1**: πέμπει δεῦρο ἄνδρα πευσόμενον τοῦ ἐξηγητοῦ ὅτι χρείη ποιεῖν. (= "he sent a man here for the purpose of inquiring from the exegete what he should do"). (Here πέμπει is an historical present.)

3. Participles have four basic uses:

(a) **Attributive** participles function like attributive adjectives, usually with the article. A noun may be expressed as in **1.1**: οἱ νενικηκότες ᾿Αθηναῖοι, but more often attributive participles act as noun substitutes, see **4.1**: ὁ τεθνεώς = "the dead man," ὁ ἀποθανών = "the victim," ὁ κτείνας = "the killer."

(b) **Circumstantial** participles are used adverbially, without an article. They can substitute for virtually all types of subordinate clauses, relative, temporal, conditional, causal, purpose, means or manner, concessive, or any attendant circumstance. See **4.1**: συνδήσας, καταβαλών (temporal), ἐπεξιών (means), συνειδώς, παροινήσας, ὀργισθείς (attendant circumstance); **4.2**· ὑβρισθείς (conditional or temporal), ποιοῦντος (concessive), λαβών, παθών (causal). Since these categories are labelled after the fact, they will often overlap.

Genitive Absolute: a participle usually with (but sometimes without) an accompanying noun may stand in the genitive when it is grammatically independent from the rest of the sentence. These constructions may express any kind of circumstance. See **4.2**: πάντα ποιοῦντος τούτου; **4.3**: γυναικὸς δούσης πέλεκυν.

Accusative absolute: neuter singular participles of impersonal verbs and of passive participles regularly occur in the accusative case in a construction analogous to the genitive absolute. It is not found before the fifth century and is restricted to prose writers (see **Smyth** §2077). See **4.1**: οὐδὲν ὂν πρᾶγμα.

A number of adverbs regularly appear with circumstantial participles:

ὡς is sometimes added to the participle to indicate an alleged or stated purpose of the subject; it means "on the grounds that" or "for the purpose of" (see **2.1**: ὡς ἀποκτενῶν).

ἅτε, οἷον, or **οἷα** may occur with causal participles to mean "inasmuch as" or "seeing as." These latter adverbs express the authority of the writer, in contrast to ὡς which expresses an alleged reason that the writer does not necessarily endorse.

ὥσπερ expresses comparison, meaning "as," or "as it were."

καίπερ = "although" and **ὅμως** = "nevertheless" often introduce concessive participles. Concession is discussed more fully in Chapter Fourteen, 9.

(c) **Supplementary** participles extend or complete the meaning of a verb by providing a reference for its action.[1] They may agree with the subject or the object of the main verb. Verbs that regularly require a supplementary participle include: (1) τυγχάνω, λανθάνω, and φθάνω (see **2.1**: παρὼν ἐτύγχανε); (2) Verbs meaning to begin, continue, cease, endure; (3) Verbs of sense perception when they denote a physical as opposed to a mental perception. For example, ἠκούσαμεν Δημοσθένους λέγοντος = "we heard (i.e., with our ears) Demosthenes speaking." (4) With verbs of emotion the participle often provides the cause (see **4.4**: χαίρουσι συγκατακείμενοι).

---

[1] Some verbs may take either a supplementary participle or an infinitive with some differences in meaning, for example, παύω (= "cause to cease") with a participle = "stop what is happening," but with an infinitive = "prevent something from happening," while παύομαι = "cease." Therefore, ἔπαυσε Δημοσθένην λέγοντα = "he put an end to Demosthenes speaking," ἔπαυσε Δημοσθένην λέγειν = "he prevented Demosthenes from speaking," while Δημοσθένης ἐπαύσατο λεγών = "Demosthenes ceased speaking." φαίνομαι with a participle means that something is evidently true, with an infinitive, that it appears to be true. For a list of such distinctions, see **Smyth** §§2123-2145.

(d) Participles are also used in a manner analogous to the infinitive in indirect speech, where they represent a dependent statement and the original tense of the finite verb (insofar as possible). Verbs of knowing, being ignorant, forgetting, remembering, showing, or appearing take this construction, though they may also take dependent constructions with ὅτι or ὡς followed by the indicative or optative. Verbs of sense perception take a participle in indirect speech when they refer to mental or intellectual rather than physical perception; in this case, ἠκούσαμεν Δημοσθένην λέγοντα would mean "we heard (i.e., were informed) that Demosthenes was speaking." See **4.2**: καὶ σφόδρ' ἐσπούδασεν, ἐφ' οἷς ἠδικημένῳ μοι συνῄδει; **5.5**: Περικλῆς δὲ ὁρῶν μὲν αὐτοὺς πρὸς τὸ παρὸν χαλεπαίνοντας καὶ οὐ τὰ ἄριστα φρονοῦντας. . .ἐκκλησίαν τε οὐκ ἐποίει αὐτῶν.

READINGS:

4.1 Plato, **Euthyphro** §4b7-d5. The **Euthyphro** is one of Plato's earliest dialogues, in which Socrates is engaged in inquiring about the nature of piety. Euthyphro is a rather foolish young man who is lodging a complaint against his father, because his father had bound up and cast into a ditch a servant who had killed another man in a drunken rage. As a result of this treatment the servant died of exposure.

γελοῖον, ὦ Σώκρατες, ὅτι οἴει τι διαφέρειν εἴτε ἀλλότριος εἴτε

οἰκεῖος ὁ **τεθνεώς**, ἀλλ' οὐ τοῦτο μόνον δεῖν φυλάττειν, εἴτε ἐν

δίκῃ ἔκτεινεν ὁ **κτείνας** εἴτε μή, καὶ εἰ μὲν ἐν δίκῃ, ἐᾶν, εἰ δὲ μή,

ἐπεξιέναι, ἐάνπερ ὁ **κτείνας** συνέστιός σοι καὶ ὁμοτράπεζος ᾖ· ἴσον

γὰρ τὸ μίασμα γίγνεται ἐὰν συνῇς τῷ τοιούτῳ **συνειδὼς** καὶ μὴ

ἀφοσιοῖς σεαυτόν τε καὶ ἐκεῖνον τῇ δίκῃ **ἐπεξιών**. ἐπεὶ ὅ γε

ἀποθανὼν πελάτης τις ἦν ἐμός, καὶ ὡς ἐγεωργοῦμεν ἐν τῇ Νάξῳ,

ἐθήτευεν ἐκεῖ παρ' ἡμῖν. **παροινήσας** οὖν καὶ **ὀργισθεὶς** τῶν

οἰκετῶν τινι τῶν ἡμετέρων ἀποσφάττει αὐτόν. ὁ οὖν πατὴρ

συνδήσας τοὺς πόδας καὶ τὰς χεῖρας αὐτοῦ, **καταβαλὼν** εἰς τάφρον τινά, πέμπει δεῦρο ἄνδρα **πευσόμενον** τοῦ ἐξηγητοῦ ὅτι χρείη ποιεῖν. ἐν δὲ τούτῳ τῷ χρόνῳ **τοῦ δεδεμένου** ὠλιγώρει τε καὶ ἠμέλει ὡς ἀνδροφόνου καὶ οὐδὲν **ὂν** πρᾶγμα εἰ καὶ ἀποθάνοι, ὅπερ οὖν καὶ ἔπαθεν· ὑπὸ γὰρ λιμοῦ καὶ ῥίγους καὶ τῶν δεσμῶν ἀποθνῄσκει πρὶν τὸν ἄγγελον παρὰ τοῦ ἐξηγητοῦ ἀφικέσθαι.

4.2 Demosthenes, **Against Meidias** §§1-2. Meidias was an extremely wealthy Athenian who had apparently victimized Demosthenes on several occasions at the time when he (Demosthenes) had undertaken to produce a dithyrambic chorus for the Dionysia. This is the opening of Demosthenes' speech in complaint.

τὴν μὲν ἀσέλγειαν, ὦ ἄνδρες δικασταί, καὶ τὴν ὕβριν, ᾗ πρὸς ἅπαντας ἀεὶ χρῆται Μειδίας, οὐδέν' οὐθ' ὑμῶν οὔτε τῶν ἄλλων πολιτῶν ἀγνοεῖν οἴομαι. ἐγὼ δ', ὅπερ ἂν καὶ ὑμῶν ἕκαστος **ὑβρισθεὶς** προείλετο πρᾶξαι, τοῦτο καὶ αὐτὸς ἐποίησα, καὶ προὐβαλόμην ἀδικεῖν τοῦτον περὶ τὴν ἑορτήν, οὐ μόνον πληγὰς ὑπ' αὐτοῦ **λαβὼν** τοῖς Διονυσίοις, ἀλλὰ καὶ ἄλλα πολλὰ καὶ βίαια **παθὼν** παρὰ πᾶσαν τὴν χορηγίαν. ἐπειδὴ δὲ καλῶς καὶ τὰ δίκαια **ποιῶν** ὁ δῆμος ἅπας οὕτως ὠργίσθη καὶ παρωξύνθη καὶ σφόδρ' ἐσπούδασεν, ἐφ' οἷς **ἠδικημένῳ** μοι συνῄδει, ὥστε πάντα **ποιοῦντος** τούτου καί τινων ἄλλων ὑπὲρ αὐτοῦ οὐκ ἐπείσθη οὐδ' ἀπέβλεψεν εἰς τὰς οὐσίας τὰς τούτων οὐδὲ τὰς ὑποσχέσεις, ἀλλὰ μιᾷ γνώμῃ κατεχειροτόνησεν αὐτοῦ, πολλοί μοι **προσιόντες**, ὦ ἄνδρες δικασταί, καὶ τῶν ἐν τῷ δικαστηρίῳ νῦν **ὄντων** ὑμῶν καὶ τῶν ἄλλων πολιτῶν ἠξίουν καὶ παρεκελεύοντ' ἐπεξελθεῖν καὶ παραδοῦναι τοῦτον εἰς ὑμᾶς . . . .

4.3 Thucydides 2.4.3-4 (with an omission). This is from the section describing the escape from the beseiged city of Plataea.

τῶν δὲ Πλαταιῶν τις τὰς πύλας ᾗ ἐσῆλθον καὶ αἵπερ ἦσαν μόναι **ἀνεῳγμέναι** ἔκλῃσε..., ὥστε μηδὲ ταύτῃ ἔξοδον ἔτι εἶναι. **δι-**

ωκόμενοι δὲ κατὰ τὴν πόλιν οἱ μέν τινες αὐτῶν ἐπὶ τὸ τεῖχος
ἀναβάντες ἔρριψαν ἐς τὸ ἔξω σφᾶς αὐτοὺς καὶ διεφθάρησαν οἱ
πλείους, οἱ δὲ κατὰ πύλας ἐρήμους γυναικὸς δούσης πέλεκυν
λαθόντες καὶ διακόψαντες τὸν μοχλὸν ἐξῆλθον οὐ πολλοί
(αἴσθησις γὰρ ταχεῖα ἐπεγένετο), ἄλλοι δὲ ἄλλῃ τῆς πόλεως
σποράδες ἀπώλλυντο.

4.4 Plato, **Symposium** §§191e6-192a5. This is Aristophanes' outrageous explanation of the origins of sexual desire. He claims that
humankind was originally spherical with four arms, four legs, two
faces, and two sets of genitalia, but as a punishment for hubris,
Zeus ordered them cut in half to produce the species we are
familiar with. Love is, therefore, one of the original halves
seeking its mate. Since these creatures came in three kinds—man-
woman, man-man, and woman-woman, this model accounts for
both homo- as well as heterosexual desire.

ὅσοι δὲ ἄρρενος τμῆμά εἰσι, τὰ ἄρρενα διώκουσι, καὶ τέως μὲν ἂν
παῖδες ὦσιν, ἅτε τεμάχια **ὄντα** τοῦ ἄρρενος, φιλοῦσι τοὺς ἄνδρας
καὶ χαίρουσι **συγκατακείμενοι** καὶ **συμπεπλεγμένοι** τοῖς ἀν-
δράσι, καί εἰσιν οὗτοι βέλτιστοι τῶν παίδων καὶ μειρακίων, ἅτε
ἀνδρειότατοι **ὄντες** φύσει. φασὶ δὲ δή τινες αὐτοὺς ἀναισχύντους
εἶναι, **ψευδόμενοι·** οὐ γὰρ ὑπ' ἀναισχυντίας τοῦτο δρῶσιν ἀλλ'
ὑπὸ θάρρους καὶ ἀνδρείας καὶ ἀρρενωπίας, τὸ ὅμοιον αὐτοῖς **ἀσ-
παζόμενοι.**

4.5 Plato, **Apology** §38d3-e2. Socrates argues that he has not been
convicted because he was unable to speak suitably, but because he
lacked the shamelessness to say whatever was necessary to gain
acquital.

ἴσως με οἴεσθε, ὦ ἄνδρες Ἀθηναῖοι, ἀπορίᾳ λόγων ἑαλωκέναι
τοιούτων οἷς ἂν ὑμᾶς ἔπεισα, εἰ ᾤμην δεῖν ἅπαντα ποιεῖν καὶ
λέγειν¹ ὥστε ἀποφυγεῖν τὴν δίκην. πολλοῦ γε δεῖ. ἀλλ' ἀπορίᾳ
μὲν ἑάλωκα, οὐ μέντοι λόγων, ἀλλὰ τόλμης καὶ ἀναισχυντίας καὶ

τοῦ μὴ ἐθέλειν λέγειν πρὸς ὑμᾶς τοιαῦτα οἷ᾽ ἂν ὑμῖν μὲν ἥδιστα ἦν

ἀκούειν ᾧ θρηνοῦντός τέ μου καὶ ὀδυρομένου καὶ ἄλλα

ποιοῦντος καὶ λέγοντος πολλὰ καὶ ἀνάξια ἐμοῦ, ὡς ἐγώ φημι,

οἷα δὴ καὶ εἴθισθε ὑμεῖς τῶν ἄλλων ἀκούειν.

1 The construction is an unreal condition in a relative clause.

EXERCISES:

1. Rewrite **4.3**, changing all of the conjugated verbs from past to present tense. What changes, if any, will you need to make in the participles to make the story coherent?

2. Write in Greek, using participles as often as possible. Consider in each sentence what tense and aspect of each participle is needed:

A Sentences:

1. I will pass over the injustices committed against me by Meidias.
2. They happened to open the gates after the Plataeans had entered the city.
3. There was nothing else for a man angered and insulted by Meidias' injustices to do.
4. Being unaware of the number of the Plataeans, the women opened the gates.
5. Some ran into the city, others scaled the wall; all were destroyed by the Plataeans.
6. Our servant cast my father, bound hand and foot, into a ditch.
7. We sent three men into the city to find out what ought to be done.
8. Since there was no longer any way out of the city, he cast himself over the wall.
9. The dead man happened to be my kinsman, not yours.
10. The city had a gate, but no bolt.
11. We heard Socrates saying these things to escape death.
12. Being angry at Socrates, they were persuaded to act badly.
13. Seeing as they were slices of the male, they behaved boldly, not shamefully.

14. They heard him making a great many unworthy remarks, when he was trying to escape punishment.
15. The Plataeans sent a man to Athens in order to learn about their laws.

B Sentences:

1. The many were not persuaded by my father's money, since they condemned him by a unanimous vote. He was angry at all of those who condemned him for neglecting his servant, seeing as he (the servant) was not a member of his family.

2. The most courageous of boys are those who were originally slices of the male. They pursue men, not from a desire for wealth or from shamelessness, but because they wish to embrace that which is most like themselves. This behavior is, therefore, admirable and worthy of praise.

3. Many of you happened to come up to me when I hauled Meidias into court. You were concerned about the wealth of his friends, but you were persuaded neither by their promises nor by their threats. Nor did you consider my wealth but only the blows I suffered from him. Afterwards, some of the citizens decided to put a stop to Meidias' violent and lawless behavior. First they bound him, then they cut his throat. But in doing these things they were neglectful of any pollution they might incur.

CHAPTER FIVE—INFINITIVES[1]

1. The infinitive is both a noun and a verb. As a noun it may stand as the subject or object of a finite verb, and it may be qualified by a neuter singular definite article. As a verb it may be modified by adverbs. Infinitives may be active, middle, or passive in voice, and present, aorist, perfect, or future in tense.

They may be used in both direct and indirect speech with some differences. In direct speech, present and aorist infinitives are most commonly used, with the tense of the infinitive indicating aspect. The negative is μή.

Since present and aorist infinitives can refer to future events, the **future** infinitive is rarely used except in indirect speech. The following distinction between direct speech (ἐλπίζω ταύτῃ τῇ ἡμέρᾳ ἀφικέσθαι ="I hope to arrive today") and indirect speech (ἐλπίζω αὐτὸν ἀφίξεσθαι ="I hope that he will arrive") is usually drawn.

The infinitive in indirect speech represents the original tense of the finite verb insofar as it is possible. The imperfect indicative is represented by a present infinitive and pluperfect by a perfect infinitive. The negative form of the direct statement is retained (usually οὐ).

2. An infinitive may be used as a substantive, to represent an indicative statement in indirect speech, to complete the meaning of a noun, adjective, or finite verb, or absolutely.

(a) The infinitive may stand as the subject or object of a finite verb, particularly with impersonal verbs like ἔξεστι, δεῖ, χρή, πρέπει, e.g., χρὴ αὐτοὺς τρέχειν = "they must run." It may also stand in apposition to a noun in the nominative or accusative.

---

[1] For further discussion see **Smyth** §§1966-2038, **GG** §§1520-1559 and **MT** §§741-810.

(b) The addition of the neuter singular forms of the definite article to the infinitive extended its flexibility and allowed it to be used after prepositions. This construction, called the **articular infinitive**, is very common in Attic prose. It may be quite extensive, with subject, object, prepositional and adverbial qualifiers all attached to the article-verb unit. If the subject of the articular infinitive is the same as the leading verb, it is normally nominative; otherwise it is accusative. The negative is μή. Consider the following examples:

(1) Plato, **Crito** §50b7-9: ἴσως ἂν εἴποιεν (sc. οἱ νόμοι) ὅτι "ὦ Σώκρατες, μὴ θαύμαζε τὰ λεγόμενα, ἀλλ' ἀποκρίνου, ἐπειδὴ καὶ εἴωθας χρῆσθαι **τῷ ἐρωτᾶν τε καὶ ἀποκρίνεσθαι.**" "Perhaps the laws would say: 'Socrates, don't be surprised at these remarks, but answer, seeing as you are in the habit of employing questioning and answering.' "

(2) Demosthenes, **Against Meidias** §37: τίς γὰρ οὐκ οἶδεν ὑμῶν **τοῦ μὲν πολλὰ τοιαῦτα γίγνεσθαι τὸ μὴ κολάζεσθαι τοὺς ἐξαμαρτάνοντας** αἴτιον ὄν, **τοῦ δὲ μηδέν' ὑβρίζειν τὸ λοιπὸν τὸ δίκην τὸν ἀεὶ ληφθένθ',** ἣν προσήκει, διδόναι μόνον αἴτιον ἂν γενόμενον; "For who of you is unaware that the reason for many of these kinds of outrages happening (τοῦ μὲν πολλὰ τοιαῦτα γίγνεσθαι) is the failure to chastise the offenders (τὸ μὴ κολάζεσθαι τοὺς ἐξαμαρτάνοντας), and the single way of discouraging anyone from committing assault in the future (τοῦ δὲ μηδέν' ὑβρίζειν τὸ λοιπὸν) would be (ἂν γενόμενον = potential optative after a verb of knowing) the exacting of a suitable punishment from anyone who is ever caught (τὸ δίκην τὸν ἀεὶ ληφθένθ', ἣν προσήκει, διδόναι) ."

Here the two articular infinitives are subjects with αἴτιον as predicate: τὸ μὴ κολάζεσθαι τοὺς ἐξαμαρτάνοντας and τὸ δίκην τὸν ἀεὶ ληφθέντ', ἣν προσήκει, διδόναι; there are also two articular infinitives in the genitive with αἴτιον: τοῦ μὲν πολλὰ τοιαῦτα γίγνεσθαι and τοῦ δὲ μηδέν' ὑβρίζειν τὸ λοιπὸν.

The articular infinitive when following a preposition may express **purpose**. The most common prepositions used are ἕνεκα (= "for the sake of") and ὑπέρ (= "on behalf of") + the genitive; ἐπί (= "to" or "for") + the dative.

Isocrates, **To Demonicus** §19: μὴ κατόκνει μακρὰν ὁδὸν πορεύεσθαι πρὸς τοὺς διδάσκειν τι χρήσιμον ἐπαγγελλομένους· αἰσχρὸν γὰρ τοὺς μὲν ἐμπόρους τηλικαῦτα πελάγη διαπερᾶν **ἕνεκα τοῦ πλείω ποιῆσαι τὴν ὑπάρχουσαν οὐσίαν,** τοὺς δὲ νεωτέρους μηδὲ τὰς κατὰ γῆν πορείας ὑπομένειν **ἐπὶ τῷ βελτίω καταστῆναι τὴν αὐτῶν διάνοιαν.** "Do not shrink from making a long journey to those who claim to teach something useful; for it is shameful for merchants to cross a vast sea for the sake of increasing their wealth, while the young do not even abide land journeys in order to improve their understanding."

Thucydides uses the articular infinitive in the genitive, without a preposition, and frequently in its negative form to express purpose, e.g., τοῦ or τοῦ μή + infinitive; see below 5.4. See also below (d 5).

(c) An infinitive phrase may be used with a verb of saying or thinking, e.g., τοῦτ᾽ εἰπεῖν τὸν Πλάτωνα πιστεύομεν ("We believe that Plato said this"). This use is called indirect statement and will be discussed below, Chapter Eighteen.

The subject of an infinitive in indirect statement is normally in the accusative case, unless it is the same as the subject of the main verb, e.g., ἔφασαν καλὸν κἀγαθὸν αὐτὸν εἶναι = "they said he was a gentleman," but καλὸς κἀγαθὸς ἔφη εἶναι = "he said he was a gentleman." However, pronoun subjects, if they are expressed, are regularly accusative, e.g., ἡγησάμενος ἐμαυτὸν καλὸν κἀγαθὸν εἶναι = "considering **myself** to be a gentleman."

(d) A wide range of verbs take a so-called "object" infinitive, that is, an infinitive to complete their meaning or to define their goal. The range is similar to English. Present or aorist tenses are most commonly used. They include:

(1) Verbs expressing will or desire, choosing, commanding, daring, deciding, entrusting, forbidding, preferring, or verbs denoting some ability. Verbs of will or desire behave in a way analogous to verbs of effort in that they may also take ὅπως with the future indicative or subjunctive (see Chapter Eight).

With respect to verbs of ordering or commanding (see 1.1: κήρυκας ἐξέπεμψεν εἰς τὴν Ἑλλάδα, **προστάξας** εἰς πάσας τὰς πόλεις **ἰέναι** καὶ τοὺς Ἕλληνας **αἰτεῖν** ὕδωρ καὶ γῆν), note that Latin usage differs from Greek in that a subjunctive construction (ut + the subjunctive) follows most verbs of ordering.

Nouns, adjectives, or adverbs expressing similar relations as the verbs listed above, particularly words denoting ability, fitness, or necessity, e.g., δυνατὸς μάχεσθαι, δεινὸς λέγειν, ἀνάγκη ἐστὶ τοῦτο ποιῆσαι.

(2) Verbs expressing hoping, promising, expecting or swearing may take an "object" infinitive or an infinitive in indirect statement, see example of ἐλπίζω above, 1.

(3) Occasionally the infinitive is used to limit the meaning of a noun, adjective, adverb, or even another verb to a particular action or circumstance. The infinitive is usually active or middle in form. This is called "epexegetic," and while it is found more frequently in poetry it also occurs in prose. For example, Homer **Od.** 8.366: θαῦμα ἰδέσθαι = "a marvel to see"; Xen., **Mem.** 1.6.9: χαλεπώτατα εὑρεῖν = "hardest to find."

(4) The infinitive is used after ὥστε to express a natural result (see Chapter Eleven).

(5) Occasionally an infinitive (without an article) is used to express purpose after verbs meaning to give, entrust, appoint, take, or receive. These verbs may also take a future participle or a dependent clause (ἵνα etc. + subjunctive) with the same sense (see Chapter Ten).

(e) The infinitive can be used absolutely, that is, without a leading verb, in certain idiomatic expressions: ὡς ἔπος εἰπεῖν = "as one might say"; ὡς ἐμοὶ δοκεῖν = "it seems to me"; ὀλίγου δεῖν = "almost " (literally, "lacking little"); ἑκὼν εἶναι = "willingly."

READINGS:

5.1 Thucydides 6.47.1: The Athenians have just launched the ruinous Sicilian expedition of 415 B.C. Three ships that had been sent ahead to Egesta have now sent news that the promised amounts of money from plunder did not exist. Nicias and his generals at Rhegium are debating what to do. Nicias' advice is as follows.

καὶ Νικίου μὲν ἦν γνώμη **πλεῖν** ἐπὶ Σελινοῦντα πάσῃ τῇ στρατιᾷ, ἐφ' ὅπερ μάλιστα ἐπέμφθησαν, καὶ ἢν (= ἐὰν) μὲν παρέχωσι χρήματα παντὶ τῷ στρατεύματι Ἐγεσταῖοι, πρὸς ταῦτα **βουλεύεσθαι**, εἰ δὲ μή, ταῖς ἑξήκοντα ναυσίν, ὅσασπερ ᾐτήσαντο, ἀξιοῦν **διδόναι** αὐτοὺς τροφήν, καὶ παραμείναντας Σελινουντίους ἢ βίᾳ ἢ ξυμβάσει **διαλλάξαι** αὐτοῖς, καὶ οὕτω παραπλεύσαντας τὰς ἄλλας πόλεις καὶ ἐπιδείξαντας μὲν τὴν δύναμιν τῆς Ἀθηναίων πόλεως, δηλώσαντας δὲ τὴν ἐς τοὺς φίλους καὶ ξυμμάχους προθυμίαν, **ἀποπλεῖν** οἴκαδε, ἢν (= ἐὰν) μή τι δι' ὀλίγου καὶ ἀπὸ τοῦ ἀδοκήτου ἢ Λεοντίνους οἷοί τε ὦσιν **ὠφελῆσαι** ἢ τῶν ἄλλων τινὰ πόλεων **προσαγαγέσθαι**, καὶ τῇ πόλει δαπανῶντας τὰ οἰκεῖα μὴ **κινδυνεύειν**.

5.2 Lysias, **Against Eratosthenes** §§1-2. Lysias was a member of a prominent resident alien family in Athens—his father and brothers are characters in Plato's **Republic**—that was proscribed during the reign of the Thirty tyrants. When the democracy was re-established, Lysias prepared this legal attack against Eratosthenes, one of the Thirty tyrants. This is the opening of the speech.

οὐκ **ἄρξασθαί** μοι δοκεῖ ἄπορον **εἶναι**, ὦ ἄνδρες δικασταί, τῆς κατηγορίας, ἀλλὰ **παύσασθαι** λέγοντι· τοιαῦτα αὐτοῖς τὸ μέγεθος καὶ τοσαῦτα τὸ πλῆθος εἴργασται, ὥστε μήτ' ἂν[1] ψευδόμενον δεινότερα τῶν ὑπαρχόντων **κατηγορῆσαι**, μήτε τἀληθῆ βουλόμενον **εἰπεῖν** ἅπαντα **δύνασθαι**, ἀλλ' ἀνάγκη ἢ τὸν κατήγορον **ἀπειπεῖν** ἢ τὸν χρόνον **ἐπιλιπεῖν**. τοὐναντίον δέ μοι δοκοῦμεν **πείσεσθαι** ἢ ἐν τῷ πρὸ τοῦ χρόνῳ. πρότερον μὲν γὰρ ἔδει τὴν ἔχθραν τοὺς κατηγοροῦντας **ἐπιδεῖξαι**, ἥτις εἴη πρὸς τοὺς φεύγοντας· νυνὶ δὲ παρὰ τῶν φευγόντων χρὴ **πυνθάνεσθαι** ἥτις ἦν αὐτοῖς πρὸς τὴν πόλιν ἔχθρα, ἀνθ' ὅτου τοιαῦτα ἐτόλμησαν εἰς αὐτὴν **ἐξαμαρτάνειν**. οὐ μέντοι ὡς οὐκ ἔχων οἰκείας ἔχθρας καὶ συμφορὰς τοὺς λόγους ποιοῦμαι, ἀλλ' ὡς ἅπασι πολλῆς ἀφθονίας οὔσης ὑπὲρ τῶν ἰδίων ἢ ὑπὲρ τῶν δημοσίων **ὀργίζεσθαι**.

[1]The addition of ἄν to the infinitive makes the statement potential (see Chapter Thirteen).

5.3 Plato, **Apology** §29a4-b9. Socrates is talking about the reason that men fear death.

τὸ γάρ τοι θάνατον **δεδιέναι**, ὦ ἄνδρες, οὐδὲν ἄλλο ἐστὶν ἢ **δοκεῖν** σοφὸν **εἶναι** μὴ ὄντα· **δοκεῖν** γὰρ **εἰδέναι** ἐστὶν ἃ οὐκ οἶδεν. οἶδε μὲν γὰρ οὐδεὶς τὸν θάνατον οὐδ' εἰ τυγχάνει τῷ ἀνθρώπῳ πάντων μέγιστον ὂν τῶν ἀγαθῶν, δεδίασι δ' ὡς εὖ εἰδότες ὅτι μέγιστον τῶν κακῶν ἐστι. καίτοι πῶς οὐκ ἀμαθία ἐστὶν αὕτη ἡ ἐπονείδιστος, ἡ τοῦ **οἴεσθαι εἰδέναι** ἃ οὐκ οἶδεν; ἐγὼ δ', ὦ ἄνδρες, τούτῳ. . .ἴσως διαφέρω τῶν πολλῶν ἀνθρώπων, καὶ εἰ δή τῳ σοφώτερός του φαίην εἶναι, τούτῳ ἄν, ὅτι οὐκ εἰδὼς ἱκανῶς περὶ τῶν ἐν Ἅιδου οὕτω καὶ οἴομαι οὐκ **εἰδέναι**· τὸ δὲ **ἀδικεῖν** καὶ **ἀπειθεῖν** τῷ βελτίονι καὶ θεῷ καὶ ἀνθρώπῳ, ὅτι κακὸν καὶ αἰσχρόν ἐστιν οἶδα. πρὸ οὖν τῶν κακῶν ὧν οἶδα ὅτι κακά ἐστιν, ἃ μὴ οἶδα εἰ καὶ ἀγαθὰ ὄντα τυγχάνει, οὐδέποτε φοβήσομαι οὐδὲ φεύξομαι.

5.4 Thucydides 2.22.1. At the beginning of the Peloponnesian war, Pericles decides that public sentiments are too volatile and chooses not to call an Athenian assembly.

Περικλῆς δὲ ὁρῶν μὲν αὐτοὺς πρὸς τὸ παρὸν χαλεπαίνοντας καὶ οὐ τὰ ἄριστα φρονοῦντας, πιστεύων δὲ ὀρθῶς γιγνώσκειν περὶ τοῦ μὴ ἐπεξιέναι, ἐκκλησίαν τε οὐκ ἐποίει αὐτῶν οὐδὲ ξύλλογον οὐδένα, τοῦ μὴ ὀργῇ τι μᾶλλον ἢ γνώμῃ ξυνελθόντας ἐξαμαρτεῖν, τήν τε πόλιν ἐφύλασσε καὶ δι' ἡσυχίας μάλιστα ὅσον ἐδύνατο εἶχεν.

EXERCISES:

Write in Greek, using an infinitive construction whenever possible:

A sentences:

1. It was not the asking of a question but the answering that he found difficult.
2. A good man should not fear death.
3. It was not his plan to provide their army with money, but to sail back to the city.
4. They did not appear to grow angry at his hostility to the prosecutor.
5. It was unnecessary to tell everything done by the defendant in the past.
6. Seeming to know is better than seeming not to know.
7. We wish to be able to accuse the defendants of what they actually did, not what they only appear to have done.
8. The army did not wish to be abandoned by Nicias, but they did not dare to anger him.
9. Because of their fear of death, they will commit more injustices than it is possible to mention.
10. Because of the anger of the people, he was unable to help those in the city.
11. Sailing around to all their cities, he displayed the might of the Athenians.

12. When the citizens of Selinous saw the whole fleet sailing past, they urged each other not to risk their city or their property by injuring the Athenians.

13. They wished him to hold an assembly, but he wished to protect the city from their anger.

14. Well begun is half done.

15. I was unable to recount the depth of their villainy in the time allotted.

B Sentences:

1. I am at a loss to accuse this man who has committed crimes of such magnitude. I have heard many others accusing him of great crimes but they have not been able to tell all that he has done. Nevertheless, I shall demonstrate to you his great hatred of the city on account of which he did not cease to commit crimes against her.

2. We will not make those who profess to teach angry because we do not seem to know the answer. Only those who pretend to know something when they do not anger their teachers, because such students are unable to improve their understanding. For teachers themselves do not know everything that it is possible to know. But only the teacher who is wise can admit this.

3. You will not wish to risk losing all your money by doing us an injustice. For you will be unable to protect your property or yourself if we become angry. Further, it is shameful for you to become angry at us because we are expecting you to obey the laws. Rather, you should not fear experiencing injustice, but committing injustice. It is best to avoid what is shameful and to do what you know to be good. By doing this you will improve your understanding.

CHAPTER SIX—QUESTIONS[1]

1. In Greek, as in English, questions may occur in any tense, though present, aorist, and future are the most common. Questions can be either direct or indirect. The latter are discussed in Chapter Nineteen. They may use indicative, subjunctive, or optative moods.

(a) Ordinary questions are found in the **indicative**, e.g., τίς ἐποίησεν; = "Who did it?" or ποῦ οἰκεῖς; = "Where do you live?"

(b) Questions about what is to be done are called **deliberative**. When concerned with the **present or future**, they take the **subjunctive**, e.g., **12.3**: μὴ ἀποκρίνωμαι. . .ἀλλ᾽ ἕτερον εἴπω; = "am I not to answer, but to say something else?" Normally they occur in the first person, or occasionally in the third, usually in a context where the speaker is referring to himself or herself in the third person. As with infinitives, choice between present or aorist subjunctive is one of aspect.

Deliberative questions about the **past** are expressed in the **indicative with a verb of necessity** or possibility, e.g., τί ἔδει ποιεῖν; = "What should she have done?" or with ἔμελλον + an infinitive, or the verbal adjective (-τέον) (see Chapter Eight).

(c) The **potential optative or indicative** + ἄν is very commonly used in questions, e.g., Pl. *Sym.* § 198B5: τίς οὐκ ἂν ἐξεπλάγη ἀκούων; = "who would not have been amazed at hearing?" For potential optative see Chapter Thirteen.

(d) An interrogative may be used with a participle, for example, τί βουλόμενος ἦλθες; = "wishing what," i.e., "with what purpose did you come?" or τί ποιήσαντες πείσομέν σε; = "having done what," i.e., "by what action shall we persuade you?"

---

[1]For further discussion see **Smyth** §§2636-2662, **GG** §§1601-1606, 1367, 1490.

2. Questions may be introduced in a number of ways:

(a) Those demanding the answer "yes" or "no" may take the form of statements with interrogative inflexion, e.g., ἐποίησας; = "you did it?" or οὐκ ἐποίησας; = "Didn't you do it?"

With οὐ a positive answer seems to be invited or even demanded, e.g., **6.1**: ταῦτα οὐχὶ καλῶς λέγεται; KP. καλῶς. (= "Is this not a fair statement?"   Cr.   "Yes it is.")

With μή the meaning is "can it be that?" See **7.2**: ἆρά γε μὴ ἐμοῦ προμηθῇ; = "Can it be that you are concerned for me?" **Note** that μή does not mean that a negative answer is expected as is often stated in textbooks. See Denniston **Greek Particles** p. 47 (5).

(b) Questions are also introduced by the interrogative particles, usually ἆρα (not to be confused with ἄρα) and sometimes ἦ. These words are untranslatable; they behave like question marks set at the beginning instead of at the end of a written question. They are often combined with οὐ and μή without altering the meaning, e.g., ἆρα τοῦτ' ἐποίησας; = "Did you do this?" or ἆρ' οὐ τοῦτ' ἐποίησας; = "Didn't you do this?"

(c) πότερον (or πότερα) . . . ἤ (= Latin utrum . . .an) offers the listener two alternatives, πότερον λέγεις τοῦτ' ἢ ἐκεῖνο; = "are you saying this or that?"   ἤ alone may introduce the second question, e.g., λέγεις τοῦτ' ἢ ἐκεῖνο;

3. Sometimes it is clear from the context that a question does not expect an answer (since the speaker already knows the answer), but is being asked for emphasis or color. These are called **rhetorical questions.** Virtually any form of question may be used rhetorically.

READINGS:

6.1 Plato, **Crito** §47a2-c4: Socrates is arguing in this passage that it is not necessary to listen to men's opinions in general, but only the opinions of those who have some expert or useful knowledge.

σκόπει δήφούχ ἱκανῶς δοκεῖ σοι λέγεσθαι ὅτι οὐ πάσας χρὴ τὰς δόξας τῶν ἀνθρώπων τιμᾶν ἀλλὰ τὰς μέν, τὰς δ' οὔ, οὐδὲ πάντων ἀλλὰ τῶν μέν, τῶν δ' οὔ; τί φής; ταῦτα οὐχὶ καλῶς λέγεται;

ΚΡ. καλῶς.

ΣΩ. οὐκοῦν τὰς μὲν χρηστὰς τιμᾶν, τὰς δὲ πονηρὰς μή;

ΚΡ. ναί.

ΣΩ. χρησταὶ δὲ οὐχ αἱ τῶν φρονίμων, πονηραὶ δὲ αἱ τῶν ἀφρόνων;

ΚΡ. πῶς δ' οὔ;

ΣΩ. φέρε δή, πῶς αὖ τὰ τοιαῦτα ἐλέγετο; γυμναζόμενος ἀνὴρ καὶ τοῦτο πράττων πότερον παντὸς ἀνδρὸς ἐπαίνῳ καὶ ψόγῳ καὶ δόξῃ τὸν νοῦν προσέχει, ἢ ἑνὸς μόνου ἐκείνου ὃς ἂν τυγχάνῃ ἰατρὸς ἢ παιδοτρίβης ὤν;

ΚΡ. ἑνὸς μόνου.

ΣΩ. οὐκοῦν φοβεῖσθαι χρὴ τοὺς ψόγους καὶ ἀσπάζεσθαι τοὺς ἐπαίνους τοὺς τοῦ ἑνὸς ἐκείνου ἀλλὰ μὴ τοὺς τῶν πολλῶν.

ΚΡ. δῆλα δή.

ΣΩ. ταύτῃ ἄρα αὐτῷ πρακτέον καὶ γυμναστέον καὶ ἐδεστέον γε καὶ ποτέον, ᾗ ἂν τῷ ἑνὶ δοκῇ, τῷ ἐπιστάτῃ καὶ ἐπαΐοντι, μᾶλλον ἢ ᾗ σύμπασι τοῖς ἄλλοις.

ΚΡ. ἔστι ταῦτα.

ΣΩ. εἶεν. ἀπειθήσας δὲ τῷ ἑνὶ καὶ ἀτιμάσας αὐτοῦ τὴν δόξαν καὶ τοὺς ἐπαίνους, τιμήσας δὲ τοὺς τῶν πολλῶν [λόγους] καὶ μηδὲν ἐπαϊόντων, ἆρα οὐδὲν κακὸν πείσεται;

ΚΡ. πῶς γὰρ οὔ;

6.2 Lysias, Against Eratosthenes §§24-26. This is a section of Lysias' speech employing the rhetorical device of question and answer. Lysias pretends to be interrogating Eratosthenes:

ἀνάβηθι οὖν μοι καὶ ἀπόκριναι, ὅ τι ἄν σε ἐρωτῶ. ("Now step into the witness box for me and answer whatever question I ask you.")

ἀπήγαγες Πολέμαρχον ἢ οὔ;

τὰ ὑπὸ τῶν ἀρχόντων προσταχθέντα δεδιὼς ἐποίουν.

ἦσθα δ' ἐν τῷ βουλευτηρίῳ, ὅτε οἱ λόγοι ἐγίγνοντο περὶ ἡμῶν; ἦ.

πότερον συνηγόρευες τοῖς κελεύουσιν ἀποκτεῖναι ἢ ἀντέλεγες;

ἀντέλεγον.

ἵνα μὴ ἀποθάνωμεν;

ἵνα μὴ ἀποθάνητε.

ἡγούμενος ἡμᾶς ἄδικα πάσχειν ἢ δίκαια;

ἄδικα.

εἶτ', ὦ σχετλιώτατε πάντων, ἀντέλεγες μὲν ἵνα σώσειας, συνελάμβανες δὲ ἵνα ἀποκτείνῃς; καὶ ὅτε μὲν τὸ πλῆθος ἦν ὑμῶν κύριον τῆς σωτηρίας τῆς ἡμετέρας, ἀντιλέγειν φῂς τοῖς βουλομένοις ἡμᾶς ἀπολέσαι, ἐπειδὴ δὲ ἐπὶ σοὶ μόνῳ ἐγένετο καὶ σῶσαι Πολέμαρχον καὶ μή, εἰς τὸ δεσμωτήριον ἀπήγαγες; εἶθ' ὅτι μέν, ὡς φῂς, ἀντειπὼν οὐδὲν ὠφέλησας, ἀξιοῖς χρηστὸς νομίζεσθαι, ὅτι δὲ συλλαβὼν ἀπέκτεινας, οὐκ ἐμοὶ καὶ τουτοισὶ δοῦναι δίκην;

6.3 Demosthenes, Against Timocrates §§152-153. Demosthenes is discussing what he considers to be the pernicious habit of using the legally constituted right to introduce new laws or psephisms (νόμοις καὶ ψηφίσμασι) to abrogate existing laws.

ἡ γὰρ πόλις ἡμῶν, ὦ ἄνδρες δικασταί, νόμοις καὶ ψηφίσμασιν διοικεῖται. εἰ δή τις τὰ ψήφῳ κεκριμένα νόμῳ καινῷ λύσει, τί πέρας ἔσται; ἢ πῶς τοῦτον δίκαιόν ἐστι νόμον προσαγορεύειν, ἀλλ' οὐκ ἀνομίαν; ἢ πῶς οὐ τῆς μεγίστης ὀργῆς ὁ τοιοῦτος νομοθέτης ἄξιός ἐστιν; ἐγὼ μὲν γὰρ τῶν ἐσχάτων νομίζω, οὐχ ὅτι τοῦτον μόνον τὸν νόμον ἔθηκεν, ἀλλ' ὅτι καὶ τοῖς ἄλλοις ὁδὸν δείκνυσι καὶ περὶ δικαστηρίων καταλύσεως καὶ περὶ τῶν φευγόντων καθόδου καὶ περὶ τῶν ἄλλων τῶν δεινοτάτων. τί γὰρ κωλύει, ὦ ἄνδρες δικασταί, εἰ οὗτος χαίρων ἀπαλλάξει ὁ τοιοῦτον νόμον τιθείς, ἕτερον φανῆναι ἄλλο τι τῶν τῆς πόλεως ἰσχυροτάτων καταλύοντα νόμῳ καινῷ;

EXERCISES:

Write the following questions in Greek:

A Sentences:

1. Where are we to go? What friends are we to seek? How are we to escape?
2. How should we escape if you are concerned for our reputation?
3. Will you hesitate to escape? Must we suffer these things?
4. Didn't you say that no one must ever commit injustice?
5. Perhaps it is a fine thing to act unjustly towards your trainer?
6. Didn't you give him the money? Is it possible that he is telling the truth when he says he did not receive it?
7. Are we to fear the opinions of the many? Or only those of a man who knows?
8. Didn't he pay attention to the praises of his teacher?
9. Who will honor the wicked more than the just?
10. Where did he happen to exercise?
11. Will you answer whatever question I put to you?
12. Did those who were urging the death sentence for us speak against you?
13. Why did you say such unjust things as these?
14. Did they wish to be considered good citizens? Would they then have killed Polemarchus?
15. So you spoke in favor of killing us after all?

B Sentences:

1. How can a man who refuses to follow the guidance of someone who understands how to exercise the body, but instead listens to the opinions of the many not come to harm? Surely he runs the risk of serious injury? No one at all, it is clear. Well then, why do you not exercise and eat properly? Have you not been instructed wisely?

2. A. Were you one of those in the council chamber who spoke against those who would kill
    honorable citizens? B. I was.
    A. Did you then later arrest my brother Polemarchus? B. I did.
    A. Because he was guilty of a crime or not? B. He was not.
    A. Then why did you arrest him? B. Because I was afraid of the Thirty.
        A. What statements were made about us when you were present? B. How am I to answer?
        If I tell the truth you will not believe me; if I lie you will suppose I am speaking the truth.

4. What penalty do you think a man should pay for trying to overturn an existing law? A law that has been passed by a vote of the assembly when many of you were present? What are we to do to prevent such a man from destroying our city? None of you can answer me, it is clear. Then I will tell you what you can do to prevent this happening in the future.

CHAPTER SEVEN—COMMANDS[1]

Commands and prohibitions may be expressed by the following constructions in Greek:

1. The **imperative** by its nature refers to the future. Second and third person imperatives, singular and plural, active, middle, and passive forms, are used regularly. The difference between present and aorist is one of aspect or stage of action.

Present imperatives urge one to continue an action thought of as already going on, or to perform a repeated or continuous action; for example, in **7.1**, present imperatives are used for prescriptive behavior (εὐσέβει, τίμα).

Aorist imperatives urge one to begin a single momentary action (see **7.2**: ἔασον, εἰπέ μοι).

Perfect imperative commands a state or state of mind (compare English "Be prepared!"). Its use is confined to some standardized expressions, mostly in the middle voice, like μέμνησο (from μιμνήσκω) = "be mindful", ἔρρωσο (from ῥώννυμι) = "be healthy," "farewell" (like Latin *vale*), and of course ἴσθι / ἴστε (from οἶδα) = "know," "be sure."

2. The imperative has no first person singular or plural, so in contexts where a speaker wishes to command himself or herself to do something, the second person singular imperative may be used. More frequently exhortations by a speaker to himself/herself and others may be given in the first person plural of the subjunctive, present or aorist, as required. This is called the **hortatory subjunctive**. The negative is expressed with μή:

φεύγωμεν, μὴ μένωμεν = "let us flee, not stay"

---

[1] For further discussion see **Smyth** §§1820, 1835-1844, 1864, 2155 and **GG** §§1341-1354.

Occasionally the first person singular is used, e.g., εἴπω, with the sense of "let me tell you." With the negative its use is normally confined to poetry. For details see **MT** §257.

3. **Prohibitions** (negative imperatives) against continuing action are expressed by μή + present imperative forms (see **7.1**: μήτε . . .στέργε, μήτε. . .ἀποδέχου). However, for momentary action (aorist aspect), note that in prose **μή + the aorist subjunctive is always substituted** for the second person imperative form (see **7.2**: μήτε. . .ἀποκάμῃς) and usually for the third person imperative.

4. Requests that seem to be half-statement, half-question may also be made in the **future indicative**. Usage includes:

(a) The future with οὐ = "won't you?" (see **7.3**: οὔκουν καλεῖς αὐτὸν).

(b) The future with οὐ μή (a strong prohibition) = "you must not" (see **7.3**: οὔκουν . . . μὴ ἀφήσεις;).

(c) The future following ὅπως μή (a desire to avert something) ="see that you don't". ὅπως μή may sometimes be introduced by σκόπει or φυλάσσου. See also Chapter Eight.

5. Certain imperative forms like φέρε, ἄγε, or ἴθι are sometimes found in combination with other imperatives, like English "come now," "look," "consider."

In addition to imperative forms and the hortatory subjunctive, Greek has a number of expressions to indicate obligation or necessity. These are taken up in the next chapter.

READINGS:

7.1 Isocrates, **To Demonicus** §§13-16 (with omissions). This section gives advice about honoring the gods and one's parents.

πρῶτον μὲν οὖν **εὐσέβει** τὰ πρὸς τοὺς θεούς, μὴ μόνον θύων, ἀλλὰ καὶ τοῖς ὅρκοις ἐμμένων· ἐκεῖνο μὲν γὰρ τῆς τῶν χρημάτων εὐπορίας σημεῖον, τοῦτο δὲ τῆς τῶν τρόπων καλοκαγαθίας τεκμήριον. τίμα τὸ δαιμόνιον ἀεὶ μὲν, μάλιστα δὲ μετὰ τῆς πόλεως· οὕτω γὰρ δόξεις ἅμα τε τοῖς θεοῖς θύειν καὶ τοῖς νόμοις ἐμμένειν.

Τοιοῦτος **γίγνου** περὶ τοὺς γονεῖς, οἵους ἂν εὔξαιο περὶ σεαυτὸν γενέσθαι τοὺς σεαυτοῦ παῖδας. . .

Μήτε γέλωτα προπετῆ **στέργε, μήτε** λόγον μετὰ θράσους **ἀποδέχου**· τὸ μὲν γὰρ ἀνόητον, τὸ δὲ μανικόν. . .

τοὺς μὲν θεοὺς **φοβοῦ**, τοὺς δὲ γονεῖς **τίμα**, τοὺς δὲ φίλους **αἰσχύνου**, τοῖς δὲ νόμοις **πείθου**.

7.2 Plato, **Crito** §§44e1-45b9 (with omissions). Crito is trying to discover the reason why Socrates will not leave Athens after the court has voted to execute him.

ΚΡ. ταῦτα μὲν δὴ οὕτως **ἐχέτω**· τάδε δέ, ὦ Σώκρατες, **εἰπέ** μοι.

ἀρά γε μὴ ἐμοῦ προμηθῇ καὶ τῶν ἄλλων ἐπιτηδείων μή, ἐὰν σὺ ἐνθένδε ἐξέλθῃς, οἱ συκοφάνται ἡμῖν πράγματα παρέχωσιν . . ., καὶ ἀναγκασθῶμεν ἢ καὶ πᾶσαν τὴν οὐσίαν ἀποβαλεῖν ἢ συχνὰ χρή-ματα, ἢ καὶ ἄλλο τι πρὸς τούτοις παθεῖν; εἰ γάρ τι τοιοῦτον φοβῇ, **ἔασον** αὐτὸ χαίρειν. . . ἀλλ' ἐμοὶ **πείθου** καὶ μὴ ἄλλως **ποίει**.

ΣΩ. καὶ ταῦτα προμηθοῦμαι, ὦ Κρίτων, καὶ ἄλλα πολλά.

ΚΡ. **μήτε** τοίνυν ταῦτα **φοβοῦ**. . . **μήτε**, ταῦτα φοβούμενος **ἀποκάμῃς** σαυτὸν σῶσαι, **μήτε**, ὃ ἔλεγες ἐν τῷ δικαστηρίῳ, δυσχερές σοι **γενέσθω** ὅτι οὐκ ἂν ἔχοις ἐξελθὼν ὅτι χρῷο σαυτῷ.

7.3 Plato, **Symposium** §§174e12-175b3 (with omissions). Aristode-mus has just arrived at Agathon's house; Socrates was accompanying him, but became abstracted and is now standing on the neighbor's porch, lost in thought. The narrative portions are related in indirect statement, while the embedded speeches are direct statement.

"καλῶς γ'," ἔφη (sc. Agathon), "ποιῶν σύ· ἀλλὰ ποῦ ἔστιν οὗτος (sc. Socrates)";

"ὄπισθεν ἐμοῦ ἄρτι εἰσῄει· ἀλλὰ θαυμάζω καὶ αὐτὸς ποῦ ἂν εἴη."

"οὐ **σκέψῃ**," ἔφη, "παῖ, . . . καὶ **εἰσάξεις** Σωκράτη; σὺ δ'," ἦ δ' ὅς,
"Ἀριστόδημε, παρ' Ἐρυξίμαχον **κατακλίνου**." . . .
ἄλλον δέ τινα τῶν παίδων ἥκειν ἀγγέλλοντα ὅτι "Σωκράτης οὗτος
ἀναχωρήσας ἐν τῷ τῶν γειτόνων προθύρῳ ἕστηκεν, κἀμοῦ
καλοῦντος οὐκ ἐθέλει εἰσιέναι."

"ἄτοπόν γ', " ἔφη, "λέγεις· οὔκουν **καλεῖς** αὐτὸν καὶ μὴ **ἀφήσεις**";

"μηδαμῶς, ἀλλ' **ἔατε** αὐτόν. ἔθος γάρ τι τοῦτ' ἔχει. . . ἥξει δ'
αὐτίκα, ὡς ἐγὼ οἶμαι. μὴ οὖν **κινεῖτε**, ἀλλ' **ἔατε**."

7.4 Thucydides 6.34.1-3 (with omissions): Hermocrates is advising
the Syracusans what to do about the Athenian invasion.

"θαρσοῦντες οὖν τά τε αὐτοῦ **παρασκευαζώμεθα** καὶ ἐς τοὺς
Σικελοὺς πέμποντες τοὺς μὲν μᾶλλον **βεβαιωσώμεθα**, τοῖς δὲ
φιλίαν καὶ ξυμμαχίαν **πειρώμεθα** ποιεῖσθαι, ἔς τε τὴν ἄλλην
Σικελίαν **πέμπωμεν** πρέσβεις δηλοῦντες ὡς κοινὸς ὁ κίνδυνος, καὶ
ἐς τὴν Ἰταλίαν, ὅπως ἢ ξυμμαχίαν ποιώμεθα ἡμῖν ἢ μὴ δέχωνται
Ἀθηναίους. δοκεῖ δέ μοι καὶ ἐς Καρχηδόνα ἄμεινον εἶναι πέμψαι· οὐ
γὰρ ἀνέλπιστον αὐτοῖς ἀλλ' αἰεὶ διὰ φόβου εἰσὶ μή ποτε Ἀθηναῖοι
αὐτοῖς ἐπὶ τὴν πόλιν ἔλθωσιν. . . . δυνατοὶ δὲ εἰσὶ μάλιστα τῶν νῦν,
βουληθέντες· χρυσὸν γὰρ καὶ ἄργυρον πλεῖστον κέκτηνται, ὅθεν ὅ τε
πόλεμος καὶ τἆλλα εὐπορεῖ. **πέμπωμεν** δὲ καὶ ἐς τὴν
Λακεδαίμονα καὶ ἐς Κόρινθον δεόμενοι δεῦρο κατὰ τάχος βοηθεῖν
καὶ τὸν ἐκεῖ πόλεμον κινεῖν."

7.5 Thucydides 1.34.1-3: The Corcyreans are urging the Athenians to support them against the Corinthians; they claim that their actions with respect to the Corinthians were perfectly justified, because although they are a colony of Corinth, the mother city has treated them badly.

"ἢν δὲ λέγωσιν (sc. the Corinthians) ὡς οὐ δίκαιον τοὺς σφετέρους

ἀποίκους ὑμᾶς δέχεσθαι, **μαθόντων** ὡς πᾶσα ἀποικία εὖ μὲν

πάσχουσα τιμᾷ τὴν μητρόπολιν, ἀδικουμένη δὲ ἀλλοτριοῦται· οὐ γὰρ

ἐπὶ τῷ δοῦλοι, ἀλλ᾽ ἐπὶ ὁμοῖοι τοῖς λειπομένοις εἶναι ἐκπέμπονται.

ὡς δὲ ἠδίκουν σαφές ἐστιν· προκληθέντες γὰρ περὶ Ἐπιδάμνου ἐς

κρίσιν πολέμῳ μᾶλλον ἢ τῷ ἴσῳ ἐβουλήθησαν τὰ ἐγκλήματα

μετελθεῖν. καὶ ὑμῖν **ἔστω** τι τεκμήριον ἃ πρὸς ἡμᾶς τοὺς ξυγγενεῖς

δρῶσιν, ὥστε ἀπάτῃ τε μὴ παράγεσθαι ὑπ᾽ αὐτῶν δεομένοις τε ἐκ

τοῦ εὐθέος μὴ ὑπουργεῖν."

EXERCISES:

Write the following sentences in Greek; use imperative forms or hortatory subjunctives whenever possible:

A Sentences:

1. Examine the matter, my friends, in the way that seems best to you.
2. Do not obey every man who tells you such things.
3. Did you respect the praise of someone who knows nothing? You should not do that.
4. Do not pay attention to people who say that you will suffer no harm by disobeying your   physicians.
5. Do not allow sycophants to harm Socrates. Trust us to provide the means for him to leave the city and do not allow him to die.
6. Order one of the slaves to bring Socrates to us.
7. Don't keep worrying about throwing away all your money.

8. Let them order Socrates to come in.

9. Let them recline next to Socrates and let us recline next to Agathon.

10. Let him not disturb Agathon, but leave him alone.

11. Obey your parents and respect your friends.

12. Let all men honor the city's gods and let them keep their oaths.

13. Let him not deceive his friends or his relations.

14. Will you not persuade them to honor their parents?

15. Let them not disturb us with their complaints, for we will not honor them.

B Sentences:

1. Always sacrifice to the gods of the city and abide by its laws. The former is a mark of piety, the latter of good sense. Further, men who do not pay attention to religious matters run the risk of offending the gods, men who ignore the laws of their city risk offending their fellow citizens. Neither course is very wise.

2. Will you summon Socrates from the neighbor's porch and will you not let him refuse you? You must compel him to come into the house. When he arrives, let him recline next to Agathon. For Agathon is eager to converse with him about the proper concerns of a man who wishes to care for his soul.

5. Because of their friendship, the Sicilians will aid us freely now against a common enemy, but we must persuade the Spartans, who are not friendly, to come to our aid. Let them know clearly that we are making preparations for war against the Athenians. Send an envoy to them to say the following: "Do not fear the Athenians; do not fear their allies; fear only shame if you fail to aid your friends. We will not allow the Athenians to harm you."

CHAPTER EIGHT—EXPRESSIONS OF OBLIGATION, NECESSITY, EFFORT

1. Greek expresses **obligation** or necessity in the following ways:

(a) The impersonal verbs δεῖ and χρή. See **GG** §887. The person or thing obligated, if expressed, is placed in the accusative, the obligation in the infinitive, e.g., "we must aid our allies" = ἡμᾶς δεῖ (or χρὴ) τοῖς συμμάχοις βοηθεῖν. Present or aorist infinitives are most common in this construction, where the choice is a matter of aspect.

οὐ δεῖ and οὐ χρή = "need not" in contrast to δεῖ μή and χρὴ μή + infinitive = "should not"

(b) The **verbal adjective** in -τέος. See **Smyth** §§2149-2152a, **GG** §§1596-1600. This is used in two ways:

(1) In the **personal** construction, the -τέος form is passive in meaning. It modifies a noun or noun substitute, and the person obligated, if expressed, is placed in the dative without a preposition. This construction is only used with verbal adjectives formed from transitive verbs. E.g., Xen. **Anab.** 2.4.6: ποταμός. . . τις. . . ἡμῖν ἐστι διαβατέος = "we must cross a river" or literally, "a river is for us to be crossed."

(2) In the **impersonal** construction, the verbal adjective is active in meaning, usually in the neuter singular nominative (or occasionally plural), the object of the verbal adjective stands in whatever case the verb requires, the agent (or obligated party) in the dative, e.g. 8.2: ἡμῖν. . . ξύμμαχοι. . . , οὓς οὐ παραδοτέα τοῖς ᾿Αθηναίοις ἐστίν = "we have allies, whom we must not abandon to the Athenians." Agent may occasionally stand in the accusative. See **Smyth** §2152a.

2. A number of verbs that refer to mental effort ("take care," "plan," "consider") e.g., ἐπιμελοῦμαι, πρόνοιαν ἔχω, βουλεύομαι, σκοπῶ, εὐλαβοῦμαι, φροντίζω are usually followed by **ὅπως + the**

future indicative after both **primary** and **secondary** tenses (see Smyth §2210); the negative is ὅπως μή. However, these verbs may also take ἵνα or ὅπως with the subjunctive or optative, for which see the next chapter.

Note that ὅπως and ὅπως μή can also be used with the future indicative, without any main verb or introductory clause on which they depend, to denote an exhortation or warning. This usage is confined to Attic.

READINGS:

8.1 Plato, **Crito** §47a2-c4 (repeated from **6.1**).

σκόπει δήᾦοὐχ ἱκανῶς δοκεῖ σοι λέγεσθαι ὅτι οὐ πάσας **χρὴ** τὰς δόξας τῶν ἀνθρώπων τιμᾶν ἀλλὰ τὰς μέν, τὰς δ' οὔ, οὐδὲ πάντων ἀλλὰ τῶν μέν, τῶν δ' οὔ; τί φῄς; ταῦτα οὐχὶ καλῶς λέγεται;

ΚΡ. καλῶς.

ΣΩ. οὐκοῦν τὰς μὲν χρηστὰς τιμᾶν, τὰς δὲ πονηρὰς μή;

ΚΡ. ναί.

ΣΩ. χρησταὶ δὲ οὐχ αἱ τῶν φρονίμων, πονηραὶ δὲ αἱ τῶν ἀφρόνων;

ΚΡ. πῶς δ' οὔ;

ΣΩ. φέρε δή, πῶς αὖ τὰ τοιαῦτα ἐλέγετο; γυμναζόμενος ἀνὴρ καὶ τοῦτο πράττων πότερον παντὸς ἀνδρὸς ἐπαίνῳ καὶ ψόγῳ καὶ δόξῃ τὸν νοῦν προσέχει, ἢ ἑνὸς μόνου ἐκείνου ὃς ἂν τυγχάνῃ ἰατρὸς ἢ παιδοτρίβης ὤν;

ΚΡ. ἑνὸς μόνου.

ΣΩ. οὐκοῦν φοβεῖσθαι **χρὴ** τοὺς ψόγους καὶ ἀσπάζεσθαι τοὺς ἐπαίνους τοὺς τοῦ ἑνὸς ἐκείνου ἀλλὰ μὴ τοὺς τῶν πολλῶν.

ΚΡ. δῆλα δή.

ΣΩ. ταύτῃ ἄρα αὐτῷ πρακτέον καὶ γυμναστέον καὶ
ἐδεστέον γε καὶ ποτέον, ᾗ ἂν τῷ ἑνὶ δοκῇ, τῷ ἐπιστάτῃ καὶ
ἐπαΐοντι, μᾶλλον ἢ ᾗ σύμπασι τοῖς ἄλλοις.

ΚΡ. ἔστι ταῦτα.

ΣΩ. εἶεν. ἀπειθήσας δὲ τῷ ἑνὶ καὶ ἀτιμάσας αὐτοῦ τὴν δόξαν καὶ
τοὺς ἐπαίνους, τιμήσας δὲ τοὺς τῶν πολλῶν [λόγους] καὶ μηδὲν
ἐπαϊόντων, ἆρα οὐδὲν κακὸν πείσεται;

ΚΡ. πῶς γὰρ οὔ;

8.2. Thucydides 1.86.1-5. The Spartan ephor, Sthenelaidas, is
addressing the Spartan assembly about going to war with Athens.

τοὺς μὲν λόγους τοὺς πολλοὺς τῶν ᾿Αθηναίων οὐ γιγνώσκω·
ἐπαινέσαντες γὰρ πολλὰ ἑαυτοὺς οὐδαμοῦ ἀντεῖπον ὡς οὐκ
ἀδικοῦσι τοὺς ἡμετέρους ξυμμάχους καὶ τὴν Πελοπόννησον· καίτοι εἰ
πρὸς τοὺς Μήδους ἐγένοντο ἀγαθοὶ τότε, πρὸς δ᾿ ἡμᾶς κακοὶ νῦν,
διπλασίας ζημίας ἄξιοί εἰσιν, ὅτι ἀντ᾿ ἀγαθῶν κακοὶ γεγένηνται.
ἡμεῖς δὲ ὅμοιοι καὶ τότε καὶ νῦν ἐσμέν, καὶ τοὺς ξυμμάχους, ἢν
σωφρονῶμεν, οὐ περιοψόμεθα ἀδικουμένους οὐδὲ μελλήσομεν
τιμωρεῖν· οἱ δ᾿ οὐκέτι μέλλουσι κακῶς πάσχειν. ἄλλοις μὲν γὰρ
χρήματά ἐστι πολλὰ καὶ νῆες καὶ ἵπποι, ἡμῖν δὲ ξύμμαχοι ἀγαθοί,
οὓς οὐ **παραδοτέα** τοῖς ᾿Αθηναίοις ἐστίν, οὐδὲ δίκαις καὶ λόγοις
διακριτέα μὴ λόγῳ καὶ αὐτοὺς βλαπτομένους, ἀλλὰ **τιμωρητέα**
ἐν τάχει καὶ παντὶ σθένει. καὶ ὡς ἡμᾶς πρέπει βουλεύεσθαι
ἀδικουμένους μηδεὶς διδασκέτω, ἀλλὰ τοὺς μέλλοντας ἀδικεῖν
μᾶλλον πρέπει πολὺν χρόνον βουλεύεσθαι. ψηφίζεσθε οὖν, ὦ
Λακεδαιμόνιοι, ἀξίως τῆς Σπάρτης τὸν πόλεμον, καὶ μήτε τοὺς ᾿Αθ-
ηναίους ἐᾶτε μείζους γίγνεσθαι μήτε τοὺς ξυμμάχους καταπροδιδῶμεν, ἀλλὰ ξὺν τοῖς θεοῖς ἐπίωμεν ἐπὶ τοὺς ἀδικοῦντας.

8.3 Demosthenes, **On the False Embassy** §§14-16 (with an omission). Demosthenes is accusing Aeschines of misconduct on an embassy sent to Philip of Macedon. Here, Demosthenes argues that Aeschines blatantly changed sides during debate over the acceptance of terms of a treaty proposed by Philocrates.

"ἐγὼ δὲ ταύτην μὲν τὴν εἰρήνην, ἕως ἂν εἷς Ἀθηναίων λείπηται, οὐδέποτ' ἂν συμβουλεύσαιμι ποιήσασθαι τῇ πόλει, εἰρήνην μέντοι φημὶ **δεῖν** ποιεῖσθαι." . . . ὁ (sc. Aeschines) δὲ ταῦτ' εἰπὼν τῇ προτεραίᾳ πάντων ἀκουόντων ὑμῶν, εἰς τὴν ὑστεραίαν, ἐν ᾗ τὴν εἰρήνην **ἔδει** κυροῦσθαι, ἐμοῦ τῷ τῶν συμμάχων συνηγοροῦντος δόγματι καὶ τὴν εἰρήνην **ὅπως ἴση καὶ δικαία γενήσεται πράττοντος**, καὶ ὑμῶν βουλομένων ταῦτα καὶ οὐδὲ φωνὴν ἐθελόντων ἀκούειν τοῦ καταπτύστου Φιλοκράτους, ἀναστὰς ἐδημηγόρει καὶ συνηγόρει 'κείνῳ πολλῶν ἀξίους, ὦ Ζεῦ καὶ πάντες θεοί, θανάτων λόγους, ὡς οὔτε τῶν προγόνων ὑμᾶς μεμνῆσθαι **δέοι** οὔτε τῶν τὰ τρόπαια καὶ τὰς ναυμαχίας λεγόντων ἀνέχεσθαι, νόμον τε θήσειν καὶ γράψειν μηδενὶ τῶν Ἑλλήνων ὑμᾶς βοηθεῖν, ὃς ἂν μὴ πρότερος βεβοηθηκὼς ὑμῖν ᾖ. καὶ ταῦθ' ὁ σχέτλιος καὶ ἀναιδὴς οὗτος ἐτόλμα λέγειν ἐφεστηκότων τῶν πρέσβεων καὶ ἀκουόντων, οὓς ἀπὸ τῶν Ἑλλήνων μετεπέμψασθε ὑπὸ τούτου πεισθέντες, ὅτ' οὔπω πεπρακὼς αὐτὸν ἦν.

8.4. Plato, **Apology** §29d2-e2. Part of Socrates' final remarks where he claims he will never cease from practicing philosophy.

ἐγὼ (sc. Socrates) ὑμᾶς, ὦ ἄνδρες Ἀθηναῖοι, ἀσπάζομαι μὲν καὶ φιλῶ, πείσομαι δὲ μᾶλλον τῷ θεῷ ἢ ὑμῖν, καὶ ἕωσπερ ἂν ἐμπνέω καὶ οἷός τε ὦ, οὐ μὴ παύσωμαι φιλοσοφῶν καὶ ὑμῖν παρακελευόμενός τε καὶ ἐνδεικνύμενος ὅτῳ ἂν ἀεὶ ἐντυγχάνω ὑμῶν, λέγων οἷάπερ εἴωθα, ὅτι "ὦ ἄριστε ἀνδρῶν, Ἀθηναῖος ὤν, πόλεως τῆς μεγίστης καὶ εὐδοκιμωτάτης εἰς σοφίαν καὶ ἰσχύν, χρημάτων μὲν οὐκ αἰσχύνῃ **ἐπιμελούμενος ὅπως** σοι **ἔσται** ὡς πλεῖστα, καὶ δόξης καὶ τιμῆς, φρονήσεως δὲ καὶ ἀληθείας καὶ τῆς ψυχῆς ὅπως ὡς βελτίστη ἔσται οὐκ ἐπιμελῇ οὐδὲ φροντίζεις";

EXERCISES:

Write in Greek using expressions of necessity or effort as the context requires.

A Sentences:

1. Take care lest you make him angry.
2. These should not be the words of a just man.
3. Socrates strove to make both himself and the Athenians better by practicing philosophy.
4. See to it that you act justly when spending money on behalf of Socrates.
5. They happened to be listening to Socrates' arguments.
6. See to it that you (plural) are obedient to the gods and to the laws of the city.
7. He was trying to anger Socrates, but I do not think he was able to do so.
8. See to it that Socrates stops his practice of philosophy.
9. What must you answer to Socrates?
10. He should not ask such an unfair question.
11. I am concerned that Socrates must lose his life.
12. Will Socrates, who happens to be an Athenian, leave his own city?
13. The Athenians should take care that they do not execute Socrates.
14. These are the premises of scoundrels.
15. Socrates cares about justice and the soul.

B Sentences:

1. You must not forget the accomplishments of your ancestors. Therefore, you cannot make peace with men who have been their enemies in the past. If you do so, you will seem shameless cowards

both to your allies and to your sons. See to it that you do not so risk your reputations.

2. He spoke as follows: "As Spartans we need not understand the speeches of the Athenians, but need only remember that they easily change sides and are not men of honor, whereas we are ever the same, men of good sense and faithful to our friends and allies. The allies must not be betrayed, but the enemy checked as soon as possible. We must take care to act with prudence and foresight in these weighty matters."

3. You must eat and drink only what the trainer orders. See to it that you do not do otherwise. You must also exercise only in moderation. Neglecting these instructions will lead to serious injury. Do not heed what others say. They too would benefit from the advice of your trainer.

CHAPTER NINE—PURPOSE CLAUSES[1]

1. Clauses used to indicate purpose (also called "final" clauses) in Greek are introduced by the following:

ἵνα is in origin an adverb of place. As a final conjunction it is translated "so that," or "in order that." It is preferred by Aristophanes, Herodotus, Plato, and the orators, although it occurs in other writers as well. Occasionally it may be found with the indicative with its original sense of "where".

ὡς means "as." It is related to the relative ὅς and was originally a relative adverb of manner; ὡς is rare in prose except for Xenophon, but common in tragedy. You should not imitate this poetic use in these exercises.

ὅπως means "as" or "how" or "so as to." It is related to ὡς as ὁπότε to ὅτε. It is the more common final conjunction in Thucydides and Xenophon, functioning in virtually the same way as ἵνα. (Be sure to distinguish from ὅπως and its negative ὅπως μή used with the future indicative after verbs of effort.)

ἄν is occasionally found with ὡς and ὅπως in this construction in Attic prose and in Attic inscriptions. The addition of ἄν is analogous to the indefinite relative construction, and it happens because ὡς and ὅπως are relative in origin (see **Smyth** §2201 and **GG** §1387). Note that ἵνα is never used in this way.

2. Purpose clauses are formed as follows:

After **primary sequence**—ἵνα / ὅπως + subjunctive. The negative is μή.

---

[1] For further discussion see **Smyth** §§2193-2206, **GG** §§1371-1381, and **MT** §§302-388.

After **secondary** **sequence**—ἵνα / ὅπως + optative. The negative is μή.

The **subjunctive is often retained** even after secondary sequence. The usual explanations for this are (1) to set forth the purpose as originally expressed (hence retain "vividness") or (2) to indicate a purpose whose effect continues into the present. Very occasionally the optative may follow primary sequence (see **MT** §§322-323), if a reference to the past as well as the present is implied. However, you should **not** imitate this last usage in your exercises.

3. The present subjunctive and optative indicate **continuous or repeated** action; aorist subjunctive and optative indicate a **single instance** of an action. Future optative is never used in final clauses (see **MT** §§132-133).

4. Purpose clauses will very occasionally use a secondary tense of the indicative in statements that are analogous to unreal conditions to mark something as actually unattained. See **MT** §§333-337 and **Smyth** §2185c. You should distinguish this from the use of the indicative with ἵνα = "where."

> Example: Plato, **Crito** §44d6-8: εἰ γὰρ ὤφελον, ὦ Κρίτων, οἷοί τ' εἶναι οἱ πολλοὶ τὰ μέγιστα κακὰ ἐργάζεσθαι, ἵνα οἷοί τ' ἦσαν καὶ ἀγαθὰ τὰ μέγιστα. "Would that the many were capable of committing the greatest evils, **in order that they were capable** also of the greatest good." The indicative indicates that Socrates thinks that they *are not* capable of this.

5. In addition to ἵνα, ὡς, and ὅπως, a variety of other constructions may express purpose in Greek (see **Smyth** §2206):

> (a) the articular infinitive, usually when it follows a preposition like ὑπέρ, ἕνεκα, or διά.

> (b) the future participle with or without ὡς.

> (c) the infinitive after verbs meaning to give, entrust, choose, appoint, take, or receive.

(d) a relative clause (with ὅς or ὅστις) with the future indicative (see **Smyth** §2554). For an example, see below **11.3**: αἵτινες βοηθήσουσι. This use is rare, however.

READINGS:

9.1 Lysias, **Against Eratosthenes** §§24-26 (repeated from **6.2**).

ἀνάβηθι οὖν μοι καὶ ἀπόκριναι, ὅ τι ἄν σε ἐρωτῶ.

ἀπήγαγες Πολέμαρχον ἢ οὔ;

τὰ ὑπὸ τῶν ἀρχόντων προσταχθέντα δεδιὼς ἐποίουν.

ἦσθα δ' ἐν τῷ βουλευτηρίῳ, ὅτε οἱ λόγοι ἐγίγνοντο περὶ ἡμῶν; ἦ.

πότερον συνηγόρευες τοῖς κελεύουσιν ἀποκτεῖναι ἢ ἀντέλεγες;

ἀντέλεγον.

ἵνα μὴ ἀποθάνωμεν;

ἵνα μὴ ἀποθάνητε.

ἡγούμενος ἡμᾶς ἄδικα πάσχειν ἢ δίκαια;

ἄδικα.

εἶτ', ὦ σχετλιώτατε πάντων, ἀντέλεγες μὲν **ἵνα σώσειας,** συνελάμβανες δὲ **ἵνα ἀποκτείνῃς;** καὶ ὅτε μὲν τὸ πλῆθος ἦν ὑμῶν κύριον τῆς σωτηρίας τῆς ἡμετέρας, ἀντιλέγειν φῇς τοῖς βουλομένοις ἡμᾶς ἀπολέσαι, ἐπειδὴ δὲ ἐπὶ σοὶ μόνῳ ἐγένετο καὶ σῶσαι Πολέμαρχον καὶ μή, εἰς τὸ δεσμωτήριον ἀπήγαγες; εἶθ' ὅτι μέν, ὡς φῄς, ἀντειπὼν οὐδὲν ὠφέλησας, ἀξιοῖς χρηστὸς νομίζεσθαι, ὅτι δὲ συλλαβὼν ἀπέκτεινας, οὐκ ἐμοὶ καὶ τουτοισὶ δοῦναι δίκην;

9.2. Thucydides 6.18.1,4 (with omissions). Alcibiades is urging the Athenians to undertake the Sicilian expedition.

οὐ γὰρ **ἵνα** δεῦρο **ἀντιβοηθῶσι** προσεθέμεθα αὐτούς, ἀλλ' **ἵνα** τοῖς ἐκεῖ ἐχθροῖς ἡμῶν λυπηροὶ ὄντες δεῦρο **κωλύωσιν** αὐτοὺς ἐπιέναι. . . . λογισάμενοι οὖν τάδε (= our power at home) μᾶλλον

αὐξήσειν, ἐπ' ἐκεῖνα ἦν (= ἐὰν) ἴωμεν, ποιώμεθα τὸν πλοῦν, **ἵνα**

Πελοποννησίων τε **στορέσωμεν** τὸ φρόνημα, εἰ δόξομεν ὑπεριδόντες

τὴν ἐν τῷ παρόντι ἡσυχίαν καὶ ἐπὶ Σικελίαν πλεῦσαι.

9.3 Plato, **Symposium** §213b4-e5 (with omissions). Alcibiades has
just entered the party being given by Agathon to celebrate his
victory in the tragic contest. Alcibiades sits down on the couch
between Agathon and Socrates, but without recognizing the latter
(Alcibiades is very drunk).

Agathon: ὑπολύετε, παῖδες, ᾿Αλκιβιάδην, **ἵνα** ἐκ τρίτων

κατακέηται.

Alcibiades: πάνυ γε, ἀλλὰ τίς ἡμῖν ὅδε τρίτος συμπότης; (He looks

around and recognizes Socrates). ὦ ῾Ηράκλεις, τουτὶ τί ἦν;

Σωκράτης οὗτος; ἐλλοχῶν αὖ με ἐνταῦθα κατέκεισο, ὥσπερ

εἰώθεις ἐξαίφνης ἀναφαίνεσθαι ὅπου ἐγὼ ᾤμην ἥκιστά σε ἔσεσθαι.

καὶ νῦν τί ἥκεις; καὶ τί αὖ ἐνταῦθα κατεκλίνης; ὡς οὐ παρὰ

᾿Αριστοφάνει οὐδὲ εἴ τις ἄλλος γελοῖος ἔστι τε καὶ βούλεται, ἀλλὰ

διεμηχανήσω **ὅπως** παρὰ τῷ καλλίστῳ τῶν ἔνδον **κατακείσῃ.**

Socrates: ᾿Αγάθων, ὅρα εἴ μοι ἐπαμύνεις· ὡς ἐμοὶ ὁ τούτου ἔρως τοῦ

ἀνθρώπου οὐ φαῦλον πρᾶγμα γέγονεν. ἀπ' ἐκείνου γὰρ τοῦ χρόνου,

ἀφ' οὗ τούτου ἠράσθην, οὐκέτι ἔξεστίν μοι οὔτε προσβλέψαι οὔτε δι-

αλεχθῆναι καλῷ οὐδ' ἑνί, ἢ οὑτοσὶ ζηλοτυπῶν με καὶ φθονῶν

θαυμαστὰ ἐργάζεται καὶ λοιδορεῖταί τε καὶ τὼ χεῖρε μόγις

ἀπέχεται. ὅρα οὖν μή τι καὶ νῦν ἐργάσηται, ἀλλὰ διάλλαξον ἡμᾶς,

ἢ ἐὰν ἐπιχειρῇ βιάζεσθαι, ἐπάμυνε, ὡς ἐγὼ τὴν τούτου μανίαν τε

καὶ φιλεραστίαν πάνυ ὀρρωδῶ.

Alcibiades: ἀλλ' οὐκ ἔστι ἐμοὶ καὶ σοὶ διαλλαγή. ἀλλὰ τούτων

μὲν εἰς αὖθίς σε τιμωρήσομαι· νῦν δέ μοι, ᾿Αγάθων, μετάδος τῶν

ταινιῶν, **ἵνα ἀναδήσω** καὶ τὴν τούτου ταυτηνὶ τὴν θαυμαστὴν κεφαλήν, καὶ μή μοι μέμφηται ὅτι σὲ μὲν ἀνέδησα, αὐτὸν δὲ νικῶντα ἐν λόγοις πάντας ἀνθρώπους, οὐ μόνον πρῴην ὥσπερ σύ, ἀλλ' ἀεί, ἔπειτα οὐκ ἀνέδησα.

9.4 Lysias, The Murder of Eratosthenes §40 The speaker, who has killed a man named Eratosthenes when finding him with his wife, argues that if he had been planning to murder him he certainly would not have invited him to dinner. (This is not the same Eratosthenes as in 9.1).

εἰ ἐν ἐκείνῃ τῇ νυκτὶ ἐγὼ ἐπεβούλευον Ἐρατοσθένει, πότερον ἦν μοι κρεῖττον αὐτῷ ἑτέρωθι δειπνεῖν ἢ τὸν συνδειπνήσοντά μοι εἰσαγαγεῖν; οὕτω γὰρ ἂν ἧττον ἐτόλμησεν ἐκεῖνος εἰσελθεῖν εἰς τὴν οἰκίαν. εἶτα δοκῶ ἂν ὑμῖν τὸν συνδειπνοῦντα ἀφεὶς μόνος καταλειφθῆναι καὶ ἔρημος γενέσθαι, ἢ κελεύειν ἐκεῖνον μεῖναι, **ἵνα** μετ' ἐμοῦ τὸν μοιχὸν **ἐτιμωρεῖτο;**

EXERCISES:

Write in Greek:

A Sentences:

1. Did you believe that I plotted against Eratosthenes in order to kill him?
2. To avenge themselves against their enemies, they denounced them in the council room.
3. Let him recline next to Socrates, so that we may continue our conversation.
4. Will you arrest Polemarchus to save his life?
5. He urged the Athenians to sail to Sicily to increase their own power and to stop the Peloponnesians from increasing theirs.
6. The Athenians did not send aid to their former allies in order to punish them but to put an end to the war.
7. We will pay a great deal of money for you not to denounce us to our enemies.

8. He had the audacity to enter my house and share my supper in order to corrupt my wife.

9. In order not to do wrong, Socrates was willing to die.

→ 10. But Crito tried to persuade Socrates to leave Athens so he would not die.

11. Alcibiades came to Agathon's house in order to recline next to Socrates.

12. Alcibiades invited Socrates to dinner, in order to converse with him.

13. Do you dare to come into my house in order to shame me?

14. We must prevent them from becoming enemies of Athens.

15. Mount the dais in order to answer my questions.

B Sentences:

1. Let us sail in order to aid our allies as soon as possible. It is also important for us to sail so that we might cause grief to our enemies. For our friends will come to harm if we do not save them, and our enemies will increase in strength if we do not hinder them. In order to be considered honorable men, we must act now. I trust you will support me and vote to go to war.

2. Alcibiades wished to invite Socrates to dinner in order to discuss philosophy with him. He instructed his slaves to greet Socrates when he arrived and remove his sandals so that he might recline next to him (sc. Alcibiades). Socrates, however, had taken up a position on the neighbor's porch to contemplate the heavens and was refusing to enter Alcibiades' house. What were they to do? Alcibiades would be angry with them if Socrates did not appear, but Socrates would be angry at being interrupted.

3. Alcibiades believed that Socrates was in love with him and he himself was certainly devoted to the philosopher. He always attended the same parties as Socrates, to try to prevent him from speaking to other good-looking young men. But Socrates frequently escaped his notice doing this. Socrates was particularly fond of Agathon, and once attended a party in order to converse with him. Alcibiades discovered them reclining together on the same couch and took care to plot a suitable revenge.

CHAPTER TEN—EXPRESSIONS OF FEARING[1]

Verbs or phrases that indicate fear or hesitation use the following constructions in Greek.

1. Constructions with μή and μή οὐ:

(a) Fear of **what is happening** or **has happened** is expressed by μή + the **indicative**; fear of what is not happening or has not happened by μή οὐ + the **indicative**. E.g., φόβουμαι μή τι νέον βουλεύει = "I am afraid that he is devising a new scheme," ἐφοβούμην μή οὐ τι νέον ἐβούλευε = "I was afraid that he was not devising a new scheme."

(b) Fear expressed about an event in the **future** is expressed by μή + the **subjunctive** or **optative** to indicate fear of what may happen; μὴ οὐ + subjunctive or optative to indicate fear of what may not happen. E.g., φόβουμαι μή τι νέον βουλεύῃ = "I am afraid that he may devise a new scheme", φόβουμαι μὴ οὐ τι νέον βουλεύῃ = "I am afraid that he may not devise a new scheme," ἐφοβούμην μή τι νέον βούλευοι = "I was afraid that he might devise a new scheme."

You will often find the archaic English word **lest** used to translate μή in this construction, e.g., "I am afraid **lest** he devise a new scheme."

As with purpose clauses, **subjunctive** follows a leading verb in **primary** sequence; the **optative** a leading verb in **secondary** sequence. However, the subjunctive is very frequently retained in secondary sequence. In fact, so few examples of μὴ οὐ + the optative occur that there is doubt whether this was ever part of regular Attic usage. If exercises seem to require this construction, you should retain the subjunctive.

---

[1] For further discussion see **Smyth** §§2221-2239, **GG** §§1389-1391, and **MT** §§365-376.

2. In fifth and fourth century prose the **future indicative** is rare after verbs of fearing with μή and the future optative even rarer (three examples). In later prose the situation is not so straightforward, nor is it well analyzed. In writing exercises, ignore this option.

3. As in English, expressions of fear or hesitation may take an **infinitive** (e.g., φοβοῦμαι ἀδικεῖν = "I am afraid to do wrong") or a direct object (e.g., φοβοῦμαι αὐτόν = "I am afraid of him," φοβοῦμαι τὸ ἀδικεῖν = "I am afraid of wrong-doing").

4. Expressions of fear or hesitation may also be followed by an **indirect question** (i.e., "I doubt whether"), **causal ὅτι and causal participles** (i.e., "I am afraid because"), or **indirect statement**, usually, when the leading verb is negative ("I am not afraid that"). See **Smyth** §§2234-2239.

5. Apart from the verbs and noun + verb combinations that actually mean "fear" in Greek, a variety of verbs that express wariness or precaution also take the construction with μή. Note that the expressions with ὁράω, σκοπέω, ἐννοέω, εὐλαβοῦμαι, φροντίζω, φυλάττω may take a construction analogous to verbs of fearing (see **9.3**: ὅρα μὴ . . . ἐργάσηται), with a meaning of "watch out in case" or ὅπως μή + future indicative = "see to it that. . . not"

READINGS:

10.1 Thucydides 6.34.1-3 (repeated from **7.4**).

"θαρσοῦντες οὖν τά τε αὐτοῦ παρασκευαζώμεθα καὶ ἐς τοὺς Σικελοὺς πέμποντες τοὺς μὲν μᾶλλον βεβαιωσώμεθα, τοῖς δὲ φιλίαν καὶ ξυμμαχίαν πειρώμεθα ποιεῖσθαι, ἔς τε τὴν ἄλλην Σικελίαν πέμπωμεν πρέσβεις δηλοῦντες ὡς κοινὸς ὁ κίνδυνος, καὶ ἐς τὴν Ἰταλίαν, ὅπως ἢ ξυμμαχίαν ποιώμεθα ἡμῖν ἢ μὴ δέχωνται Ἀθηναίους. δοκεῖ δέ μοι καὶ ἐς Καρχηδόνα ἄμεινον εἶναι πέμψαι· οὐ γὰρ ἀνέλπιστον αὐτοῖς ἀλλ' αἰεὶ **διὰ φόβου εἰσὶ** μή ποτε Ἀθηναῖοι αὐτοῖς ἐπὶ τὴν πόλιν **ἔλθωσιν**. . . . δυνατοὶ δέ εἰσι μάλιστα τῶν νῦν, βουληθέντες· χρυσὸν γὰρ καὶ ἄργυρον πλεῖστον κέκτηνται, ὅθεν ὅ τε πόλεμος καὶ τἆλλα εὐπορεῖ. πέμπωμεν δὲ καὶ ἐς τὴν Λακεδαίμονα καὶ ἐς Κόρινθον δεόμενοι δεῦρο κατὰ τάχος βοηθεῖν καὶ τὸν ἐκεῖ πόλεμον κινεῖν."

10.2 Demosthenes, On the Crown §§175-176. Demosthenes is explaining why Philip has occupied Elatea and what the consequences will be for the Athenians if they do not respond promptly.

τί οὖν βούλεται, καὶ τίνος εἵνεκα τὴν 'Ελάτειαν κατείληφεν; πλησίον δύναμιν δείξας καὶ παραστήσας τὰ ὅπλα τοὺς μὲν ἑαυτοῦ φίλους ἐπᾶραι καὶ θρασεῖς ποιῆσαι, τοὺς δ' ἐναντιουμένους κατ-απλῆξαι, ἵν' ἢ συγχωρήσωσι **φοβηθέντες** ἃ νῦν οὐκ ἐθέλουσιν, ἢ βιασθῶσιν. εἰ μὲν τοίνυν προαιρησόμεθ' ἡμεῖς. . . ἐν τῷ παρόντι, εἴ τι δύσκολον πέπρακται Θηβαίοις πρὸς ἡμᾶς, τούτου μεμνῆσθαι καὶ ἀπιστεῖν αὐτοῖς ὡς ἐν τῇ τῶν ἐχθρῶν οὖσιν μερίδι, πρῶτον μὲν ἂν (= ἃ ἂν) εὔξαιτο Φίλιππος ποιήσομεν, εἶτα **φοβοῦμαι μὴ** προσδε-ξαμένων τῶν νῦν ἀνθεστηκότων αὐτῷ καὶ μιᾷ γνώμῃ πάντων φιλιππισάντων, εἰς τὴν 'Αττικὴν **ἔλθωσιν** ἀμφότεροι.

10.3 Plato, Crito §§44e2-45b9 (repeated from 7.2).

ἆρά γε μὴ ἐμοῦ **προμηθῇ** καὶ τῶν ἄλλων ἐπιτηδείων μή, ἐὰν σὺ ἐνθένδε ἐξέλθῃς, οἱ συκοφάνται ἡμῖν πράγματα **παρέχωσιν**. . . , **καὶ ἀναγκασθῶμεν** ἢ καὶ πᾶσαν τὴν οὐσίαν ἀποβαλεῖν ἢ συχνὰ χρήματα, ἢ καὶ ἄλλο τι πρὸς τούτοις παθεῖν; εἰ γάρ τι τοιοῦτον **φοβῇ**, ἔασον αὐτὸ χαίρειν. . . . ἀλλ' ἐμοὶ πείθου καὶ μὴ ἄλλως ποίει.

ΣΩ. καὶ ταῦτα προμηθοῦμαι, ὦ Κρίτων, καὶ ἄλλα πολλά.

ΚΡ. **μήτε** τοίνυν ταῦτα **φοβοῦ**. . . μήτε, ταῦτα **φοβούμενος** ἀποκάμῃς σαυτὸν σῶσαι, μήτε, ὃ ἔλεγες ἐν τῷ δικαστηρίῳ, δυσχερές σοι γενέσθω ὅτι οὐκ ἂν ἔχοις ἐξελθὼν ὅτι χρῷο σαυτῷ.

EXERCISES:

Write in Greek:

A Sentences:

1. Are you afraid that you will suffer misfortunes greater than the present ones?
2. All good men fear that they will do evil while they are still alive, with the result that they themselves will suffer evil in the life hereafter.
3. Let them not fear telling the truth more than lying.
4. Do not be afraid that you will lose all your property.
5. They were afraid that the Athenians had already entered their city.
6. Do not worry that I will be compelled to suffer dreadful things.
7. In our fear we agreed to support Philip.
8. Philip did not fear Theban power, but he did fear that of the Athenians.
9. They were afraid he would laugh at Aristophanes' story.
10. For the present, Philip lives in fear of Athens.
11. He lived in constant fear that they would send aid to the Thebans.
12. They sent ambassadors to Italy in fear of Philip's power.
13. We listened fearfully lest Philip invade Attica.
14. Athenians feared Philip more than their other enemies.
15. Let them not be afraid to support Philip.

B Sentences:

1. Philip is not afraid that we will come to the aid of those who oppose him in Elataea. You, I know, believe that Philip fears us,

on account of our armies and our wealth. Indeed, he does not. Rather he fears what others in Greece will think if he is unwilling to risk provoking us. Therefore we must consider how best to meet his attack.

2. Socrates was concerned about his friends in the city, fearing that the sycophants might do them great harm. But Crito tried to persuade him that his fears were of no account. For they possessed considerable wealth about which the sycophants were unaware. All this they were willing to place at Socrates' disposal.

3. In your fear of the Athenians, you have failed to consider their strengths and their weaknesses. At this point let us do this, so that we might prepare for the future not in doubt but in full confidence of our own judgment. The Athenians too fear war. But if we prepare quickly and secure the aid of our allies, we need not fear that they can defeat us.

CHAPTER ELEVEN—RESULT CLAUSES[1]

1. Result clauses are also called **consecutive** clauses, because they express the consequence of the main clause. They are introduced by a relative, usually ὥστε (ὡς + τε), frequently with a demonstrative pronoun (e.g., τοσοῦτος) or adverb (e.g., οὕτως) in the principal clause. In English they are often translated "and so" in contrast to the "so that" of purpose clauses. For examples, see **11.1** and **11.4** below.

Result may be expressed as **natural** (or rational) or **actual**:

Natural result expresses what **may** or **could** or **might be expected** to result from the action of the leading verb. This may or may not express a fact, that is, something that really does happen, but for the purposes of the author the event is conceived of as potential, not real. Natural result is expressed by the infinitive; μή is used to negate a natural result, because it is the normal negative for an infinitive that is not in indirect discourse.

Actual result emphasizes what **does (or did) in fact take place** as a consequence of the leading verb. Any construction that can stand as an independent sentence may follow ὥστε as an actual result. The negative is οὐ for indicative verbs.

2. The construction with ἐφ' ᾧ and ἐφ' ᾧτε, which is analogous to result, takes the infinitive with the meaning of "on the condition that." Sometimes ἐπὶ τούτῳ is placed proleptically in the preceding clause. For example:

Plato, **Apology** §29c6-8: ὦ Σώκρατες, νῦν μὲν 'Ανύτῳ οὐ πεισόμεθα ἀλλ' ἀφίεμέν σε, **ἐπὶ τούτῳ** μέντοι, **ἐφ' ᾧτε** μηκέτι ἐν ταύτῃ τῇ ζητήσει διατρίβειν μηδὲ φιλοσοφεῖν. "Socrates, for the present we will not obey Anytus, but will let you go, **on this condition** however, **that** you no longer spend your time in this search nor in the pursuit of wisdom."

---

[1] For further discussion see **Smyth** §§2249-2278, **GG** §§1466-1476, and **MT** §§582-606.

let you go, **on this condition** however, **that** you no longer spend your time in this search nor in the pursuit of wisdom."

This construction may very occasionally appear with a future indicative following ἐφ' ᾧτε, see **Smyth** §2279.

3. ὥστε in indirect discourse will be discussed separately, see below Chapter Eighteen.

READINGS:

11.1 Plato, **Apology** §25d8-e7 Socrates is arguing that no one would willingly attempt to corrupt another, since the corrupted person might bring harm to the corrupter. Hence, if he corrupted the youth of the city as charged, it must have been unintentional.

τί δῆτα, ὦ Μέλητε; **τοσοῦτον** σὺ ἐμοῦ σοφώτερος εἶ τηλικούτου ὄντος τηλικόσδε ὤν, **ὥστε** σὺ μὲν **ἔγνωκας** ὅτι οἱ μὲν κακοὶ κακόν τι ἐργάζονται ἀεὶ τοὺς μάλιστα πλησίον ἑαυτῶν, οἱ δὲ ἀγαθοὶ ἀγαθόν, ἐγὼ δὲ δὴ **εἰς τοσοῦτον ἀμαθίας ἥκω ὥστε** καὶ τοῦτ' **ἀγνοῶ**, ὅτι ἐάν τινα μοχθηρὸν ποιήσω τῶν συνόντων, κινδυνεύσω κακόν τι λαβεῖν ὑπ' αὐτοῦ, **ὥστε** τοῦτο ⟨τὸ⟩ τοσοῦτον κακὸν ἑκὼν **ποιῶ**, ὡς φὴς σύ; ταῦτα ἐγώ σοι οὐ πείθομαι, ὦ Μέλητε, οἶμαι δὲ οὐδὲ ἄλλον ἀνθρώπων οὐδένα· ἀλλ' ἢ οὐ διαφθείρω, ἢ εἰ διαφθείρω, ἄκων, **ὥστε** σύ γε κατ' ἀμφότερα ψεύδῃ.

11.2 Thucydides 1.34.1-3 (repeated from **7.5**). The Corcyreans are speaking.

ἢν (= ἐὰν) δὲ λέγωσιν (sc. the Corinthians) ὡς οὐ δίκαιον τοὺς σφετέρους ἀποίκους ὑμᾶς δέχεσθαι, μαθόντων ὡς πᾶσα ἀποικία εὖ μὲν πάσχουσα τιμᾷ τὴν μητρόπολιν, ἀδικουμένη δὲ ἀλλοτριοῦται· οὐ γὰρ ἐπὶ τῷ δοῦλοι, ἀλλ' ἐπὶ ὁμοῖοι τοῖς λειπομένοις εἶναι

ἐκπέμπονται. ὡς δὲ ἠδίκουν σαφές ἐστιν· προκληθέντες γὰρ περὶ
'Επιδάμνου ἐς κρίσιν πολέμῳ μᾶλλον ἢ τῷ ἴσῳ ἐβουλήθησαν τὰ
ἐγκλήματα μετελθεῖν. καὶ ὑμῖν ἔστω τι τεκμήριον ἃ πρὸς ἡμᾶς (=
the Corcyreans) τοὺς ξυγγενεῖς δρῶσιν, **ὥστε** ἀπάτῃ τε **μ ὴ
παράγεσθαι** ὑπ' αὐτῶν δεομένοις τε ἐκ τοῦ εὐθέος **μ ὴ
ὑπουργεῖν.**

11.3 Lysias, **In Defense of Mantitheus** §§16-17. Manitheus has
been elected to serve in the council and must undergo an
examination to discover if there is any reason why he should not
serve. As part of this examination he must defend his military
service under the Thirty tyrants. This incident is designed to show
his bravery.

καὶ οὐ πολλαῖς ἡμέραις ὕστερον μετὰ ταῦτα ἐν Κορίνθῳ χωρίων
ἰσχυρῶν κατειλημμένων, **ὥστε** τοὺς πολεμίους **μὴ δύνασθαι**
παριέναι, 'Αγησιλάου δ' εἰς τὴν Βοιωτίαν ἐμβαλόντος,
ψηφισαμένων τῶν ἀρχόντων ἀποχωρίσαι τάξεις αἵτινες βοηθήσουσι,
φοβουμένων ἁπάντων (εἰκότως, ὦ βουλή· δεινὸν γὰρ ἦν ἀγαπητῶς
ὀλίγῳ πρότερον σεσωσμένους ἐφ' ἕτερον κίνδυνον ἰέναι), προσελθὼν
ἐγὼ τὸν ταξίαρχον ἐκέλευον ἀκληρωτὶ τὴν ἡμετέραν τάξιν
πέμπειν. **ὥστ'** εἴ τινες ὑμῶν ὀργίζονται τοῖς τὰ μὲν τῆς πόλεως
ἀξιοῦσι πράττειν, ἐκ δὲ τῶν κινδύνων ἀποδιδράσκουσιν, **οὐκ ἂν
δικαίως περὶ ἐμοῦ τὴν γνώμην ταύτην ἔχοιεν**· οὐ γὰρ μόνον
τὰ προσταττόμενα ἐποίουν προθύμως, ἀλλὰ καὶ κινδυνεύειν
ἐτόλμων.

11.4 Lysias, **Against Eratosthenes** §§1-2 (repeated from **5.2**).
οὐκ ἄρξασθαί μοι δοκεῖ ἄπορον εἶναι, ὦ ἄνδρες δικασταί, τῆς
κατηγορίας, ἀλλὰ παύσασθαι λέγοντι· **τοιαῦτα** αὐτοῖς τὸ
μέγεθος καὶ **τοσαῦτα** τὸ πλῆθος εἴργασται, **ὥστε μήτ' ἂ ν**
ψευδόμενον δεινότερα τῶν ὑπαρχόντων **κατηγορῆσαι, μήτε**

τἀληθῆ βουλόμενον εἰπεῖν ἅπαντα **δύνασθαι**, ἀλλ' ἀνάγκη ἢ τὸν κατήγορον ἀπειπεῖν ἢ τὸν χρόνον ἐπιλιπεῖν. τοὐναντίον δέ μοι δοκοῦμεν πείσεσθαι ἢ ἐν τῷ πρὸ τοῦ χρόνῳ. πρότερον μὲν γὰρ ἔδει τὴν ἔχθραν τοὺς κατηγοροῦντας ἐπιδεῖξαι, ἥτις εἴη πρὸς τοὺς φεύγοντας· νυνὶ δὲ παρὰ τῶν φευγόντων χρὴ πυνθάνεσθαι ἥτις ἦν αὐτοῖς πρὸς τὴν πόλιν ἔχθρα, ἀνθ' ὅτου τοιαῦτα ἐτόλμησαν εἰς αὐτὴν ἐξαμαρτάνειν. οὐ μέντοι ὡς οὐκ ἔχων οἰκείας ἔχθρας καὶ συμφορὰς τοὺς λόγους ποιοῦμαι, ἀλλ' ὡς ἅπασι πολλῆς ἀφθονίας οὔσης ὑπὲρ τῶν ἰδίων ἢ ὑπὲρ τῶν δημοσίων ὀργίζεσθαι.

EXERCISES:

Write in Greek:

A Sentences:

1. They were Athenians, so they did not fear death.
2. Socrates made trouble for the Athenians, so they put him to death.
3. The Thirty were so corrupt that no one could describe adequately their crimes; in order to make their full extent clear to you, I was afraid that I had exceeded my time limit.
4. See to it that Socrates does not escape from prison.
5. He committed crimes so numerous that we cannot remember them all.
6. I am so foolish that I did not realize that evil men do harm to those around them.
7. They did not honor their mother city; the result was that they suffered many evils.
8. Are you so wise that you can accuse Socrates of such terrible crimes?
9. The Athenians reached such an extreme of baseness that they executed Socrates.
10. We made so many complaints about him that he was unable to answer the accusations.

11. We came to the rescue of the men in Boeotia, on the condition that they themselves would not try to evade the danger.

12. A little later I was chosen by the taxiarch to lead the troops against the enemy, with the result that I was not in Athens when Socrates was executed.

13. Are you incensed at those who try to evade dangers in order to save their own lives?

14. The commander decided to send some troops to the rescue with the result that those in Boeotia are now safe.

15. They fled so swiftly that they escaped.

B Sentences:

1. The colony was treated so badly by its mother city that it decided to revolt. So they sent envoys to Athens to ask for help. These men spoke so eloquently in the assembly that the Athenians immediately voted to send both ships and men to support them in their struggle for independence.

2. Do you think that Socrates was so foolish that he willingly committed the crimes they accused him of? Surely he did not. For he was wiser than his accusers who were so envious that they tried to destroy a good man. Evil men do harm to those around them, with the result that no one wants them for neighbors.

3. I am afraid that even a Demosthenes would be unable to express the heinousness of the crimes of the Thirty. Not only did they kill the innocent in order to take their money, but they reached such a level of criminal behavior that they betrayed their own friends and relations even more quickly than their enemies. In fact, their corruption was so extensive that the Thirty even began to prey upon their own members.

CHAPTER TWELVE—WISHES[1]

As with many other constructions in Greek, expressions of wishing are divided into (1) wishes that look to the future and (2) wishes expressed about the present or past that remain unfulfilled, e.g., "I wish you were here" (but you are not). By far the greatest number of examples of wishes occur in the poets; the construction is rare in historical prose, only slightly more frequent in Plato and in the orators.

1. Wishes for the future, for good or evil, are expressed with the **optative**, either alone or with εἰ, εἰ γάρ, or εἴθε. The negative of both is μή.

(a) The **optative may be used independently**, for example, εὐδαιμονοῖτε = "may you be happy!" or ὄλοιο = "may you perish!"

In the orators, this optative occurs in the relative phrase ὃ μὴ γένοιτο, e.g., Dem. **Against Aphobus I** §67: ἂν γὰρ ἀποφύγῃ μ' οὗτος, ὃ μὴ γένοιτο, τὴν ἐπωβελίαν ὀφλήσω μνᾶς ἑκατόν. "If he is acquitted—which heaven forbid!—I will owe a fine of 100 minas."

(b) A wish introduced by εἰ, εἰ γάρ or εἴθε is in essence the **protasis of a future less vivid condition** with the apodosis suppressed. εἰ γὰρ γένοιτο (= if it would happen!), but conventionally translated "would that it might happen!"

2. Unattainable wishes are also divided into two categories:

(a) The wish may be expressed with ✕ εἰ γάρ, or εἴθε + the **imperfect or aorist indicative.** Again, these behave like the **protases to unreal conditions:** the imperfect is used to express a wish for the present, the aorist for the past, for example, εἴθε

---

[1] For further discussion see **Smyth** §§1780-1782, 1814-1823, **GG** §§1355-1361; **MT** §§720-740 gives the most coherent account.

παρῆσθα = "I wish that you were here" or εἴθε μὴ ἀπέθανες = "if only you had not died."

(b) Alternatively, ὤφελον + an infinitive may be used to express an unattainable wish. ὤφελον is the aorist of ὀφείλω (= owe), and it is conjugated. This construction then is literally "I/he ought to have done this" (= ὤφελον/ε ποιῆσαι τοῦτο, normally translated as "would that I/he had done this"). εἰ or εἰ γάρ may also be used with ὤφελον. More rarely ἐβουλόμην + an infinitive may be used analogously to ὤφελον to express an unattainable wish. The negative is expressed by ὤφελον μή, see **Smyth** §1781.

Example: Plato, **Crito** §44d6-8: εἰ γὰρ ὤφελον, ὦ Κρίτων, οἷοί τ' εἶναι οἱ πολλοὶ τὰ μέγιστα κακὰ ἐργάζεσθαι, ἵνα οἷοί τ' ἦσαν καὶ ἀγαθὰ τὰ μέγιστα. "**Would that** the many were capable of committing the greatest evils, in order that they were capable also of the greatest good."

READINGS:

12.1 Demosthenes, **On the Crown** §288: Demosthenes is explaining why he was chosen to give the funeral oration over the war dead instead of Aeschines.

διὰ ταῦτ' ἔμ' ἐχειροτόνησαν καὶ οὐχ ὑμᾶς. καὶ οὐχ ὁ μὲν δῆμος οὕτως, οἱ δὲ τῶν τετελευτηκότων πατέρες καὶ ἀδελφοὶ οἱ ὑπὸ τοῦ δήμου τόθ' αἱρεθέντες ἐπὶ τὰς ταφὰς ἄλλως πως, ἀλλὰ δέον ποιεῖν αὐτοὺς τὸ περίδειπνον ὡς παρ' οἰκειοτάτῳ τῶν τετελευτηκότων, ὥσπερ τἄλλ' εἴωθε γίγνεσθαι, τοῦτ' ἐποίησαν παρ' ἐμοί. εἰκότως· γένει μὲν γὰρ ἕκαστος ἑκάστῳ μᾶλλον οἰκεῖος ἦν ἐμοῦ, κοινῇ δὲ πᾶσιν οὐδεὶς ἐγγυτέρω· ᾧ γὰρ ἐκείνους σωθῆναι καὶ κατορθῶσαι μάλιστα διέφερεν, οὗτος καὶ παθόντων **ἃ μήποτ' ὤφελον** τῆς ὑπὲρ ἁπάντων λύπης πλεῖστον μετεῖχεν.

12.2 Plato, **Protagoras** §310d2-e1. Socrates is teasing Hippocrates, because he is very eager to study with the sophist Protagoras, who has just arrived in Athens.

καὶ ἐγὼ γιγνώσκων αὐτοῦ τὴν ἀνδρείαν καὶ τὴν πτοίησιν, "τί οὖν σοι," ἦν δ᾽ ἐγώ, "τοῦτο; μῶν τί σε ἀδικεῖ Πρωταγόρας"; καὶ ὃς γελάσας, "νὴ τοὺς θεούς," ἔφη, "ὦ Σώκρατες, ὅτι γε μόνος ἐστὶ σοφός, ἐμὲ δὲ οὐ ποιεῖ." "ἀλλὰ ναὶ μὰ Δία," ἔφην ἐγώ, "ἂν (= ἐὰν) αὐτῷ διδῷς ἀργύριον καὶ πείθῃς ἐκεῖνον, ποιήσει καὶ σὲ σοφόν." "εἰ γάρ," ἦ δ᾽ ὅς, "ὦ Ζεῦ καὶ θεοί, ἐν τούτῳ εἴη."

12.3: Xenophon, **Cyropaedia** 6.1.37-39: Araspas has disobeyed Cyrus' orders about the oversight of a beautiful female captive; Cyrus, instead of punishing Araspas, suggests that he might do him a favor by pretending to defect to the enemy.

καὶ ὁ Ἀράσπας ὑπολαβὼν εἶπεν· ἀλλὰ σὺ μέν, ὦ Κῦρε, καὶ ταῦτα ὅμοιος εἶ οἷόσπερ καὶ τἆλλα, πρᾶός τε καὶ συγγνώμων τῶν ἀνθρωπίνων ἁμαρτημάτων· ἐμὲ δ᾽, ἔφη, καὶ οἱ ἄλλοι ἄνθρωποι καταδύουσι τῷ ἄχει. ὡς γὰρ ὁ θροῦς διῆλθε τῆς ἐμῆς συμφορᾶς, οἱ μὲν ἐχθροὶ ἐφήδονταί μοι, οἱ δὲ φίλοι προσιόντες συμβουλεύουσιν ἐκποδὼν ἔχειν ἐμαυτόν, μή τι καὶ πάθω ὑπὸ σοῦ, ὡς ἠδικηκότος ἐμοῦ μεγάλα. καὶ ὁ Κῦρος εἶπεν· εὖ τοίνυν ἴσθι, ὦ Ἀράσπα, ὅτι ταύτῃ τῇ δόξῃ οἷός τ᾽ εἶ ἐμοί τε ἰσχυρῶς χαρίσασθαι καὶ τοὺς συμμάχους μεγάλα ὠφελῆσαι. εἰ γὰρ γένοιτο, ἔφη ὁ Ἀράσπας, ὅ τι ἐγώ σοι ἐν καιρῷ ἂν γενοίμην [αὖ χρήσιμος]. εἰ τοίνυν, ἔφη, προσποιησάμενος ἐμὲ φεύγειν ἐθέλοις εἰς τοὺς πολεμίους ἐλθεῖν, οἴομαι ἄν σε πιστευθῆναι ὑπὸ τῶν πολεμίων. ἔγωγε ναὶ μὰ Δί᾽, ἔφη ὁ Ἀράσπας, καὶ ὑπὸ τῶν φίλων οἶδα ὅτι ὡς σὲ πεφευγὼς λόγον ἂν [παρ]έχοιμι.

EXERCISES:

Write in Greek:

A Sentences:

1. Would that this had never happened, Cyrus.
2. May they perish before they are allowed to destroy the city.
3. I wish they were the sort of men who would be inclined to do good instead of ill to their fellows, as you are.
4. I wish that the Athenians had never executed Socrates.
5. Would that loving women instead of boys was not bad for the soul.
6. Let Protagoras make him wise, if he is able.
7. When Araspas heard about these events (would that they had never happened!) he left Cyrus in distress to go over to the enemy.
8. I wish that Protagoras might be the sort of man to make others wise, for then he would not be taking their money in vain.
9. Would that I had met Protagoras before I began to converse with Socrates.
10. Would that even my enemies had never suffered what I have suffered.

B Sentences:

1. I wish that Socrates had been able to leave the city. He was truly wiser than any of the citizens, for he knew what he knew and refused to pretend that he knew what he did not. Nor would he act unjustly through ignorance. Would that such a man were alive today!

2. They were afraid to allow Aeschines to deliver the funeral oration (ἐπιτάφιος λόγος) for those who had died in battle the year before—if only they had not died!—because he was too friendly towards Philip. Instead, the assembly chose Demosthenes, who was both a political opponent of Aeschines and a zealous defender of Athens against the incursions of Philip's armies. I wish we could have heard his speech.

3. A. "I wish I had known Protagoras, for they say that he was the wisest of the philosophers of that time. But he only arrived in Athens after I left to go to Sicily. I only learned about his teachings from Socrates. "

B. "If only Socrates had never met Protagoras! He was a sophist, you know, and later on the Athenians came to despise the sophists and to believe that Socrates was one of them."

CHAPTER THIRTEEN—POTENTIAL EXPRESSIONS[1]

1. In Greek the optative + ἄν and the indicative + ἄν are used to express a wide range of feelings held by the speaker, from vague possibility to strong expectation. These constructions are the grammatical equivalent of apodoses of future less vivid and contrary-to-fact conditions and are translated into English by the auxiliaries "would," "may," "might," "can," "could." The construction occurs very frequently as a question, as the examples demonstrate. The negative is οὐ.

(a) The optative + ἄν is used in expressions about the **future**. The usual tenses are present and aorist optative; perfect optative occurs rarely.

Example: Plato, **Republic** §328e4-5: καὶ δὴ καὶ σοῦ ἡδέως ἂν πυθοίμην. "And I would like to ask you. . . ."

(b) The imperfect indicative + ἄν is used for the **present**. Present potential expresses **what could or would be true now**. It is hypothetical in that it can imply (but need not) that the potential situation is untrue, that it is possible, but is not actually happening.

Example: Demosthenes, **On the Crown** §24: τί γὰρ καὶ βουλόμενοι μετεπέμπεσθ' ἂν αὐτοὺς ἐν τούτῳ τῷ καιρῷ; "What would be the point of your sending for them at this moment?"

(c) The imperfect or aorist indicative + ἄν is used for expressions about the past. This has the same meaning as the present potential, but now shifted into the past. Here the difference in tense is one of aspect.

---

[1] For further discussion see **Smyth** §§1761-1834, **GG** §§1299-1315, and **MT** §§192-229, 233-249.

2. The particle ἄν is postpositive and will naturally gravitate toward the opening of the sentence or phrase. It is particularly attracted to interrogatives, negatives, or adverbs. Often with potential optatives in indirect discourse the ἄν will precede the verb of speaking and appear to be attached to it.

Example: Plato, **Republic** §332c7-8: τί ἄν οἴει ἡμῖν αὐτὸν ἀποκρίνασθαι; "What answer do you suppose he would give us?"

3. When a potential construction is reported in indirect speech after a verb requiring the accusative + infinitive (or participle) construction, the verb expressing potential (whether optative or indicative) will be represented by the corresponding tense of the infinitive (or participle) **and the ἄν is retained.** Because present optative **and** imperfect indicative become present infinitives, and aorist optative **and** aorist indicative become aorist infinitives the distinction of direct discourse is lost; only context can determine whether optative or indicative was originally intended.

READINGS:

13.1 Plato, **Republic** §374c2-d7. Socrates is arguing that people have more aptitude for one skill than another and that excellence at a particular skill requires both aptitude and training. Skills are not interchangeable.

τὰ δὲ δὴ περὶ τὸν πόλεμον πότερον οὐ περὶ πλείστου ἐστὶν εὖ ἀπερ-

γασθέντα; ἢ οὕτω ῥᾴδιον, ὥστε καὶ γεωργῶν τις ἅμα πολεμικὸς

ἔσται καὶ σκυτοτομῶν καὶ ἄλλην τέχνην ἡντινοῦν ἐργαζόμενος,

πεττευτικὸς δὲ ἢ κυβευτικὸς ἱκανῶς οὐδ' **ἂν εἷς γένοιτο** μὴ αὐτὸ

τοῦτο ἐκ παιδὸς ἐπιτηδεύων, ἀλλὰ παρέργῳ χρώμενος; καὶ ἀσπίδα

μὲν λαβὼν ἤ τι ἄλλο τῶν πολεμικῶν ὅπλων τε καὶ ὀργάνων

αὐθημερὸν ὁπλιτικῆς ἤ τινος ἄλλης μάχης τῶν κατὰ πόλεμον ἱκανὸς

ἔσται ἀγωνιστής, τῶν δὲ ἄλλων ὀργάνων οὐδὲν οὐδένα δημιουργὸν

οὐδὲ ἀθλητὴν ληφθὲν ποιήσει, οὐδ' ἔσται χρήσιμον τῷ μήτε τὴν ἐπιστήμην ἑκάστου λαβόντι μήτε τὴν μελέτην ἱκανὴν παρασχομένῳ;

πολλοῦ γὰρ **ἄν, ἦ δ' ὅς, τὰ ὄργανα ἦν ἄξια.**

13.2 Plato, Crito §44b5-c5. Crito is begging Socrates to save himself and go into exile rather than stay in Athens and face execution.

ἀλλ', ὦ δαιμόνιε Σώκρατες, ἔτι καὶ νῦν ἐμοὶ πιθοῦ καὶ σώθητι· ὡς ἐμοί, ἐὰν σὺ ἀποθάνῃς, οὐ μία συμφορά ἐστιν, ἀλλὰ χωρὶς μὲν τοῦ ἐστερῆσθαι τοιούτου ἐπιτηδείου οἷον ἐγὼ οὐδένα μή ποτε εὑρήσω, ἔτι δὲ καὶ πολλοῖς δόξω, οἳ ἐμὲ καὶ σὲ μὴ σαφῶς ἴσασιν, ὡς οἷός τ' ὤν σε σῴζειν εἰ ἤθελον ἀναλίσκειν χρήματα, ἀμελῆσαι. καίτοι **τίς ἂν αἰσχίων εἴη ταύτης δόξα** ἢ δοκεῖν χρήματα περὶ πλείονος ποιεῖσθαι ἢ φίλους; οὐ γὰρ πείσονται οἱ πολλοὶ ὡς σὺ αὐτὸς οὐκ ἠθέλησας ἀπιέναι ἐνθένδε ἡμῶν προθυμουμένων.

13.3 Lucian, Judgment of the Goddesses §§7-8 (with an omission). Hermes has been instructed by Zeus to take Athena, Hera, and Aphrodite to the young shepherd, Paris, who is to sit in judgment on them. Paris is here arguing with Hermes that he is suited to judge the beauty of goats or heifers, but not immortal goddesses.

πῶς **ἂν** οὖν, ὦ δέσποτα Ἑρμῆ, **δυνηθείην** ἐγὼ θνητὸς αὐτὸς καὶ ἄγροικος ὢν δικαστὴς γενέσθαι παραδόξου θέας καὶ μείζονος ἢ κατὰ βουκόλον; τὰ γὰρ τοιαῦτα κρίνειν τῶν ἁβρῶν μᾶλλον καὶ ἀστικῶν· τὸ δὲ ἐμόν, αἶγα μὲν αἰγὸς ὁποτέρα ἡ καλλίων καὶ δά- μαλιν ἄλλης δαμάλεως, τάχ' **ἂν δικάσαιμι** κατὰ τὴν τέχνην· αὗται δὲ πᾶσαί τε ὁμοίως καλαὶ καὶ οὐκ οἶδ' ὅπως **ἄν** τις ἀπὸ τῆς ἑτέρας ἐπὶ τὴν ἑτέραν **μεταγάγοι** τὴν ὄψιν ἀποσπάσας· οὐ γὰρ ἐθέλει ἀφίστασθαι ῥᾳδίως, ἀλλ' ἔνθα **ἂν ἀπερείσῃ** τὸ πρῶτον, τούτου ἔχεται καὶ τὸ παρὸν ἐπαινεῖ. . .καὶ ὅλως περικέχυταί μοι τὸ κάλλος αὐτῶν καὶ ὅλον περιείληφέ με καὶ ἄχθομαι, ὅτι μὴ[1] καὶ αὐτὸς ὥσπερ ὁ ΄Αργος ὅλῳ βλέπειν δύναμαι τῷ σώματι. δοκῶ δ᾽ ἄν μοι καλῶς δικάσαι πάσαις ἀποδοὺς τὸ μῆλον.

[1]Lucian frequently uses ὅτι μὴ where ὅτι οὐ would be expected in the classical period.

In these last two readings consider the fine line between the potential use of ἄν and its use in the apodoses to future less vivid and contrafactual conditions. In 13.4, for example, does it alter either the meaning or the translation if you consider the final two questions to be independent potential optatives or part of a series of apodoses to the condition εἰ συνέβη τόθ᾽ ἁλῶναι? In 13.5 do we regard ἄν. . . ἐθελήσειαν as a potential optative or the apodosis of a condition, the apodosis of which is expressed as a participle (νομίσαντες)?

13.4 Demosthenes, **Against Androtion** §2. Demosthenes complains that Androtion had accused him falsely of charges so heinous that, if they were true, no one would have wished to know him.

αἰτιασάμενος γάρ με ἃ καὶ λέγειν ἂν ὀκνήσειέ τις, εἰ μὴ τύχοι προσόμοιος ὢν τούτῳ, τὸν πατέρ᾽ ὡς ἀπέκτον᾽ ἐγὼ τὸν ἐμαυτοῦ, καὶ κατασκευάσας ἀσεβείας γραφήν, οὐκ ἐπ᾽ ἐμέ, ἀλλ᾽ ἐπὶ τὸν θεῖόν μου, γράψας ἀσεβεῖν ἐμοὶ συνιόντ᾽ εἰς ταὐτὸ ὡς πεποιηκότι ταῦτα, εἰς ἀγῶνα κατέστησεν, ὃν εἰ συνέβη τόθ᾽ ἁλῶναι, τίς ἂν ἀθλιώτερ᾽ ἐμοῦ **πεπονθὼς ἦν** ὑπὸ τούτου; τίς γὰρ **ἂν** ἢ φίλος ἢ ξένος εἰς ταὐτό ποτ᾽ ἐλθεῖν **ἠθέλησεν** ἐμοί; τίς δ᾽ **ἂν εἴασε** πόλις που παρ᾽ ἑαυτῇ γενέσθαι τὸν τὸ τοιοῦτ᾽ ἀσέβημα δοκοῦντ᾽ εἰργάσθαι; οὐκ ἔστιν οὐδεμία.

13.5 Thucydides 6.34.2-4: Hermocrates is advising the Syracusans what to do about the Athenian invasion.

δοκεῖ δέ μοι καὶ ἐς Καρχηδόνα ἄμεινον εἶναι πέμψαι· οὐ γὰρ ἀνέλπιστον αὐτοῖς ἀλλ᾽ αἰεὶ διὰ φόβου εἰσὶ μή ποτε ᾿Αθηναῖοι αὐτοῖς ἐπὶ τὴν πόλιν ἔλθωσιν ὥστε τάχ᾽ **ἂν** ἴσως νομίσαντες, εἰ τάδε προήσονται, κἂν σφεῖς ἐν πόνῳ εἶναι, **ἐθελήσειαν** ἡμῖν ἤτοι

κρύφα γε ἢ φανερῶς ἢ ἐξ ἑνός γέ του τρόπου ἀμῦναι. δυνατοὶ δὲ εἰσὶ
μάλιστα τῶν νῦν, βουληθέντες· χρυσὸν γὰρ καὶ ἄργυρον πλεῖστον
κέκτηνται, ὅθεν ὅ τε πόλεμος καὶ τἆλλα εὐπορεῖ. πέμπωμεν δὲ καὶ
ἐς τὴν Λακεδαίμονα καὶ ἐς Κόρινθον δεόμενοι δεῦρο κατὰ τάχος βοηθεῖν καὶ τὸν ἐκεῖ πόλεμον κινεῖν. ὃ δὲ μάλιστα ἐγώ τε νομίζω
ἐπίκαιρον ὑμεῖς τε διὰ τὸ ξύνηθες ἥσυχον ἥκιστ' ἂν ὀξέως
πείθοισθε, ὅμως εἰρήσεται. Σικελιῶται γὰρ εἰ ἐθέλοιμεν ξύμπαντες, εἰ δὲ μή, ὅτι πλεῖστοι μεθ' ἡμῶν, καθελκύσαντες ἅπαν τὸ
ὑπάρχον ναυτικὸν μετὰ δυοῖν μηνοῖν τροφῆς ἀπαντῆσαι 'Αθηναίοις
ἐς Τάραντα καὶ ἄκραν 'Ιαπυγίαν, καὶ δῆλον ποιῆσαι αὐτοῖς ὅτι οὐ
περὶ τῆς Σικελίας πρότερον ἔσται ὁ ἀγὼν ἢ τοῦ ἐκείνους
περαιωθῆναι τὸν 'Ιόνιον, μάλιστ' ἂν αὐτοὺς ἐκπλήξαιμεν καὶ ἐς
λογισμὸν καταστήσαιμεν ὅτι ὁρμώμεθα μὲν ἐκ φιλίας χώρας
φύλακες (ὑποδέχεται γὰρ ἡμᾶς Τάρας), τὸ δὲ πέλαγος αὐτοῖς πολὺ
περαιοῦσθαι μετὰ πάσης τῆς παρασκευῆς, χαλεπὸν δὲ διὰ πλοῦ
μῆκος ἐν τάξει μεῖναι, καὶ ἡμῖν ἂν εὐεπίθετος εἴη, βραδεῖά τε καὶ
κατ' ὀλίγον προσπίπτουσα.

EXERCISES:

Write in Greek using potential constructions wherever possible.

A Sentences:

1. What could we answer?
2. Would they have spoken in favor of killing your brother?
3. You could give him the money.
4. I wouldn't do such unjust things, nor would she.
5. Neither of them could pay attention to the teacher.
6. What would you want us to do about it?
7. The Athenians would not have crossed the sea easily.
8. We must remain at Tarentum and await their arrival.
9. What would be the point of stopping them?
10. Socrates lacked the words that would have persuaded the court.

B Sentences:

1. Why would they hesitate to tell the truth? If only I had known what they thought before I entered the court. At least I would have been prepared to endure their hatred and contempt. Has anyone hated you as they have hated me? Surely no one has. What could I have done to avoid this misfortune?

2. Now, Crito, you must not be afraid that the many would despise you for neglecting me when I was in the greatest peril. Do you really believe that I have been convicted because you and my other friends would not have paid sufficient money to my jailers? Neither your money nor our friendship could have saved me. For my deity has urged me to say or do nothing contrary to its instruction, even if obedience should mean death. How could I not perish if the god so wishes?

3. It would be better to have the Athenians as allies than as enemies, but since this is no longer possible, I would advise you to prepare for war. You ought already to have sent envoys to the Carthaginians and to any other Greeks who might be well disposed towards us, in order to persuade them to support us, or at least not to enter into an alliance with the Athenians. As I said, you should have done this before making any other preparations. But since things are as they are, I would strengthen our navy, increase the provisions and the number of rowers, and be prepared for an early attack. The Athenians say that they are not at war with us and that they would, like us, prefer peace, but I, at least, am not inclined to trust them.

CHAPTER FOURTEEN—CONDITIONS AND CONCESSIONS[1]

1. **Conditional** sentences, have two parts, the names of which derive from ancient grammarians: the **protasis** (πρότασις = that which is put forward) sets forth the condition (= "if. . ."), and the **apodosis** (ἀπόδοσις = the giving back or return) functions as the main clause of the condition ("then such-and-such will/has/may/might/could happen/be happening/happened"). In Greek, the protasis is regularly introduced by εἰ or ἐάν (= εἰ + ἄν, and sometimes contracted to ἤν or ἄν), or in its negative form, εἰ μή or ἐὰν μή (= "if not" or "unless"). Since the apodosis is the main clause, any independent construction found in Greek can function as an apodosis (see below 4c for examples). The negative is normally οὐ unless the construction requires μή.

2. Conditions have been categorized in a variety of ways—by **time** (that is, whether they refer to present, past or future events), by **fulfillment vs. non-fulfillment** (whether or not they express wishes about something that can happen or has, in fact, not happened), by **form** of protasis and apodosis (that is, whether they require εἰ or ἐάν in the protasis, ἄν in the apodosis); the names may vary accordingly, see **Smyth** §§2289-2297. The scheme below is organized by time:

	PROTASIS	APODOSIS
PRESENT		
A. OPEN	εἰ + present indicative	present indicative
B. CONTRAFACTUAL	εἰ + imperf. indic.	imperf. indic.+ ἄν
C. GENERAL	ἐάν + subjunctive	present indicative
PAST		
A. OPEN	εἰ + past indicative	past indicative

---

[1] For further discussion see **Smyth** §§2289-2368, **GG** §§1392-1450, and **MT** §§ 378-513.

B. CONTRAFACTUAL ἄν	εἰ + aorist indicative	aorist indicative +
C. GENERAL	εἰ + optative	imperfect indicative
FUTURE		
A. MOST VIVID	εἰ + future indicative	future indicative
B. MORE VIVID	ἐάν + subjunctive	future indicative
C. LESS VIVID	εἰ + optative	optative + ἄν

Open (also called **simple** or **real**) conditions express **no expecta-tions** about the reality or probability of the protasis. They may use any of the indicative tenses, though present, imperfect, and aorist are the most common. Example: "If he is late, they are waiting for him." "If he was late, they did not wait for him."

Contrafactual (also called **unreal** or **hypothetical**) conditions assume in the protasis what **is not** or **was not** the case, e.g., "If I were you, I would not do that." "If he had been late, they would have waited for him." Aorist and imperfect indicative are the usual tenses.

General conditions express circumstances that **continually** or **fre-quently happen** or happened. They refer to past and present events. In general conditions, the introductory particles (εἰ, ἐάν) are often translated "if ever" or "whenever." E.g., "Whenever he is late, they wait for him." "Whenever he was late, they did not wait for him."

Conditions that express expectations for the **future** are usually called "vivid" in grammar books. While in practice they show some correspondence with the open and contrary-to-fact conditions of the present and past, they also show a few differences.

The **Most Vivid** condition is usually threatening or advising in tone, e.g., "If he will be late (i.e., persist in being late), they will wait for him" (or else!).

The **More Vivid** condition behaves like an open condition in future, e.g., "If he is late, they will wait for him," but it can also behave like a general condition in the future, e.g, "**Whenever** he is late, they will wait for him"; only context can make it clear how you should translate into English.

The **Less Vivid** condition (also called a should-would condition) expresses a doubt or hesitancy about the likelihood of what is expressed in the protasis, e.g., "If he **should** be late, then then **would** wait for him" (but I doubt he will be late).

3. As in English, conditions may have **more than one protasis** connected to a single apodosis. εἰ μὲν . . . εἰ δέ or just εἰ . . . εἰ introduce co-ordinate protases (see **14.1, 14.2, 14.5** below for examples); but εἴτε . . . εἴτε, translated "whether. . .or," introduce alternative indirect questions (see **14.4**) and below Chapter Nineteen.

4. Conditions may appear in the above listed "pure" forms or they may show any of the following variations:

(a) Conditions may **mix protases of one form with apodoses of another**. This is extremely common, especially in contrary-to-fact conditions. See below **14.5**: εἰ γὰρ ἐκ τοῦ παρεληλυθότος χρόνου τὰ δέοντα οὗτοι **συνεβούλευσαν**, οὐδὲν ἂν ὑμᾶς νῦν **ἔδει** βουλεύεσθαι.

(b) **Participial constructions may substitute for either protasis or apodosis or both**. A participle substituting for a protasis is negated by μή. See below **14.2**: μὴ ἀφιέντων 'Αθηναίων (protasis); ἀποκτεινύντων καὶ ἀναβιωσκομένων γ' ἂν (apodosis), **14.5**: πρῶτος ἀναστὰς (protasis).

(c) The **apodosis** may be phrased as a **question, command, wish, or potential optative**. For an example see below **14.2**: ἐὰν μὲν φαίνηται δίκαιον, πειρώμεθα, εἰ δὲ μή, ἐῶμεν (hortatory subjunctive), **18.5**: εἴ σοι εἶπεν. . .τί ἂν αὐτῷ εἶπες πρὸς ταῦτα; (question), see above **10.3**: εἰ γάρ τι τοιοῦτον φοβῇ, ἔασον αὐτὸ χαίρειν. (command).

(d) The **apodosis** may become **an infinitive**. See Chapter Eighteen for a discussion of conditions in indirect statement. See below **14.2**: πότερον δίκαιον ἐμὲ ἐνθένδε πειρᾶσθαι ἐξιέναι μὴ ἀφιέντων 'Αθηναίων ἢ οὐ δίκαιον, **14.4**: εἰ μὲν ἐν δίκῃ, ἐάν, εἰ δὲ μή, ἐπεξιέναι, **13.5**: εἰ τάδε προήσονται, κἂν σφεῖς ἐν πόνῳ εἶναι.

(e) The **protasis** may lack its verb or be **implied** in some other form of expression, e.g., **Third Olynthiac** 3.14 where the phrase εἵνεκά γε ψηφισμάτων substitutes for a protasis: πάλαι γὰρ ἂν εἵνεκά γε ψηφισμάτων ἐδεδώκει δίκην = "if decrees were of any avail, he would long ago have paid the penalty." The potential construction may be thought of as the equivalent of certain types of conditions with the if-clause suppressed, e.g., "I wouldn't do that" (sc. "If I were you"), see Chapter Thirteen.

(f) The **apodosis** may be missing (said to be **suppressed** or in ellipse). Example: "If I were you" (sc. I wouldn't do that). Grammatically, this is the equivalent of a wish, see Chapter Twelve.

(g) The apodosis of a contrary-to-fact condition sometimes contains a verb that indicates **necessity, propriety, or obligation,** e.g., χρῆν, ἐξῆν, ἔδει, εἰκὸς ἦν. With these words which normally represent an unrealized action the ἄν is often omitted.

9. **Concessive** clauses[1] are a type of condition in which something is granted or conceded, in spite of the force of the main clause. The apodosis has an adversative force, sometimes marked by ὅμως, "nevertheless." Concessive clauses are usually introduced by "although" or "though" in English. They show the same range of tenses and moods as conditions. There are two ways of expressing concession in Greek:

(a) They may be introduced by εἰ καί or ἐὰν καί, usually translated "although," or "even though," or by καὶ εἰ (κεἰ) or καὶ ἐάν (κἄν), usually translated "even if." "Not even if" is expressed by οὐδ' εἰ, οὐδ' ἐάν. The difference between εἰ καί and καὶ εἰ is a matter of emphasis: εἰ καί introduces a concession conceived of as a real possibility, though of no importance for the writer's conclusion; καὶ εἰ introduces an extreme concession, scarcely imagined as a possible outcome.

However, not all instances of εἰ καί and καὶ εἰ are concessive; occasionally καί will exert its usual linking force as in

---

[1] For further discussion see **Smyth** §§2369-2382 and **GG** §§1435-1436.

14.2 below where καὶ ἐάν and κἄν mean "and if." Context should make the concessive force clear.

Examples: Plato **Apology** §38c3-4: φήσουσι γὰρ δὴ σοφὸν εἶναι, **εἰ καὶ** μή εἰμι, οἱ βουλόμενοι ὑμῖν ὀνειδίζειν. "For they will say that I (sc. Socrates) am wise, **although** I am not, those who wish to find fault with you."

Demosthenes **Against Meidias**, §199: τίς γάρ ἐστιν ὅστις καταχειροτονηθὲν αὐτοῦ, καὶ ταῦτ' ἀσεβεῖν περὶ τὴν ἑορτήν, **εἰ καὶ** μηδεὶς ἄλλος ἐπῆν ἀγὼν ἔτι μηδὲ κίνδυνος, οὐκ ἂν ἐπ' αὐτῷ τούτῳ κατέδυ καὶ μέτριον παρέσχεν ἑαυτὸν τόν γε δὴ μέχρι τῆς κρίσεως χρόνον, **εἰ καὶ** μὴ πάντα; οὐδεὶς ὅστις οὐκ ἄν. "Who is there who, if a verdict of guilty had been recorded against him, and that was for outrages during the festival—**even though** there had been no further suit pending nor further danger—would not have effaced himself and behaved circumspectly, at least until the time of the trial—**even though** not forever? There is no one who would not."

Plato **Symposium** §182d5-6: ἐνθυμηθέντι γὰρ ὅτι λέγεται κάλλιον τὸ φανερῶς ἐρᾶν τοῦ λάθρᾳ, καὶ μάλιστα τῶν γενναιοτάτων καὶ ἀρίστων, **κἂν** αἰσχίους ἄλλων ὦσι. . . . "To someone considering the fact that to be in love openly is said to be a better thing than to be in love secretly, especially with the naturally better sort of boy, **even if** they are less attractive. . ."

(b) Concessions may be introduced by καίπερ, καί or καὶ ταῦτα [-947 Nope] with a participle.

Examples: Demosthenes **Against Meidias** §72: οὐδὲ τὸ τύπτεσθαι τοῖς ἐλευθέροις ἐστὶ δεινόν, **καίπερ ὂν δεινόν**, ἀλλὰ τὸ ἐφ' ὕβρει. "It is not the being struck that is a terrible thing for a free man—**though** it is terrible—but the being struck in insolence."

Demosthenes **Against Meidias**, §199: τίς γάρ ἐστιν ὅστις καταχειροτονηθὲν αὐτοῦ, **καὶ ταῦτ'** ἀσεβεῖν περὶ τὴν ἑορτήν. . . . "Who is there that, if a verdict of guilty had been recorded against him, **and that** was for outrages during the festival. . . ."

READINGS:

14.1 Thucydides 1.53.3-4: The Athenians respond to the Corinthians about their willingness to aid the Corcyreans.

οἱ δὲ Ἀθηναῖοι τοιάδε ἀπεκρίναντο. "οὔτε ἄρχομεν πολέμου, ὦ ἄνδρες Πελοποννήσιοι, οὔτε τὰς σπονδὰς λύομεν, Κερκυραίοις δὲ τοῖσδε ξυμμάχοις οὖσι βοηθοὶ ἤλθομεν. εἰ μὲν οὖν ἄλλοσέ ποι βούλεσθε πλεῖν, οὐ κωλύομεν· εἰ δὲ ἐπὶ Κέρκυραν πλευσεῖσθε ἢ ἐς τῶν ἐκείνων τι χωρίων, οὐ περιοψόμεθα κατὰ τὸ δυνατόν."

14.2 Plato, **Crito** §48b11-d5 (with omissions). Socrates argues that it is necessary to consider whether his leaving the city after the Athenians have condemned him to death is a just or an unjust act.

οὐκοῦν ἐκ τῶν ὁμολογουμένων τοῦτο σκεπτέον, πότερον **δίκαιον ἐμὲ ἐνθένδε πειρᾶσθαι ἐξιέναι μὴ ἀφιέντων** Ἀθηναίων **ἢ οὐ δίκαιον· καὶ ἐὰν μὲν φαίνηται δίκαιον, πειρώμεθα, εἰ δὲ μή, ἐῶμεν.** ἃς δὲ σὺ λέγεις τὰς σκέψεις περί τε ἀναλώσεως χρημάτων καὶ δόξης καὶ παίδων τροφῆς, μὴ ὡς ἀληθῶς ταῦτα, ὦ Κρίτων, σκέμματα ἦ[1] τῶν ῥᾳδίως **ἀποκτεινύντων καὶ ἀναβιωσκομένων** γ᾽ ἄν, εἰ οἷοί τ᾽ ἦσαν. ... ἡμῖν δ᾽ ... μὴ οὐδὲν ἄλλο σκεπτέον ἦ ἢ ὅπερ νυνδὴ ἐλέγομεν, πότερον δίκαια πράξομεν ... ἢ τῇ ἀληθείᾳ **ἀδικήσομεν πάντα ταῦτα ποιοῦντες. κἂν φαινώμεθα** ἄδικα αὐτὰ ἐργαζόμενοι, μὴ οὐ δέῃ ὑπολογίζεσθαι οὔτ᾽ **εἰ ἀποθνήσκειν δεῖ** παραμένοντας καὶ ἡσυχίαν ἄγοντας, οὔτε ἄλλο ὁτιοῦν πάσχειν πρὸ τοῦ ἀδικεῖν.

[1] μὴ + the independent subjunctive is used to indicate "doubtful assertion," that is, what the speaker suspects, but does not know for sure. The construction is common in Plato, but rare elsewhere.

14.3 Thucydides 1.86.1-5 (repeated from 8.2).

τοὺς μὲν λόγους τοὺς πολλοὺς τῶν Ἀθηναίων οὐ γιγνώσκω· ἐπαινέσαντες γὰρ πολλὰ ἑαυτοὺς οὐδαμοῦ ἀντεῖπον ὡς οὐκ ἀδικοῦσι τοὺς ἡμετέρους ξυμμάχους καὶ τὴν Πελοπόννησον· καίτοι **εἰ πρὸς τοὺς Μήδους ἐγένοντο ἀγαθοὶ τότε, πρὸς δ' ἡμᾶς κακοὶ νῦν, διπλασίας ζημίας ἄξιοί εἰσιν**, ὅτι ἀντ' ἀγαθῶν κακοὶ γεγένηνται. ἡμεῖς δὲ ὅμοιοι καὶ τότε καὶ νῦν ἐσμέν, καὶ **τοὺς ξυμμάχους, ἢν σωφρονῶμεν, οὐ περιοψόμεθα ἀδικουμένους οὐδὲ μελλήσομεν τιμωρεῖν**· οἱ δ' οὐκέτι μέλλουσι κακῶς πάσχειν. ἄλλοις μὲν γὰρ χρήματά ἐστι πολλὰ καὶ νῆες καὶ ἵπποι, ἡμῖν δὲ ξύμμαχοι ἀγαθοί, οὓς οὐ παραδοτέα τοῖς Ἀθηναίοις ἐστίν, οὐδὲ δίκαις καὶ λόγοις διακριτέα μὴ λόγῳ καὶ αὐτοὺς βλαπτομένους, ἀλλὰ τιμωρητέα ἐν τάχει καὶ παντὶ σθένει. καὶ ὡς ἡμᾶς πρέπει βουλεύεσθαι ἀδικουμένους μηδεὶς διδασκέτω, ἀλλὰ τοὺς μέλλοντας ἀδικεῖν μᾶλλον πρέπει πολὺν χρόνον βουλεύεσθαι. ψηφίζεσθε οὖν, ὦ Λακεδαιμόνιοι, ἀξίως τῆς Σπάρτης τὸν πόλεμον, καὶ μήτε τοὺς Ἀθηναίους ἐᾶτε μείζους γίγνεσθαι μήτε τοὺς ξυμμάχους καταπροδιδῶμεν, ἀλλὰ ξὺν τοῖς θεοῖς ἐπίωμεν ἐπὶ τοὺς ἀδικοῦντας.

14.4 Plato Euthyphro §4b7-c3 (repeated from 4.1).

γελοῖον, ὦ Σώκρατες, ὅτι οἴει τι διαφέρειν εἴτε ἀλλότριος εἴτε οἰκεῖος ὁ τεθνεώς, ἀλλ' οὐ τοῦτο μόνον δεῖν φυλάττειν, εἴτε ἐν δίκῃ ἔκτεινεν ὁ κτείνας εἴτε μή, **καὶ εἰ μὲν ἐν δίκῃ, ἐᾶν, εἰ δὲ μή, ἐπεξιέναι, ἐάνπερ ὁ κτείνας συνέστιός σοι καὶ ὁμοτράπεζος ᾖ**· ἴσον γὰρ τὸ μίασμα γίγνεται **ἐὰν συνῇς** τῷ τοιούτῳ συνειδὼς καὶ **μὴ ἀφοσιοῖς** σεαυτόν τε καὶ ἐκεῖνον τῇ δίκῃ ἐπεξιών.

14.5 Demosthenes, First Philippic §1. Demosthenes explains at the beginning of this speech why he has risen to speak before more senior and distinguished men.

εἰ μὲν περὶ καινοῦ τινος πράγματος προυτίθετ', ὦ ἄνδρες Ἀθηναῖοι, λέγειν, ἐπισχὼν ἂν ἕως οἱ πλεῖστοι τῶν εἰωθότων γνώμην ἀπεφήναντο, εἰ μὲν ἤρεσκέ τί μοι τῶν ὑπὸ τούτων ῥηθέντων, ἡσυχίαν ἂν ἦγον, εἰ δὲ μή, τότ' ἂν αὐτὸς ἐπειρώμην ἃ γιγνώσκω λέγειν· ἐπειδὴ δὲ περὶ ὧν πολλάκις εἰρήκασιν οὗτοι πρότερον συμβαίνει καὶ νυνὶ σκοπεῖν, ἡγοῦμαι καὶ πρῶτος ἀναστὰς εἰκότως ἂν συγγνώμης τυγχάνειν. εἰ γὰρ ἐκ τοῦ παρεληλυθότος χρόνου τὰ δέονθ' οὗτοι συνεβούλευσαν, οὐδὲν ἂν ὑμᾶς νῦν ἔδει βουλεύεσθαι.

14.6 Plato Symposium §§182d5-183a8. The speech of Pausanias in which he argues that Athenian custom permits those in love to behave in ways that would be considered shameful if the individual so acting were engaged in any other activity.

ἐνθυμηθέντι[1] γὰρ ὅτι λέγεται κάλλιον τὸ φανερῶς ἐρᾶν τοῦ λάθρᾳ, καὶ μάλιστα τῶν γενναιοτάτων καὶ ἀρίστων, κἂν αἰσχίους ἄλλων ὦσι, καὶ ὅτι αὖ ἡ παρακέλευσις τῷ ἐρῶντι παρὰ πάντων θαυμαστή, οὐχ ὥς τι αἰσχρὸν ποιοῦντι, καὶ ἑλόντι τε καλὸν δοκεῖ εἶναι καὶ μὴ ἑλόντι αἰσχρόν, καὶ πρὸς τὸ ἐπιχειρεῖν ἑλεῖν ἐξουσίαν ὁ νόμος δέδωκε τῷ ἐραστῇ θαυμαστὰ ἔργα ἐργαζομένῳ ἐπαινεῖσθαι, ἃ εἴ τις τολμῴη ποιεῖν ἄλλ' ὁτιοῦν διώκων καὶ βουλόμενος διαπράξασθαι πλὴν τοῦτο, τὰ μέγιστα καρποῖτ' ἂν ὀνείδη· εἰ γὰρ ἢ χρήματα βουλόμενος παρά του λαβεῖν ἢ ἀρχὴν ἄρξαι ἤ τινα ἄλλην δύναμιν ἐθέλοι ποιεῖν οἷάπερ οἱ ἐρασταὶ πρὸς τὰ παιδικά, ἱκετείας τε καὶ ἀντιβολήσεις ἐν ταῖς δεήσεσιν ποιούμενοι, καὶ ὅρκους ὀμνύντες, καὶ κοιμήσεις ἐπὶ θύραις, καὶ ἐθέλοντες δουλείας δουλεύειν οἵας οὐδ' ἂν δοῦλος οὐδείς, ἐμποδίζοιτο ἂν μὴ πράττειν οὕτω τὴν πρᾶξιν καὶ ὑπὸ φίλων καὶ ὑπὸ ἐχθρῶν. . . .

[1]Pausanias breaks off his thought before completing it; there is nothing in the sentence to govern ἐνθυμηθέντι.

14.7 Demosthenes, **First Olynthiac** §§25-26. Demosthenes is urging the Athenians to enter into an alliance with Olynthus against Philip of Macedon in order to halt Philip's progress into Greece at that northern territory.

ἔτι τοίνυν, ὦ ἄνδρες 'Αθηναῖοι, μηδὲ τοῦθ' ὑμᾶς λανθανέτω, ὅτι νῦν

αἵρεσίς ἐστιν ὑμῖν πότερ' ὑμᾶς ἐκεῖ χρὴ πολεμεῖν ἢ παρ' ὑμῖν

ἐκεῖνον (= Philip). **ἐὰν μὲν γὰρ ἀντέχῃ** τὰ τῶν 'Ολυνθίων,

ὑμεῖς ἐκεῖ **πολεμήσετε** καὶ τὴν (sc. γῆν) ἐκείνου **κακῶς**

ποιήσετε, τὴν ὑπάρχουσαν καὶ τὴν οἰκείαν ταύτην ἀδεῶς καρ-

πούμενοι· **ἂν (= ἐὰν) δ' ἐκεῖνα Φίλιππος λάβῃ**, τίς αὐτὸν

κωλύσει δεῦρο βαδίζειν; Θηβαῖοι; μὴ λίαν πικρὸν εἰπεῖν ἦ ᾧ καὶ

συνεισβαλοῦσιν ἑτοίμως. ἀλλὰ Φωκεῖς; οἱ τὴν οἰκείαν οὐχ οἷοί τε

ὄντες φυλάττειν, **ἐὰν μὴ βοηθήσηθ' ὑμεῖς**. ἢ ἄλλος τις; ἀλλ', ὦ

τᾶν, οὐχὶ βουλήσεται. **τῶν ἀτοπωτάτων μέντἂν εἴη, εἰ, ἃ**

νῦν ἄνοιαν ὀφλισκάνων ὅμως ἐκλαλεῖ, ταῦτα δυνηθεὶς **μὴ**

πράξει.

EXERCISES

Write in Greek using conditions wherever possible:

A Sentences:

1. If we had kept quiet, Philip would have been able to launch an attack against Greece.
2. If the laws should speak to Socrates, what would they say?
3. Is it necessary to prosecute your father if he killed someone unjustly?
4. Let us consider nothing else but whether Socrates committed an unjust act; if he did, let us execute him, if not, let us release him.

5. If you were wise, you would consider the doing of injustice worse than the being a victim of injustice.

6. Whenever Socrates meets an Athenian who prefers the making of money to the care of his soul, he exhorts him in his customary way.

7. If the Athenians willingly kill Socrates, what are we to think about their laws and their city?

8. For the Athenians who killed Socrates was the pollution the same, whether they did it willingly or unwillingly?

9. If he could have, would Demosthenes have prevented the unification of Greece?

10. If the Athenians were unwilling, should Socrates have tried to escape?

11. Even if the usual speaker had been willing to come forward, Demosthenes would still have spoken.

12. We will pardon our allies for giving us poor advice, even if they did so deliberately.

13. If you wish to stay in Athens we will allow it, even though we prefer that you leave the city.

14. We are going to give you advice, even though you may not listen.

15. If you were to do the sort of things that lovers do in pursuit of their beloved, we would have to send you out of the city.

B Sentences:

1. Now if Meidias had insulted me as a private citizen, I would have considered it appropriate to accuse him before you and would have expected that, if I proved my case, you, men of Athens, in accordance with your sworn oaths, would have exacted a suitable punishment. But as it is, he stands accused not of insult, but of sacrilege (if it is proper to consider my person, which he outraged, sacred for the period of the festival), a crime far more heinous, and far more worthy of condemnation and death. (For vocabulary see **4.2** and **13.4**.)

2. Soc. If you are wise, my friend, you will be able to answer my questions.

Friend. If I were wise, Socrates, I would already have left this party. For this I know well: whenever other men turn their thoughts to pleasure, you desire only to engage in serious discussion. If anyone is willing to encourage you, you will spend the night in talk.

Soc. Can it be that you know me too well to answer me anything? Or is it that you are afraid to appear foolish?

Friend. Not only would I appear to be foolish, I would certainly prove myself to be so, if I were to try to engage in debate with you.

3. Whenever Alcibiades was in love, he was accustomed to do the most outrageous things for his beloved. He would sleep in doorways, make all sorts of empty promises, give away any amount of money in order to persuade his quarry to return his affections. Now whenever Socrates saw him engaging in this behavior, he tried to persuade him that these actions damaged his soul. But this only caused Alcibiades to fall in love with Socrates.

CHAPTER FIFTEEN—RELATIVE CLAUSES[1]

The term "relative clause" can designate any subordinate clause introduced by a relative pronoun, pronominal adjective, or adverbial expression of time, place, or manner. For convenience relative clauses can be divided into (i) those with a **definite** referent and (ii) those with an **indefinite** referent. **Definite** relative clauses refer to a **specific** person, place, time, object, or event. Usually these take **indicative tenses** of the verb, but they may also take **any construction** that appears in an independent sentence. (For example, in **4.5** the relative clause contains the apodosis to an unreal condition.) Their negative is in accord with the construction that appears. The specific behavior of indefinite relative clauses is set out in the next chapter; the rules for agreement and the behavior of relatives with respect to their referents, set forth below, are the same for both types.

1. The following classes of pronoun or adverb introduce such clauses:

(a) **relative pronouns**, either definite (ὅς, ἥ, ὅ), ὅσπερ, or indefinite (ὅστις, ἥτις, ὅτι, which may be written as ὅ τι or ὅ, τι to distinguish it from ὅτι = that).

(b) **pronominal adjectives**, some of which are called "correlatives" because they have related forms which are used as interrogative or demonstrative pronouns (see **Smyth** §340). The most common are: ὅσος (= as much as, related to the demonstrative τοσοῦτος, and the interrogative πόσος); οἷος (= such a kind as, related to τοιοῦτος, ποῖος); ἡλίκος (= as old [large] as, related to τηλικόσδε, τηλικοῦτος, πηλίκος).

---

[1] For further discussion see **Smyth** §§2488-2559, **G G** §§1437-146, and Goodwin **MT** §§514-537.

(c) **adverbs**, e.g., οὗ (= where); οἷ (= whither); ᾗ (= in which way); ὅθεν (= whence); ὡς (= as, how), see **Smyth** §346. For adverbial expressions of time see Chapter Seventeen, 3.

2. The relative pronoun will **agree with its referent in number and gender**, but its **case will be determined by its use in the relative clause**. In **15.1** below, for example, εἴ τίς ἐστιν ἐπαΐων, ὃν δεῖ καὶ αἰσχύνεσθαι καὶ φοβεῖσθαι, ὅν is masculine, singular in agreement with its antecedent τις; it is accusative because in the relative clause it serves as the object of αἰσχύνεσθαι καὶ φοβεῖσθαι; ᾧ in the next clause has the same antecedent (τις ἐπαΐων), but now is dative, because it serves as the object of ἀκολουθήσομεν.

(a) As in English, the **referent** of the relative (definite or indefinite) **is often omitted** if it can be supplied from context.

Example: Demosthenes **Against Meidias** §24: βούλομαι δὲ πρὸ τούτων εἰπεῖν οἷς ἐπιχειρήσειν αὐτὸν ἀκήκο' ἐξαπατᾶν ὑμᾶς. "Before I come to these matters (πρὸ τούτων), I want to talk about the deceptions which I have heard he will try to use on you."

(b) The **relative** which stands as the object of a verb in the accusative case **may be attracted to the case of its referent** when the referent stands in either the genitive or dative. See **Smyth** §2522.

(c) If the omitted referent would have been in either the genitive or dative case, the relative may be attracted into that case. E.g., Xenophon **Cyropaedia** 5.1.8: ἀμελήσας ὧν (= ἐκείνων ἃ) με δεῖ πράττειν. Note however, that masculine and feminine nominative relatives, or those following prepositions will not be attracted.

(d) Frequently the referent will be **incorporated into the relative clause**, e.g, οὐκ ἀπεκρύπτετο ἣν εἶχε γνώμην (for τὴν γνώμην ἣν) = "He did not hide the opinion he held."

(e) Occasionally a relative pronoun will introduce a clause that is **coordinate** instead of subordinate. In this case the relative pronoun is the equivalent of a demonstrative. (Compare coordinating *qui = et is* in Latin). This construction is more common in later prose than in the classical period, see below 15.3.

(f) Often the **relative clause precedes its referent**. See, e.g., **1.2**: ἃ μὲν ἐπίστασαι, ταῦτα διαφύλαττε ταῖς μελέταις, ἃ δὲ μὴ μεμάθηκας, προσλάμβανε ταῖς ἐπιστήμαις.

3. Relative clauses may substitute for final or result clauses:

(a) Relative final clauses in Attic take the future indicative after both primary and secondary sequence. The subjunctive is never used for this construction in Attic Greek, though it is common in Homer. The antecedent is usually indefinite; the negative is μή. But this construction is much rarer than the future participle to express purpose. See **Smyth** §2554, **GG** §§1454-1456 and **MT** §§565-574.

Example: Plato, **Apology** §37c4: οὐ γὰρ ἔστι μοι χρήματα ὁπόθεν ἐκτείσω. "For I do not have the money to pay the fine with."

(b) Consecutive relative clauses normally take the indicative; the negative is οὐ when the clause approximates an actual result, μή when it approximates an intended or anticipated result. οἷος, ὅσος, and phrases like οὐκ ἔστιν ὅστις, εἰσιν οἵ, οὐκ ἔστιν ὅπως often introduce consecutive result clauses. For further discussion see **Smyth** §§2556-2559, **GG** §§1457-1460, **MT** §§575-581.

READINGS:

15.1 Plato, **Crito** §§47c8-48a1. Socrates is trying to persuade Crito that following the opinions of the many does not necessarily lead to just behavior.

ΣΩ. καλῶς λέγεις. οὐκοῦν καὶ τἆλλα, ὦ Κρίτων, οὕτως, ἵνα μὴ

πάντα διίωμεν, καὶ δὴ καὶ περὶ τῶν δικαίων καὶ ἀδίκων καὶ

αἰσχρῶν καὶ καλῶν καὶ ἀγαθῶν καὶ κακῶν, **περὶ ὧν νῦν ἡ**

βουλὴ ἡμῖν ἐστιν, πότερον τῇ τῶν πολλῶν δόξῃ δεῖ ἡμᾶς ἕπεσθαι

καὶ φοβεῖσθαι αὐτὴν ἢ τῇ τοῦ ἑνός, εἴ τίς ἐστιν ἐπαΐων, **ὃν δεῖ καὶ** αἰσχύνεσθαι καὶ φοβεῖσθαι μᾶλλον ἢ σύμπαντας τοὺς ἄλλους; ᾧ εἰ μὴ ἀκολουθήσομεν, διαφθεροῦμεν ἐκεῖνο καὶ λωβησόμεθα, ὃ τῷ μὲν δικαίῳ βέλτιον ἐγίγνετο τῷ δὲ ἀδίκῳ ἀπώλλυτο. ἢ οὐδέν ἐστι τοῦτο;

ΚΡ. οἶμαι ἔγωγε, ὦ Σώκρατες.

ΣΩ. φέρε δή, ἐὰν τὸ ὑπὸ τοῦ ὑγιεινοῦ μὲν βέλτιον γιγνόμενον, ὑπὸ τοῦ νοσώδους δὲ διαφθειρόμενον διολέσωμεν πειθόμενοι μὴ τῇ τῶν ἐπαϊόντων δόξῃ, ἆρα βιωτὸν ἡμῖν ἐστιν διεφθαρμένου αὐτοῦ; ἔστι δέ που τοῦτο σῶμα· ἢ οὐχί;

ΚΡ. ναί.

ΣΩ. ἆρ' οὖν βιωτὸν ἡμῖν ἐστιν μετὰ μοχθηροῦ καὶ διεφθαρμένου σώματος;

ΚΡ. οὐδαμῶς.

ΣΩ. ἀλλὰ μετ' ἐκείνου ἆρ' ἡμῖν βιωτὸν διεφθαρμένου, ᾧ τὸ ἄδικον μὲν λωβᾶται, τὸ δὲ δίκαιον ὀνίνησιν; ἢ φαυλότερον ἡγούμεθα εἶναι τοῦ σώματος ἐκεῖνο, ὅτι ποτ' ἐστὶ τῶν ἡμετέρων, περὶ ὃ ἥ τε ἀδικία καὶ ἡ δικαιοσύνη ἐστίν;

15.2 Plato, **Phaedo** §58a10-b4. Phaedo is describing the ship that must sail to Delos and return before Socrates can be executed.

τοῦτ' ἔστι τὸ πλοῖον, ὥς φασιν 'Αθηναῖοι, ἐν ᾧ Θησεύς ποτε εἰς Κρήτην τοὺς "δὶς ἑπτὰ" ἐκείνους ᾤχετο ἄγων καὶ ἔσωσέ τε καὶ αὐτὸς ἐσώθη. τῷ οὖν 'Απόλλωνι ηὔξαντο ὡς λέγεται τότε, εἰ σωθεῖεν, ἑκάστου ἔτους θεωρίαν ἀπάξειν εἰς Δῆλον· ἣν δὴ ἀεὶ καὶ νῦν ἔτι ἐξ ἐκείνου κατ' ἐνιαυτὸν τῷ θεῷ πέμπουσιν.

15.3 Diodorus 19.2.2-7. This is an incident from the early Hellenistic period concerning the exposure of a child.

Καρκῖνος ὁ 'Ρηγῖνος φυγὰς γενόμενος ἐκ τῆς πατρίδος κατῴκησεν ἐν Θέρμοις τῆς Σικελίας, τεταγμένης τῆς πόλεως ταύτης ὑπὸ Καρχηδονίους. ἐμπλακεὶς δὲ τῶν ἐγχωρίων τινὶ γυναικὶ καὶ ποιήσας αὐτὴν ἔγκυον συνεχῶς κατὰ τοὺς ὕπνους ἐταράττετο. διόπερ ἀγωνιῶν ὑπὲρ τῆς παιδοποιίας ἔδωκεν ἐντολὰς Καρχηδονίοις τισὶ θεωροῖς ἀναγομένοις εἰς Δελφοὺς ἐπερωτῆσαι τὸν θεὸν περὶ τοῦ γεννηθησομένου βρέφους. ὧν ἐπιμελῶς τὸ παρακληθὲν πραξάντων ἐξέπεσε χρησμὸς ὅτι μεγάλων ἀτυχημάτων ὁ γεννηθεὶς αἴτιος ἔσται Καρχηδονίοις καὶ πάσῃ Σικελίᾳ. ἃ δὴ πυθόμενος καὶ φοβηθεὶς ἐξέθηκε τὸ παιδίον δημοσίᾳ. . . . διελθουσῶν δέ τινων ἡμερῶν τὸ μὲν οὐκ ἀπέθνῃσκεν, οἱ τεταγμένοι δ' ἐπὶ τῆς φυλακῆς ὠλιγώρουν. καθ' ὃν δὴ χρόνον ἡ μήτηρ νυκτὸς παρελθοῦσα λάθρᾳ τὸ παιδίον ἀνείλετο καὶ πρὸς αὐτὴν μὲν οὐκ ἀπήνεγκε, φοβουμένη τὸν ἄνδρα, πρὸς δὲ τὸν ἀδελφὸν 'Ηρακλείδην καταθεμένη προσηγόρευσεν 'Α-γαθοκλέα, τὴν ὁμωνυμίαν εἰς τὸν ἑαυτῆς ἀνενέγκασα πατέρα. παρ' ᾧ τρεφόμενος ὁ παῖς ἐξέβη τήν τε ὄψιν εὐπρεπὴς καὶ τὸ σῶμα εὔρωστος πολὺ μᾶλλον ἢ κατὰ τὴν ἡλικίαν. ἑπταετοῦς δ' ὄντος αὐτοῦ παρακληθεὶς ὁ Καρκῖνος ὑφ' 'Ηρακλείδου πρός τινα θυσίαν καὶ θεασάμενος τὸν 'Αγαθοκλέα παίζοντα μετά τινων ἡλικιωτῶν ἐθαύμαζε τό τε κάλλος καὶ τὴν ῥώμην, τῆς τε γυναικὸς εἰπούσης ὅτι τηλικοῦτος ἂν ἦν ὁ ἐκτεθείς, εἴπερ ἐτράφη, μεταμέλεσθαί τε ἔφη τοῖς πραχθεῖσι καὶ συνεχῶς ἐδάκρυεν. εἶθ' ἡ μὲν γνοῦσα τὴν ὁρμὴν τἀνδρὸς συμφωνοῦσαν τοῖς πεπραγμένοις ἐξέθηκε πᾶσαν τὴν ἀλήθειαν. ὁ δ' ἀσμένως προσδεξάμενος τοὺς λόγους τὸν μὲν υἱὸν ἀπέλαβε, τοὺς δὲ Καρχηδονίους φοβούμενος μετῴκησεν εἰς Συρακούσσας πανοίκιος· πένης δ' ὢν ἐδίδαξε τὸν 'Αγαθοκλέα τὴν κεραμευτικὴν τέχνην ἔτι παῖδα τὴν ἡλικίαν ὄντα.

15.4 Isocrates, **Panegyricus** §§28-29 (repeated from 2.3).

Πρῶτον μὲν οὖν, οὗ πρῶτον ἡ φύσις ἡμῶν ἐδεήθη, διὰ τῆς πόλεως τῆς ἡμετέρας ἐπορίσθη· καὶ γὰρ εἰ μυθώδης ὁ λόγος γέγονεν, ὅμως αὐτῷ καὶ νῦν ῥηθῆναι προσήκει. Δήμητρος γὰρ ἀφικομένης εἰς τὴν χώραν ὅτ' ἐπλανήθη τῆς Κόρης ἁρπασθείσης, καὶ πρὸς τοὺς προγόνους ἡμῶν εὐμενῶς διατεθείσης ἐκ τῶν εὐεργεσιῶν **ἃς** οὐχ οἷόν τ' ἄλλοις ἢ τοῖς μεμυημένοις ἀκούειν, καὶ δούσης δωρεὰς διττὰς αἵπερ μέγισται τυγχάνουσιν οὖσαι, τούς τε καρπούς, **οἳ** τοῦ μὴ θηριωδῶς ζῆν ἡμᾶς αἴτιοι γεγόνασι, καὶ τὴν τελετήν, **ἧς** οἱ μετασχόντες περί τε τῆς τοῦ βίου τελευτῆς καὶ τοῦ σύμπαντος αἰῶνος ἡδίους τὰς ἐλπίδας ἔχουσιν, οὕτως ἡ πόλις ἡμῶν οὐ μόνον θεοφιλῶς ἀλλὰ καὶ φιλανθρώπως ἔσχεν, ὥστε κυρία γενομένη τοσούτων ἀγαθῶν οὐκ ἐφθόνησε τοῖς ἄλλοις, ἀλλ' **ὧν** ἔλαβεν ἅπασι μετέδωκεν. καὶ τὰ μὲν ἔτι καὶ νῦν καθ' ἕκαστον τὸν ἐνιαυτὸν δείκνυμεν, τῶν δὲ συλλήβδην τάς τε χρείας καὶ τὰς ἐργασίας καὶ τὰς ὠφελείας τὰς ἀπ' αὐτῶν γιγνομένας ἐδίδαξεν.

15.5 Demosthenes, **Second Olynthiac** §§18-19 (with an omission). Demosthenes portrays Philip of Macedon as a man who excludes all decent and honest men from his company and prefers to be surrounded by low life.

εἰ μὲν γάρ τις ἀνήρ ἐστιν ἐν αὐτοῖς **οἷος ἔμπειρος πολέμου καὶ ἀγώνων**, τούτους μὲν φιλοτιμίᾳ πάντας ἀπωθεῖν αὐτὸν ἔφη, βουλόμενον πάνθ' αὐτοῦ δοκεῖν εἶναι τἄργα· ... εἰ δέ τις σώφρων ἢ δίκαιος ἄλλως, τὴν καθ' ἡμέραν ἀκρασίαν τοῦ βίου καὶ μέθην καὶ κορδακισμοὺς οὐ δυνάμενος φέρειν, παρεῶσθαι καὶ ἐν οὐδενὸς εἶναι μέρει τὸν τοιοῦτον. λοιποὺς δὴ περὶ αὐτὸν εἶναι λῃστὰς καὶ κόλακας καὶ τοιούτους ἀνθρώπους **οἵους μεθυσθέντας ὀρχεῖσθαι** τοιαῦθ' **οἷ'** ἐγὼ ὀκνῶ πρὸς ὑμᾶς ὀνομάσαι. δῆλον

δ' ὅτι ταῦτ' ἐστὶν ἀληθῆ· καὶ γὰρ οὓς ἐνθένδε πάντες
ἀπήλαυνον ὡς πολὺ τῶν θαυματοποιῶν ἀσελγεστέρους ὄντας,
Καλλίαν ἐκεῖνον τὸν δημόσιον καὶ τοιούτους ἀνθρώπους, μίμους
γελοίων καὶ ποιητὰς αἰσχρῶν ᾀσμάτων, ὧν εἰς τοὺς συνόντας
ποιοῦσιν ἕνεκα τοῦ γελασθῆναι, τούτους ἀγαπᾷ καὶ περὶ αὐτὸν
ἔχει.

EXERCISES:

Write in Greek using relative clauses wherever possible:

A Sentences:

1. What makes a man just is the soul.
2. Apollo was the god to whom the Athenians sent the festival.
3. Even just men fear sickness which destroys the body.
4. By whom were the fourteen youths saved?
5. Was Theseus the sort whom the Athenians would send to Apollo?
6. He told us what he saw.
7. She gave the child to her brother, by whom it was reared and for whom it was named.
8. She was afraid that the man to whom her husband gave the child might harm him.
9. He was a fugitive from his own country against which he had waged a war.
10. If the father had not wept continuously over the loss of his child, the mother would not have returned it to him.
11. The oracle will make clear what harm the child will do to the Carthaginians.
12. What this city provides for each of us the myth makes clear.
13. Demeter, whose daughter, Kore, was carried off by a god, wandered throughout Greece in order to find her.
14. What they received from the gods, they shared with others.
15. Have you heard about the things the initiates do?

B Sentences:

①. We Athenians have received two great benefits from the goddess Demeter, who was very grateful for the city's help in the search for her daughter. She gave us agriculture, which allows us to live in towns and cities. Without this gift we would be forced to eat what wild animals eat. She also gave us the mysteries, which we have in turn dedicated to her. To the man who has been initiated into her rites, she gives eternal life.

②. Soc. Come now, let us consider what makes us healthy. What we eat, what we drink, do
  these things affect our health?
  Cr. Of course they do.
— Soc. Would you agree that if we eat something that makes us sick we do not improve our
  health.
  Cr. I would.
— Soc. And, likewise, if we drink so much that we get sick do we improve our health?
  Cr. Of course not.
— Soc. Then having agreed on this, let us consider what contributes to the health of the soul.

3. Whenever the wife of Carcinus thought about the child whom her husband had exposed she grew exceedingly angry. What she said to him on these occasions is not recorded; though it is clear that he was deeply distressed both by her anger and his own guilt. For when the child had been exposed, although she went quickly to take it up from the location in which it had been left, she was unable to recover it without attracting the attention of those who had been left to watch over it until it died.

CHAPTER SIXTEEN—INDEFINITE RELATIVE CLAUSES[1]

A relative clause whose referent is an indefinite or indeterminate person, place, object, time, or event has a conditional force. These clauses are introduced by (1) the range of words that may introduce definite relatives (see previous chapter) or (2) a special set of pronouns, adjectives, and adverbs used for indefinite constructions. e.g., ὅστις, ἥτις, ὅ τι, ὁπόσος, ὁποῖος, ὅποι, ὅπου, ὁπόθεω, ὅπως. For adverbial expressions of time see below Chapter Seventeen, 3. Indefinite relative clauses behave like the protases of conditions, and are usually schematized in a way analogous to conditions:

OPEN: ἅ(ττ’) ἔχει, ταῦτα δίδωσιν.=He gives me what(ever) he has.

ἅ μὴ εἶχε, ταῦτ’ οὐκ ἔδωκεν.=He didn't give me what he didn't have.

These state suppositions about the present or past, which may or may not be true. The indicative is used in such relative clauses; in the positive form they are undistinguishable from definite relative clauses; it is only in the negative form that the indefinite nature becomes clear.

> Example: Plato, **Apology** 21d7: ἃ μὴ οἶδα, οὐδὲ οἴομαι εἰδέναι. "What I do not know, I do not even think I know."

> Antiphon 5.19: ἃ γάρ τις μὴ προσεδόκησεν, οὐδὲ φυλάξασθαι ἐγχωρεῖ. "There is not even the opportunity to protect oneself against what no one expected."

---

[1] For further discussion see **Smyth** §§2560-2573, GG §§1441-1450, and **MT** §§514-537.

CONTRARY-TO-FACT:

> ἅ(ττ') ἐνόμιζε, ταῦτ' ἂν ἔλεγεν. = He would be saying what(ever) he would be thinking.   (But he is not,)

> ἅ(ττ') ἐνόμισε, ταῦτ' ἂν εἶπεν.= He would have said what(ever) he thought.   (But he did not.)

This relative, like its analogous condition, assumes something that is not or was not the case. Normally a past tense of the indicative (or the equivalent) + ἄν is found in the **main** clause. Examples of this type are less common than other indefinites.

Example: Lysias, **Against Eratosthenes** §98: οἱ δὲ παῖδες ὑμῶν, ὅσοι μὲν ἐνθάδε ἦσαν, ὑπὸ τούτων ἂν ὑβρίζοντο. . . . "Your children, as many as were present, would be outraged by these men . . . ." (But in fact no children were present).

FUTURE MORE VIVID:

> ἅ(ττ') **ἂν** **νομίζῃ**, ταῦτα ἐρεῖ.= He will say what(ever) he thinks.

FUTURE LESS VIVID:

> ἅ(ττα) **νομίζοι**, ταῦτ' εἴποι ἄν.= What(ever) he should think, he would say.

These relatives refer to the future, and take either ἄν (= ἐάν) + subjunctive or optative **without ἄν** in the relative clause, depending on whether the event is conceived of as more or less likely to happen. The relative that is analogous to the more vivid condition is quite common.

Example: Demosthenes, **Against Meidias** §130: λέξω δ' ὅ τι ἂν πρῶτον ἀκούειν βουλομένοις ὑμῖν ᾖ. "I shall tell you whatever you want to hear first."

GENERAL:

PRESENT:

ἅ(ττ’) ἂν νομίζῃ, ταῦτα λέγει.= He says what(ever) he thinks.

PAST:

ἅ(ττα) νομίζοι, ταῦτα ἔλεγεν= He said what(ever) he thought.

In relatives analogous to general conditions, the relative clause sets out the general circumstance; the main clause a repeated or customary action. The present occurs more frequently than the past.

Example: Plato **Symposium** 190e2-5: ὅντινα δὲ τέμοι, τὸν Ἀπόλλω ἐκέλευεν τό τε πρόσωπον μεταστρέφειν καὶ τὸ τοῦ αὐχένος ἥμισυ πρὸς τὴν τομήν, ἵνα θεώμενος τὴν αὑτοῦ τμῆσιν κοσμιώτερος εἴη ὁ ἄνθρωπος. "Whomever he (sc. Zeus) cut, he ordered Apollo to turn the face and the half of the neck toward the cut, so that by gazing at his own slicing, man might be more orderly."

READINGS (Both definite and indefinite relatives are in bold):

16.1 Plato **Crito** §51c6-e4. The laws are speaking to Socrates and explaining that every citizen is given the opportunity (τῷ ἐξουσίαν πεποιηκέναι) to accept or reject the conditions of citizenship at the time of entry into the citizen rolls (ἐπειδὰν δοκιμασθῇ).

"σκόπει τοίνυν, ὦ Σώκρατες," φαῖεν ἂν ἴσως οἱ νόμοι, "εἰ ἡμεῖς ταῦτα ἀληθῆ λέγομεν, ὅτι οὐ δίκαια ἡμᾶς ἐπιχειρεῖς δρᾶν **ἃ νῦν ἐπιχειρεῖς**. ἡμεῖς γάρ σε γεννήσαντες, ἐκθρέψαντες, παιδεύσαντες, μεταδόντες ἁπάντων **ὧν οἷοί τ’ ἦμεν** καλῶν σοὶ καὶ τοῖς ἄλλοις πᾶσιν πολίταις, ὅμως προαγορεύομεν τῷ ἐξουσίαν πεποιηκέναι Ἀθηναίων τῷ βουλομένῳ, ἐπειδὰν δοκιμασθῇ καὶ ἴδῃ τὰ ἐν τῇ πόλει πράγματα καὶ ἡμᾶς τοὺς νόμους, **ᾧ ἂν μὴ ἀρέσκωμεν ἡμεῖς**, ἐξεῖναι λαβόντα τὰ αὑτοῦ ἀπιέναι **ὅποι ἂν**

βούληται. καὶ οὐδεὶς ἡμῶν τῶν νόμων ἐμποδών ἐστιν οὐδ'
ἀπαγορεύει, ἐάντε τις βούληται ὑμῶν εἰς ἀποικίαν ἰέναι, εἰ μὴ
ἀρέσκοιμεν ἡμεῖς τε καὶ ἡ πόλις, ἐάντε μετοικεῖν ἄλλοσέ ποι ἐλθών,
ἰέναι ἐκεῖσε **ὅποι ἂν βούληται**, ἔχοντα τὰ αὑτοῦ. **ὃς δ' ἂν
ὑμῶν παραμείνῃ**, ὁρῶν **ὃν τρόπον** ἡμεῖς **τάς τε δίκας
δικάζομεν** καὶ τἆλλα τὴν πόλιν διοικοῦμεν, ἤδη φαμὲν τοῦτον
ὡμολογηκέναι ἔργῳ ἡμῖν **ἃ ἂν ἡμεῖς κελεύωμεν** ποιήσειν
ταῦτα."

16.2 Plato **Symposium** §181a7-b7. This is from Pausanias' speech
about the two kinds of love—the common sort (as described here)
and the proper kind that leads to self-sacrifice.

ὁ (sc. ἔρως) μέν οὖν τῆς Πανδήμου 'Αφροδίτης ὡς ἀληθῶς πάνδημός
ἐστι καὶ ἐξεργάζεται **ὅτι ἂν τύχῃ**· καὶ οὗτός ἐστιν **ὃν** (= ἐρῶτα,
a cognate accusative) οἱ **φαῦλοι** τῶν ἀνθρώπων **ἐρῶσιν**.
ἐρῶσι δὲ οἱ τοιοῦτοι πρῶτον μὲν οὐχ ἧττον γυναικῶν ἢ παίδων,
ἔπειτα **ὧν καὶ ἐρῶσι** τῶν σωμάτων μᾶλλον ἢ τῶν
ψυχῶν, ἔπειτα **ὡς ἂν δύνωνται** ἀνοητοτάτων, πρὸς τὸ
διαπράξασθαι μόνον βλέποντες, ἀμελοῦντες δὲ τοῦ καλῶς ἢ μή·
ὅθεν δὴ συμβαίνει αὐτοῖς, **ὅτι ἂν τύχωσι**, τοῦτο πράττειν, ὁμοίως
μὲν ἀγαθόν, ὁμοίως δὲ τοὐναντίον.

16.3 Thucydides 2.34.1-8: Thucydides is describing the Athenian
practice of common burial of war dead.

ἐν δὲ τῷ αὐτῷ χειμῶνι 'Αθηναῖοι τῷ πατρίῳ νόμῳ χρώμενοι
δημοσίᾳ ταφὰς ἐποιήσαντο τῶν ἐν τῷδε τῷ πολέμῳ πρώτων
ἀποθανόντων τρόπῳ τοιῷδε· τὰ μὲν ὀστᾶ προτίθενται τῶν
ἀπογενομένων πρότριτα σκηνὴν ποιήσαντες, καὶ ἐπιφέρει τῷ αὑτοῦ
ἕκαστος **ἥν τι βούληται**· ἐπειδὰν δὲ ἡ ἐκφορὰ ᾖ, λάρνακας κυπαρισσίνας ἄγουσιν ἄμαξαι, φυλῆς ἑκάστης μίαν· ἔνεστι δὲ τὰ
ὀστᾶ **ἧς ἕκαστος ἦν φυλῆς**. μία δὲ κλίνη κενὴ φέρεται

ἐστρωμένη τῶν ἀφανῶν, οἳ ἂν μὴ εὑρεθῶσιν ἐς ἀναίρεσιν. ξυνεκφέρει δὲ ὁ βουλόμενος καὶ ἀστῶν καὶ ξένων, καὶ γυναῖκες πάρεισιν αἱ προσήκουσαι ἐπὶ τὸν τάφον ὀλοφυρόμεναι. τιθέασιν οὖν ἐς τὸ δημόσιον σῆμα, ὅ ἐστιν ἐπὶ τοῦ καλλίστου προαστείου τῆς πόλεως, καὶ αἰεὶ ἐν αὐτῷ θάπτουσι τοὺς ἐκ τῶν πολέμων, πλήν γε τοὺς ἐν Μαραθῶνι· ἐκείνων δὲ διαπρεπῆ τὴν ἀρετὴν κρίναντες αὐτοῦ καὶ τὸν τάφον ἐποίησαν. ἐπειδὰν δὲ κρύψωσι γῇ, ἀνὴρ ᾑρημένος ὑπὸ τῆς πόλεως, ὃς ἂν γνώμῃ τε δοκῇ μὴ ἀξύνετος εἶναι καὶ ἀξιώσει προήκῃ, λέγει ἐπ' αὐτοῖς ἔπαινον τὸν πρέποντα· μετὰ δὲ τοῦτο ἀπέρχονται. ὧδε μὲν θάπτουσιν· καὶ διὰ παντὸς τοῦ πολέμου, ὁπότε ξυμβαίη αὐτοῖς, ἐχρῶντο τῷ νόμῳ. ἐπὶ δ' οὖν τοῖς πρώτοις τοῖσδε Περικλῆς ὁ Ξανθίππου ᾑρέθη λέγειν. καὶ ἐπειδὴ καιρὸς ἐλάμβανε, προελθὼν ἀπὸ τοῦ σήματος ἐπὶ βῆμα ὑψηλὸν πεποιημένον, ὅπως ἀκούοιτο ὡς ἐπὶ πλεῖστον τοῦ ὁμίλου, ἔλεγε τοίαδε.

16.4 Lysias, **Against Eratosthenes** §§99-100. Lysias' summation of the crimes of the Thirty tyrants.

ἀλλὰ γὰρ οὐ τὰ μέλλοντα ἔσεσθαι βούλομαι λέγειν, τὰ πραχθέντα ὑπὸ τούτων οὐ δυνάμενος εἰπεῖν· οὐδὲ γὰρ ἑνὸς κατηγόρου οὐδὲ δυοῖν ἔργον ἐστίν, ἀλλὰ πολλῶν. ὅμως δὲ τῆς ἐμῆς προθυμίας (οὐδὲν) ἐλλέλειπται, ὑπέρ ⟨τε⟩ τῶν ἱερῶν, ἃ οὗτοι τὰ μὲν ἀπέδοντο τὰ δ' εἰσιόντες ἐμίαινον, ὑπέρ τε τῆς πόλεως, ἣν μικρὰν ἐποίουν, ὑπέρ τε τῶν νεωρίων, ἃ καθεῖλον, καὶ ὑπὲρ τῶν τεθνεώτων, οἷς ὑμεῖς, ἐπειδὴ ζῶσιν ἐπαμῦναι οὐκ ἐδύνασθε, ἀποθανοῦσι βοηθήσατε. οἶμαι δ' αὐτοὺς ἡμῶν τε ἀκροᾶσθαι καὶ ὑμᾶς εἴσεσθαι τὴν ψῆφον φέροντας, ἡγουμένους, ὅσοι μὲν ἂν τούτων ἀποψηφίσησθε, αὐτῶν θάνατον κατεψηφισμένους

ἔσεσθαι, ὅσοι δ' ἂν παρὰ τούτων δίκην λάβωσιν, ὑπὲρ
αὐτῶν τιμωρίας πεποιημένους.

16.5 Demosthenes, **Against Androtion** §§51-52 Demosthenes begins
by explaining the virtue of living in a democracy, then goes on to
describe the situation under the Thirty.

εἰ γὰρ ἐθέλοιτ' ἐξετάσαι τίνος εἵνεκα μᾶλλον ἄν τις ἕλοιτο τ'ἐν
δημοκρατίᾳ ζῆν ἢ ἐν ὀλιγαρχίᾳ, τοῦτ' ἂν εὕροιτε προχειρότατον, ὅτι
πάντα πραότερ' ἐστὶν ἐν δημοκρατίᾳ. ὅτι μὲν τοίνυν τῆς ὅπου
βούλεσθ' ὀλιγαρχίας οὗτος (sc. Androtion) ἀσελγέστερος γέγονεν,
παραλείψω. ἀλλὰ παρ' ἡμῖν πότε πώποτε δεινότατ' ἐν τῇ πόλει
γέγονεν; ἐπὶ τῶν τριάκοντα, πάντες ἂν εἴποιτε. τότε τοίνυν, ὡς
ἔστιν ἀκούειν, **οὐδεὶς ἔστιν ὅστις ἀπεστερεῖτο τοῦ σωθῆναι,**
ὅστις ἑαυτὸν οἴκοι κρύψειεν, ἀλλὰ τοῦτο κατηγοροῦμεν τῶν
τριάκοντα, ὅτι τοὺς ἐκ τῆς ἀγορᾶς ἀδίκως ἀπῆγον.

EXERCISES:

Write the following sentences in Greek:

A Sentences:

1. Whatever you try to do is unjust.
2. Apollo ordered them to do whatever they wished.
3. The laws speak to whoever will listen.
4. They were accustomed to love whoever of the boys was most
beautiful.
5. Give it to whomever you chance upon.
6. Anything you can do I can do better; I can do anything better
than you.
7. Men who love whomever they chance upon endanger their own
souls.
8. They will choose as speaker whoever seems best to them.
9. Men who find the laws unsatisfactory must leave the city.

10. Whatever they obtain from the gods, they will share with others.

11. Do whatever seems best to you.

12. What you don't know won't hurt you.

13. Agathon heard whatever Socrates said to Alcibiades.

14. Who spoke against what Demosthenes proposed to prevent Philip from invading Greece?

15. The man who loves those who lack good sense is destroying his soul, whatever that is.

B Sentences:

1. Whoever of the citizens wishes to live in our city must abide by whatever laws the assembly enacts. He must obey the laws he knows as well as the laws he does not know. Therefore, as soon as he becomes a citizen he must learn what our laws are and how they are to be obeyed. Where will he find them? He should ask the interpreter to explain to him whatever he wishes to know.

2. The city had the custom of burying at state expense whoever of the citizens was killed in battle. Whoever of the relatives wished to do so attended the funeral and brought whatever was appropriate to place in the grave of the dead man. The relatives of a man who had not been found after the battle were also allowed to attend the funeral.

3. A. Whoever loves those who are sensible rather than those who are foolish improves his soul. And he should desire to make the soul of whomever he loves better.

B. But must I love the sensible even if they are not beautiful? I do not find pleasing those who are not beautiful.

A. Only the weakest of men prefer beauty in their beloved to intelligence. I fear you may be among those who desire only the bodies of those whom they love, not the minds.

B. Alas, I fear you are right.

CHAPTER SEVENTEEN—TEMPORAL CLAUSES[1]

Temporal clauses are analogous to relative clauses in construction; they may refer either to a definite or an indefinite time in the past, present, or future.

1. The conjunctions or relative expressions of time serving as conjunctions are as follows:

SAME TIME AS :	ὅτε, ἡνίκα= when
referring to actions	ὁσάκις = as often as
contemporaneous	ἕως, μέχρι, ὅσον χρόνον= so long as
with the main verb	ἕως, ἐν ᾧ= while

Example: Plato, **Republic** 340c8-9: ἔγωγε, εἶπον, ᾤμην σε τοῦτο λέγειν **ὅτε** τοὺς ἄρχοντας ὡμολόγεις οὐκ ἀναμαρτήτους εἶναι ἀλλά τι καὶ ἐξαμαρτάνειν. "I at least, I said, supposed that you were saying this **when** you acknowledged that rulers were not infallible but might also err in some respect."

TIME BEFORE:	ἐπεί, ἐπειδή= after, since
referring to actions	ὡς = since, when, as soon as
prior to that of	ἐξ οὗ, ἀφ' οὗ= since, ever since
the main verb	

Example: 2.1: **ἐπεὶ** δὲ ἐτελεύτησε Δαρεῖος καὶ κατέστη εἰς τὴν βασιλείαν Ἀρταξέρξης, Τισσαφέρνης διαβάλλει τὸν Κῦρον πρὸς τὸν ἀδελφὸν ὡς ἐπιβουλεύοι αὐτῷ. "**After** Darios died and Artaxerxes succeeded to the kingship, Tissaphernes accused Kyros to his brother of plotting against him."

---

[1]For further discussion see **Smyth** §§2383-2460, **MT** §§611-661. **GG** discusses relative and temporal sentences together §§1437-1456.

TIME AFTER:	ἕως, ἕστε (not used in prose)= until
referring to actions	μέχρι, μέχρι οὗ= until
subsequent to that of	πρίν, πρότερον ἤ= before, until
the main verb	

Example: Plato, **Republic** 344d6-e1: ὦ δαιμόνιε Θρασύμαχε, οἶον ἐμβαλὼν λόγον ἐν νῷ ἔχεις ἀπιέναι **πρὶν** διδάξαι ἱκανῶς ἢ μαθεῖν εἴτε οὕτως εἴτε ἄλλως ἔχει; "My dear Thrasymachus, after you have thrown out such an argument, are you intending to leave us **before** suitably instructing or learning whether it is true or not?"

2. Temporal clauses are found with the indicative, subjunctive + ἄν, optative, and infinitive. These uses follow the patterns set out below:

(a) The **indicative** mood refers to **present or past time** and is used for **statements of fact**. The negative is οὐ. The aorist indicative in the temporal clause marks a completed action, the present or imperfect a continuing action. The verb in the leading clause is normally in a present or past tense. For example, see below, **17.4**: ἐπειδὴ δ' ἀπεστείλατε, εἰρήνης ἐτύχεθ' ὁποίας τινὸς ἐβούλεσθε.

(b) The **subjunctive** mood + ἄν[1] refers to **future** or **general** suppositions or **customary** or **repeated** actions; usage is analogous to the protasis of the more vivid or the present general condition. The negative is μή. The verb in the leading clause is normally in the future tense or is a generalizing present. For examples, see below, **17.1**: ἀρχὴ δ' ἐστὶ τῆς θεωρίας **ἐπειδὰν ὁ ἱερεὺς τοῦ 'Απόλλωνος στέψῃ** τὴν πρύμναν τοῦ πλοίου.

(c) The **optative** mood (used without ἄν) refers to **unfulfilled** events or **future** events about which the speaker is dubious; it may also refer to **general** suppositions or **customary or repeated events in the past**. For an example of the latter, see below, **17.2**: περιεμένομεν οὖν ἑκάστοτε **ἕως ἀνοιχθείη τὸ δεσμωτήριον**. . .

---

[1] Note that ἄν tends to combine with some temporal expressions, e.g., ὅτε ἄν —> ὅταν or ἐπειδὴ ἄν —> ἐπειδάν.

. These are analogous to the use of the optative in the protasis of past general and future less vivid conditions. The negative is μή. The verb in the leading clause is usually in a past tense of the indicative (with or without ἄν) or in the optative + ἄν. The optative is very frequently used to replace the subjunctive + ἄν in secondary sequence in indirect statement, where the ἄν of the subjunctive construction is lost.

(d) The **infinitive** is used with πρίν when the conjunction means **"before" and the main clause is positive.** Here πρίν may be thought of as the equivalent of πρὸ τοῦ with the articular infinitive. The aorist infinitive is used to refer to completed action, the present to continuing action. When πρίν means **"until,"** or when the main clause is **negative** or a virtual negative, πρίν behaves like ἕως (i.e., like a normal temporal conjunction).

Example: Plato, **Republic** §354b1-5: ἀλλ᾽ ὥσπερ οἱ λίχνοι τοῦ ἀεὶ παραφερομένου ἀπογεύονται ἁρπάζοντες, **πρὶν** τοῦ προτέρου μετρίως ἀπολαῦσαι, καὶ ἐγώ μοι δοκῶ οὕτω, **πρὶν** ὃ τὸ πρῶτον ἐσκοποῦμεν εὑρεῖν. . . . "But like gluttons who snatch up and taste from the dish that is always coming by, **before** enjoying the earlier one properly, I too seem to be behaving like this, **before** finding out what I first was enquiring about. . . ."

Plato, **Phaedrus** §242a3: μήπω γε,. . . .**πρὶν** ἂν τὸ καῦμα παρέλθῃ "Not yet, **until** the heat of the day passes."

3. Note the following adverbial expressions of time:

(a) **Genitive (Smyth §1444, GG §1136);** this construction is a subclass of partitive genitive. It denotes a portion of time "within which" or "at a certain point of which" an action takes place.

ἑκάστου ἔτους = a part of each year, yearly

ἑσπέρας = of evening, at evening

(b) **Dative (Smyth §1539-42, GG §1194-1196)**; this construction is a subclass of the locative dative. It indicates the time "at which" an event takes place. Normally temporal datives are translated by "in" or "on."

τῇ προτεραίᾳ = on the day before

Sometimes this construction will also be found with the preposition ἐν (see Smyth §1542 for details). Here ἐν is added to τῷ χρόνῳ τούτῳ to indicate the period "in which" an event may be expected to happen.

(c) **Accusative (Smyth §1582-87, GG §1061)**: the accusative of "extent of time." This construction gives the duration of the event.

τὰς πρόσθεν ἡμέρας = during the preceding days

οὐ πολὺν χρόνον = for a short period of time

(d) Note also the **adverbial** expressions of time:

ἕωθεν (ἕως = dawn + θεν) = at or towards dawn

πρῷ = early (and its comparative and superlative, πρῳαίτερον, πρῳαίτατα)

τότε (correlative of ὅτε) = then

ὕστερον = later

μετὰ ταῦτα or μετὰ τοῦτο = after these things / this, next

νῦν is a temporal adverb. Distinguish it from the enclitic form νυν which is an emphasizing particle found in Homer and poetry (more than in prose), and οὖν, which is an inferential particle.

READINGS:

17.1 Plato **Phaedo** §58a10-c5. The Athenians have sent a ship on a sacred embassy to Delos. The ship must complete its journey and return to Athens before the execution of Socrates can take place.

τοῦτ' ἔστι τὸ πλοῖον, ὥς φασιν Ἀθηναῖοι, ἐν ᾧ Θησεύς ποτε εἰς Κρήτην τοὺς "δὶς ἑπτὰ" ἐκείνους ᾤχετο ἄγων καὶ ἔσωσέ τε καὶ αὐτὸς ἐσώθη. τῷ οὖν Ἀπόλλωνι ηὔξαντο ὡς λέγεται τότε, εἰ σωθεῖεν, ἑκάστου ἔτους θεωρίαν ἀπάξειν εἰς Δῆλον· ἣν δὴ ἀεὶ καὶ νῦν ἔτι ἐξ ἐκείνου κατ' ἐνιαυτὸν τῷ θεῷ πέμπουσιν. **ἐπειδὰν οὖν ἄρξωνται** τῆς θεωρίας, νόμος ἐστὶν αὐτοῖς ἐν τῷ χρόνῳ τούτῳ καθαρεύειν τὴν πόλιν καὶ δημοσίᾳ μηδένα ἀποκτεινύναι, **πρὶν ἂν εἰς Δῆλόν τε ἀφίκηται** τὸ πλοῖον καὶ πάλιν δεῦρο· τοῦτο δ' ἐνίοτε ἐν πολλῷ χρόνῳ γίγνεται, **ὅταν τύχωσιν** ἄνεμοι ἀπολάβοντες αὐτούς. ἀρχὴ δ' ἐστὶ τῆς θεωρίας **ἐπειδὰν ὁ ἱερεὺς τοῦ Ἀπόλλωνος στέψῃ** τὴν πρύμναν τοῦ πλοίου· τοῦτο δ' ἔτυχεν, ὥσπερ λέγω, τῇ προτεραίᾳ τῆς δίκης γεγονός. διὰ ταῦτα καὶ πολὺς χρόνος ἐγένετο τῷ Σωκράτει ἐν τῷ δεσμωτηρίῳ ὁ μεταξὺ τῆς δίκης τε καὶ τοῦ θανάτου.

17.2 Plato **Phaedo** §§59c8-60a8. This is a description of the last day of Socrates' life, when his friends join him in the prison and he finally drinks the hemlock.

ἐγώ σοι ἐξ ἀρχῆς πάντα πειράσομαι διηγήσασθαι. ἀεὶ γὰρ δὴ καὶ τὰς πρόσθεν ἡμέρας εἰώθεμεν φοιτᾶν καὶ ἐγὼ καὶ οἱ ἄλλοι παρὰ τὸν Σωκράτη, συλλεγόμενοι ἕωθεν εἰς τὸ δικαστήριον ἐν ᾧ καὶ ἡ δίκη ἐγένετο· πλησίον γὰρ ἦν τοῦ δεσμωτηρίου. περιεμένομεν οὖν ἑκάστοτε **ἕως ἀνοιχθείη τὸ δεσμωτήριον,** διατρίβοντες μετ' ἀλλήλων, ἀνεῴγετο γὰρ οὐ πρῴ· **ἐπειδὴ δὲ ἀνοιχθείη,** εἰσῇμεν παρὰ τὸν Σωκράτη καὶ τὰ πολλὰ διημερεύομεν μετ' αὐτοῦ. καὶ δὴ καὶ τότε πρῳαίτερον συνελέγημεν· τῇ γὰρ προτεραίᾳ [ἡμέρᾳ] ἐπειδὴ ἐξήλθομεν ἐκ τοῦ δεσμωτηρίου ἑσπέρας, ἐπυθόμεθα ὅτι τὸ πλοῖον ἐκ Δήλου ἀφιγμένον εἴη. παρηγγείλαμεν οὖν ἀλλήλοις ἥκειν ὡς πρῳαίτατα εἰς τὸ εἰωθός. καὶ ἥκομεν καὶ ἡμῖν ἐξελθὼν ὁ θυρωρός, ὅσπερ εἰώθει ὑπακούειν, εἶπεν περιμένειν καὶ μὴ πρότερον παριέναι **ἕως ἂν αὐτὸς κελεύσῃ**· "λύουσι γάρ," ἔφη, " οἱ ἕνδεκα Σωκράτη καὶ παραγγέλλουσιν ὅπως ἂν τῇδε τῇ ἡμέρᾳ τελευτᾷ." οὐ πολὺν δ' οὖν χρόνον ἐπισχὼν ἧκεν καὶ ἐκέλευεν ἡμᾶς εἰσιέναι. εἰσιόντες οὖν κατελαμβάνομεν τὸν μὲν Σωκράτη ἄρτι λελυμένον, τὴν δὲ Ξανθίππην ‐ γιγνώσκεις γάρ ‐ ἔχουσάν τε τὸ παιδίον αὐτοῦ καὶ παρακαθημένην. **ὡς οὖν εἶδεν ἡμᾶς ἡ Ξανθίππη**, ἀνηυφήμησέ τε καὶ τοιαῦτ' ἄττα εἶπεν, οἷα δὴ εἰώθασιν αἱ γυναῖκες, ὅτι " ὦ Σώκρατες, ὕστατον δή σε προσεροῦσι νῦν οἱ ἐπιτήδειοι καὶ σὺ τούτους." καὶ ὁ Σωκράτης βλέψας εἰς τὸν Κρίτωνα, "ὦ Κρίτων," ἔφη, "ἀπαγέτω τις αὐτὴν οἴκαδε."

17.3 Thucydides 2.34.1-8 (repeated from **16.3**).

ἐν δὲ τῷ αὐτῷ χειμῶνι Ἀθηναῖοι τῷ πατρίῳ νόμῳ χρώμενοι δημοσίᾳ ταφὰς ἐποιήσαντο τῶν ἐν τῷδε τῷ πολέμῳ πρώτων ἀποθανόντων τρόπῳ τοιῷδε· τὰ μὲν ὀστᾶ προτίθενται τῶν ἀπογενομένων πρότριτα σκηνὴν ποιήσαντες, καὶ ἐπιφέρει τῷ αὑτοῦ ἕκαστος ἤν τι βούληται· **ἐπειδὰν δὲ ἡ ἐκφορὰ ᾖ,** λάρνακας κυπαρισσίνας ἄγουσιν ἅμαξαι, φυλῆς ἑκάστης μίαν· ἔνεστι δὲ τὰ ὀστᾶ ἧς ἕκαστος ἦν φυλῆς. μία δὲ κλίνη κενὴ φέρεται ἐστρωμένη τῶν ἀφανῶν, οἳ ἂν μὴ εὑρεθῶσιν ἐς ἀναίρεσιν. ξυνεκφέρει δὲ ὁ βουλόμενος καὶ ἀστῶν καὶ ξένων, καὶ γυναῖκες πάρεισιν αἱ προσήκουσαι ἐπὶ τὸν τάφον ὀλοφυρόμεναι. τιθέασιν οὖν ἐς τὸ δημόσιον σῆμα, ὅ ἐστιν ἐπὶ τοῦ καλλίστου προαστείου τῆς πόλεως, καὶ αἰεὶ ἐν αὐτῷ θάπτουσι τοὺς ἐκ τῶν πολέμων, πλήν γε τοὺς ἐν Μαραθῶνι· ἐκείνων δὲ διαπρεπῆ τὴν ἀρετὴν κρίναντες αὐτοῦ καὶ τὸν τάφον ἐποίησαν. **ἐπειδὰν δὲ κρύψωσι γῇ**, ἀνὴρ ᾑρημένος ὑπὸ τῆς πόλεως, ὃς ἂν γνώμῃ τε δοκῇ μὴ ἀξύνετος εἶναι καὶ ἀξιώσει προήκῃ, λέγει ἐπ' αὐτοῖς ἔπαινον τὸν πρέποντα· μετὰ δὲ τοῦτο ἀπέρχονται. ὧδε μὲν θάπτουσιν· καὶ διὰ παντὸς τοῦ πολέμου, **ὁπότε ξυμβαίη** αὐτοῖς, ἐχρῶντο τῷ νόμῳ. ἐπὶ δ' οὖν τοῖς πρώτοις τοῖσδε Περικλῆς ὁ Ξανθίππου ᾑρέθη λέγειν. καὶ **ἐπειδὴ καιρὸς ἐλάμβανε**, προελθὼν ἀπὸ τοῦ σήματος ἐπὶ βῆμα ὑψηλὸν πεποιημένον, ὅπως ἀκούοιτο ὡς ἐπὶ πλεῖστον τοῦ ὁμίλου, ἔλεγε τοιάδε.

17.4 Demosthenes **Against Androtion** §15: Demosthenes is arguing about the value of a strong navy for Athens.

ἐκ δὲ τοῦ κακῶς (sc. κατεσκευάσθαι ναῦς) πόσα δεινά; τὰ μὲν πόλλ' ἐάσω· ἀλλ' ἐπὶ τοῦ Δεκελεικοῦ πολέμου (τῶν γὰρ ἀρχαίων ἕν, ὃ πάντες ἐμοῦ μᾶλλον ἐπίστασθε, ὑπομνήσω) πολλῶν καὶ δεινῶν ἀτυχημάτων συμβάντων τῇ πόλει, **οὐ πρότερον** τῷ πολέμῳ παρέστησαν, **πρὶν τὸ ναυτικὸν αὐτῶν ἀπώλετο**. καὶ τί δεῖ τὰ παλαιὰ λέγειν; τὸν τελευταῖον γὰρ ἴστε, τὸν πρὸς Λακεδαιμονίους πόλεμον, **ὅτε** μὲν ναῦς **οὐκ ἐδοκεῖτ'** ἀποστεῖλαι δυνήσεσθαι, πῶς διέκειθ' ἡ πόλις. ἴστ' ὀρόβους ὄντας ὠνίους. **ἐπειδὴ δ' ἀπεστείλατε**, εἰρήνης ἐτύχεθ' ὁποίας τινὸς ἐβούλεσθε.

17.5 Demosthenes **Against Aristogeiton** §§60-62. This unusual anecdote describes the character of Aristogeiton most graphically. When he was in prison, the other prisoners voted to "exile" him by denying him fire, bread, and water.

ἓν τοίνυν εἰπὼν ἔτι τῶν ἰδίων αὐτοῦ πονηρευμάτων τὰ λοίπ' ἐάσω. **πρὶν γὰρ ἐξελθεῖν** ἐκ τοῦ δεσμωτηρίου, ἐμπεσόντος ἀνθρώπου τινὸς Ταναγραίου πρὸς κατεγγύην, γραμματεῖον ἔχοντος, προσελθὼν καὶ λαλῶν ὁτιδήποθ' ὑφαιρεῖται τὸ γραμματεῖον. αἰτιωμένου δὲ καὶ δεινὰ ποιοῦντος τἀνθρώπου, καὶ λέγοντος ὅτι οὐδεὶς ἄλλος ὑφῄρηται, εἰς τοῦτ' ἀφικνεῖται βδελυρίας ὥστε τύπτειν ἐπεχείρησε τὸν ἄνθρωπον. νεαλὴς δὲ καὶ πρόσφατος ὢν ἐκεῖνος περιῆν αὐτοῦ τεταριχευμένου καὶ πολὺν χρόνον ἐμπεπτωκότος. ὡς δ' εἰς τοῦθ' ἧκεν, ἀπεσθίει τὴν ῥῖνα τἀνθρώπου. καὶ τότε μὲν περὶ τὴν γεγονυῖαν συμφορὰν ἄνθρωπος γενόμενος ἀπέστη τοῦ τὸ γραμματεῖον ἐρευνᾶν. ὕστερον δ' εὑρίσκουσι τὸ γραμματεῖον ἐν κιβωτίῳ τινί, οὗ τὴν κλεῖν οὗτος εἶχεν. καὶ μετὰ ταῦτα ψηφίζονται περὶ αὐτοῦ ταῦθ' οἱ ἐν τῷ οἰκήματι, μὴ πυρός, μὴ λύχνου, μὴ ποτοῦ, μὴ βρωτοῦ μηδενὸς μηδένα τούτῳ κοινωνεῖν, [μηδὲ λαμβάνειν, μηδ' αὐτὸν τούτῳ διδόναι]. καὶ ὅτι ταῦτ' ἀληθῆ λέγω, κάλει μοι τὸν ἄνθρωπον οὗ τὴν ῥῖν' ὁ μιαρὸς οὗτος ἐσθίων κατέφαγεν.

EXERCISES:

Write in Greek using temporal constructions wherever possible.

A Sentences

1. Before destroying your body, will you not follow the opinion of a man of the sort who knows what improves health?
2. When the ship was sent to Delos, the Athenians waited until it returned before they executed anyone who had committed a crime.
3. Since the doorman had not arrived, we were unable to spend the day conversing with Socrates.
4. I will try to tell you everything before Xanthippe arrives with Socrates' child.
5. Socrates was not freed from his bonds until the day on which he was to die.
6. Whenever we visit Socrates in order to spend the day with him, the doorman does not open the prison until we have waited for a considerable period of time.
7. When we destroy that which health improves and sickness harms, do we also destroy what men call the soul, whatever it may be?

8. Do the sort of men who love women as well as boys have a soul? If they do, surely they are heedless of what may improve it or what may harm it.

9. As long as the ship was in Delos, Socrates did not need to die. After it had returned, he was given the order to die.

10. After Xanthippe was led home by someone whom Crito knew, Socrates conversed about the soul with those who were accustomed to spend the day with him.

11. Did that scoundrel gnaw off the man's nose before you arrived at the prison, or when you yourself were present?

12. They waited until we were present before summoning the witnesses into the courtroom. After we arrived, they told their story.

13. Since the war began a great many misfortunes have befallen the city; whenever I am reminded about them, I wish that Pericles were still alive.

14. Whenever the city performed a public burial of those who had died in war, someone from the citizen body was always selected to make the appropriate remarks about the courage of the men before they were placed in the earth.

15. After he gnawed off the man's nose, his fellow prisoners decided to lock him up in a chest, the key to which they threw away.

B Sentences

1. Socrates was not condemned to death before the ship that left each year for Delos was ready to sail. Since the Athenians had the practice of not executing the condemned during the period of this sacred embassy, Socrates was held in prison until the ship returned. During that time he conversed with his friends, who were in the habit of joining him every day in the prison. They were present on the day when the ship did return and Socrates was told to drink the poison. They waited with him until he died.

2. How is it possible to believe the story Demosthenes tells about Aristogeiton? After Aristogeiton had been imprisoned, so the story goes, he stole another prisoner's account book and hid it away. When that man asked for it back, Aristogeiton gnawed off his nose! As soon as the other inmates discovered this they treated him as if he were an exile, that is, they refused to give him food or drink or anything at all. But what happened to the man who lost his nose to this scoudrel?

3. Whenever Athenians died in battle, they were buried by the state at public expense and a man who was considered preeminent in speaking was chosen to give the eulogy. Pericles was the first orator whom we know to have given such a speech, although the custom continued up until the time of Hyperides. Before a man could be selected by the assembly for this honor, he needed to have demonstrated that he was capable of giving sound advice to the state.

CHAPTER EIGHTEEN—INDIRECT STATEMENT[1]

Greek employs three different methods to report the words of others:

1. A verb of speaking or its equivalent may introduce a direct quotation:

> Example: Plato **Symposium** §173a8-b2: "ἀλλὰ τίς σοι δι-
> ηγεῖτο; ἢ αὐτὸς Σωκράτης"; "οὐ μὰ τόν Δία," ἦν δ' ἐγώ,
> "ἀλλ'... 'Αριστόδημος ἦν τις...." "But who told you? Was
> it Socrates himself?" "No, by god," I said, "it was a certain
> Aristodemus...."

2. The reported speech or thought may follow ὡς or ὅτι. In this case the tenses and **moods of the direct speech are retained** after leading verbs of speaking or thinking in **primary** tenses; after leading verbs in **secondary** tenses, verbs in the subordinate construction **may be changed to the optative** or retained in their original form in accordance with the rules set out below.

> Example: **18.1**: μετ' ἐκεῖνον δὲ Λύσανδρος ἀναστὰς ἄλλα τε
> πολλὰ **εἶπε καὶ ὅτι** παρασπόνδους ὑμᾶς ἔχοι, **καὶ ὅτι** οὐ
> περὶ πολιτείας ὑμῖν ἔσται ἀλλὰ περὶ σωτηρίας, εἰ μὴ
> ποιήσεθ' ἃ Θηραμένης κελεύει. "After him Lysander stood
> up and said many other things and that he would hold you
> to be breakers of the truce and that it will not be a matter of
> constitution for you, but of safety, unless you do what
> Theramenes urges."

---

[1]For further discussion see **Smyth** §§2589-2635, **GG** §§1490-1519, and **MT** §§662-705.

3. The reported speech or thought may be expressed with an **accusative + infinitive** construction.

> Example: Plato **Symposium** §174a3-5: ἔφη γάρ οἱ Σωκράτη ἐντυχεῖν λελουμένον τε καὶ τὰς βλαύτας ὑποδεδεμένον, ἃ ἐκεῖνος ὀλιγάκις ἐποίει· καὶ ἐρέσθαι αὐτὸν ὅποι ἴοι οὕτω καλὸς γεγενημένος. "He said that Socrates, who was bathed and wearing sandals, which he did infrequently, encountered him (οἱ). And he asked him where he was going in such a prettified state."

Indirect speech may be "virtual," that is, it may express what is in the mind of the speaker or others even without the presence of a leading verb of speaking or thinking.

Also, writers sometimes shift from reported speech after ὅτι or ὡς to an accusative + infinitive construction without any change in a leading verb; e.g., see below, **18.2**.

4. The following types of verbs commonly introduce indirect statements:

(a) verbs of **saying**: λέγω and εἶπον, usually take ὅτι or ὡς; φημί and φάσκω take the infinitive.

(b) verbs of **thinking** normally take accusative and **infinitive**; e.g., νομίζω, οἴομαι, ἡγοῦμαι, πιστεύω, ἀπιστέω. οἶδα may take infinitive, but is more commonly found with the participle. However, οἶδ' ὅτι (and sometimes δῆλον ὅτι) may be used parenthetically without affecting the construction.

(c) verbs of **sense perception** normally take a **participle** to complete their meaning, though some (e.g., ἀκούω, αἰσθάνομαι, πυνθάνομαι) will occasionally take an infinitive by analogy to verbs of thinking, see Chapter Four 3 (c) and (d).

5. Rules for indirect statements introduced by ὅτι or ὡς:

(a) After a leading verb in a **primary** tense, each verb of the indirect quotation **maintains the mood and tense of the direct speech**, though person will normally be adjusted, i.e., "I am doing this" will become "**She says** that **she** is doing this."

(b) After a leading verb in a **secondary** tense, each verb in the indirect quotation that was in a primary tense of the indicative or in the subjunctive **may be changed to the corresponding tense of the optative**. Alternatively all these tenses **may be retained in their original form** for clarity or emphasis (for the latter, see **18.1**).

(c) The **aorist indicative** may be changed to the aorist optative **only** if representing a main verb in the indirect statement, **never** in a subordinate clause. When an aorist optative occurs in a subordinate clause it may represent the subjunctive without ἄν. See below (f).

(d) **Imperfect** and **pluperfect** tenses for which there are no corresponding optatives, are retained after secondary tenses. However, occasionally, present optative can substitute for imperfect, if context permits (see **MT** § 673 for examples).

(e) After a leading verb in a secondary tense, the tenses of all **unreal conditions** (with or without ἄν) and all **optatives** (with or without ἄν) are retained without change.

(f) When **subjunctives in subordinate clauses** introduced by ἐάν, or ἄν in some combination (e.g., ὅστις ἄν, ὅταν, ἕως ἄν) are changed to the optative, the conjunctions and relatives are also changed to εἰ, ὅστις, ὅτε, ἕως etc. The ἄν is dropped.

(g) The negative of direct discourse is commonly retained.

6.   Rules for indirect statements represented by accusative and infinitive:

(a) Normally only the **leading verbs** of the original direct quotation are **represented by the infinitive** (or participle); subordinate clauses change in accordance with 5 above. In both **primary and secondary** sequence, the infinitive (or participle) takes the tense of the original verb in the direct form, regardless of the orginal mood:

> present or imperfect =present infinitive/ participle
> future=future infinitive/ participle
> aorist=aorist infinitive/ participle
> perfect or pluperfect=perfect infinitive/participle

(b) The **subject of an infinitive** will become **accusative**, unless it is identical with the subject of the introductory verb of speaking/thinking; if it is, it will remain in the nominative. In this latter respect Greek usage differs from Latin.

(d) If ἄν was joined to the original verb, then **ἄν is retained** with the infinitive or participle.

(e) Occasionally subordinate clauses attached to infinitives in indirect discourse will also be represented with an infinitive (= an original indicative or optative) by attraction. See **18.4** for an example.   If negated, the original οὐ is retained, see above section 5 (g).

7. Conditions in indirect statement follow the rules set out in 5 and 6 above, but for convenience they have been schematized below. (Relative and temporal clauses follow the same pattern.)

	ORIGINAL	AFTER εἶπεν ὅτι	AFTER ἔφη
Open:	εἰ ταῦτ' ἀκούει, λέγει	εἰ ταῦτ' ἀκούοι, λέγοι	λέγειν
Open:	εἰ ταῦτ' ἤκουε, ἔλεγε	εἰ ταῦτ' ἤκουε, ἔλεγε	λέγειν
Open:	εἰ ταῦτ' ἤκουσε, εἶπεν	εἰ ταῦτ' ἤκουσε, εἶπεν/ εἴποι	εἰπεῖν
Most Vivid:	εἰ ταῦτ'ἀκούσεται, ἐρεῖ	εἰ ταῦτ' ἀκούσοιτο, ἐροίη	ἐρεῖν
More Vivid:	ἐὰν ταῦτ' ἀκούῃ, ἐρεῖ	εἰ ταῦτ' ἀκούοι, ἐροίη	ἐρεῖν
General:	ἐὰν ταῦτ' ἀκούῃ, λέγει	εἰ ταῦτ' ἀκούοι, λέγοι	λέγειν
General:	εἰ ταῦτ' ἀκούοι, ἔλεγε	εἰ ταῦτ' ἀκούοι, ἔλεγε	λέγειν
Contra-factual:	εἰ ταῦτ' ἤκουε, ἔλεγεν ἄν	εἰ ταῦτ' ἤκουε, ἔλεγεν ἄν	λέγειν ἄν

Contra-factual:	εἰ ταῦτ' ἤκουσε, εἶπεν ἄν	εἰ ταῦτ' ἤκουσε, εἶπεν ἄν	εἰπεῖν ἄν
Less Vivid:	εἰ ταῦτ' ἀκούοι, λέγοι ἄν	εἰ ταῦτ' ἀκούοι, λέγοι ἄν	λέγειν ἄν

Note that these changes are optional; the tenses and moods of direct speech are often retained. For examples of conditions in indirect statement see **18.2, 18.3, 18.5-7**.

READINGS:

18.1 Lysias, **Against Eratosthenes** §§73-74. Lysias is, in his own voice, narrating an incident that demonstrates Theramenes' involvement with Lysander and the Spartans at the time of the defeat of Athens in the Peloponnesian war

ἀναστὰς δὲ Θηραμένης ἐκέλευσεν ὑμᾶς τριάκοντα ἀνδράσιν ἐπιτρέψαι τὴν πόλιν, καὶ τῇ πολιτείᾳ χρῆσθαι ἣν Δρακοντίδης ἀπέφαινεν. ὑμεῖς δ' ὅμως καὶ οὕτω διακείμενοι ἐθορυβεῖτε ὡς οὐ ποιήσοντες ταῦτα· ἐγιγνώσκετε γὰρ ὅτι περὶ δουλείας καὶ ἐλευθερίας ἐν ἐκείνῃ τῇ ἡμέρᾳ ἠκκλησιάζετε. Θηραμένης δέ, ὦ ἄνδρες δικασταί (καὶ τούτων ὑμᾶς αὐτοὺς μάρτυρας παρέξομαι) εἶπεν ὅτι οὐδὲν αὐτῷ μέλοι τοῦ ὑμετέρου θορύβου, ἐπειδὴ πολλοὺς μὲν 'Αθηναίων εἰδείη τοὺς τὰ ὅμοια πράττοντας αὐτῷ, δοκοῦντα δὲ Λυσάνδρῳ καὶ Λακεδαιμονίοις λέγοι. μετ' ἐκεῖνον δὲ Λύσανδρος ἀναστὰς ἄλλα τε πολλὰ εἶπε καὶ ὅτι παρασπόνδους ὑμᾶς ἔχοι, καὶ ὅτι οὐ περὶ πολιτείας ὑμῖν ἔσται ἀλλὰ περὶ σωτηρίας, εἰ μὴ ποιήσεθ' ἃ Θηραμένης κελεύει.

18.2 Lysias, **Against Eratosthenes** §§6-9. This is an incident in which the two of the so-called Thirty tyrants came to arrest Lysias.

Θέογνις γὰρ καὶ Πείσων ἔλεγον ἐν τοῖς τριάκοντα περὶ τῶν μετοίκων, ὡς εἶέν τινες τῇ πολιτείᾳ ἀχθόμενοι· καλλίστην οὖν εἶναι πρόφασιν τιμωρεῖσθαι μὲν δοκεῖν, τῷ δ' ἔργῳ χρηματίζεσθαι· πάντως δὲ τὴν μὲν πόλιν πένεσθαι, τὴν δ' ἀρχὴν δεῖσθαι χρημάτων. καὶ τοὺς ἀκούοντας οὐ χαλεπῶς ἔπειθον. . . . διαλαβόντες δὲ τὰς οἰκίας ἐβάδιζον· καὶ ἐμὲ μὲν ξένους ἑστιῶντα κατέλαβον, οὓς ἐξελάσαντες Πείσωνί με παραδιδόασιν· οἱ δὲ ἄλλοι εἰς τὸ ἐργαστήριον ἐλθόντες τὰ ἀνδράποδα ἀπεγράφοντο. ἐγὼ δὲ Πείσωνα μὲν ἠρώτων εἰ βούλοιτό με σῶσαι χρήματα λαβών· ὁ δ' ἔφασκεν, εἰ πολλὰ εἴη. εἶπον οὖν ὅτι τάλαντον ἀργυρίου ἕτοιμος εἴην δοῦναι· ὁ δ' ὡμολόγησε ταῦτα ποιήσειν.

18.3 Lysias, **Against Eratosthenes** §§12-15. Lysias explains how he escaped from one of the Thirty who was sent to arrest him.

ἐξιοῦσι δ' ἐμοὶ καὶ Πείσωνι ἐπιτυγχάνει Μηλόβιός τε καὶ Μνησιθείδης ἐκ τοῦ ἐργαστηρίου ἀπιόντες, καὶ καταλαμβάνουσι πρὸς αὐταῖς ταῖς θύραις, καὶ ἐρωτῶσιν[1] ὅπῃ βαδίζοιμεν· ὁ δ' ἔφασκεν εἰς τοῦ ἀδελφοῦ τοῦ ἐμοῦ ἵνα καὶ τὰ ἐν ἐκείνῃ τῇ οἰκίᾳ σκέψηται. ἐκεῖνον μὲν οὖν ἐκέλευον βαδίζειν, ἐμὲ δὲ μεθ' αὑτῶν ἀκολουθεῖν εἰς Δαμνίππου. Πείσων δὲ προσελθὼν σιγᾶν μοι παρεκελεύετο καὶ θαρρεῖν, ὡς ἥξων ἐκεῖσε. καταλαμβάνομεν δὲ αὐτόθι Θέογνιν ἑτέρους φυλάττοντα· ᾧ παραδόντες ἐμὲ πάλιν ᾤχοντο. (When they reach the house of Damnippos:) καλέσας δὲ Δάμνιππον λέγω πρὸς αὐτὸν τάδε· "ἐπιτήδειος μέν μοι τυγχάνεις ὤν, ἥκω δ' εἰς τὴν σὴν οἰκίαν, ἀδικῶ δ' οὐδέν, χρημάτων δ' ἕνεκα ἀπόλλυμαι. σὺ οὖν ταῦτα πάσχοντί μοι πρόθυμον παράσχου τὴν σεαυτοῦ δύναμιν εἰς τὴν ἐμὴν σωτηρίαν." ὁ δ' ὑπέσχετο ταῦτα ποιήσειν. ἐδόκει δ' αὐτῷ βέλτιον εἶναι πρὸς Θέογνιν μνησθῆναι· ἡγεῖτο γὰρ ἅπαν ποιήσειν αὐτόν, εἴ τις ἀργύριον διδοίη. ἐκείνου δὲ διαλεγομένου Θεόγνιδι (ἔμπειρος γὰρ ὢν ἐτύγχανον τῆς οἰκίας, καὶ ᾔδειν ὅτι ἀμφίθυρος εἴη) ἐδόκει μοι ταύτῃ πειρᾶσθαι σωθῆναι, ἐνθυμουμένῳ ὅτι, ἐὰν μὲν λάθω, σωθήσομαι, ἐὰν δὲ ληφθῶ, ἡγούμην μέν, εἰ Θέογνις εἴη πεπεισμένος ὑπὸ τοῦ Δαμνίππου χρήματα λαβεῖν, οὐδὲν ἧττον ἀφεθήσεσθαι, εἰ δὲ μή, ὁμοίως ἀποθανεῖσθαι.

1 ἐρωτῶσιν: the tense is an historic present, hence the indirect question ὅπῃ βαδίζοιμεν is in secondary sequence.

18.4 Plato **Symposium** §174d4-e5. The narrator encounters Socrates who is on his way to the house of the tragic poet, Agathon, to celebrate his victory in the tragic competition.

τοιαῦτ' ἄττα σφᾶς ἔφη διαλεχθέντας ἰέναι. τὸν οὖν Σωκράτη ἑαυτῷ πως προσέχοντα τὸν νοῦν κατὰ τὴν ὁδὸν πορεύεσθαι ὑπολειπόμενον, καὶ περιμένοντος οὗ κελεύειν προιέναι εἰς τὸ πρόσθεν. ἐπειδὴ δὲ γενέσθαι ἐπὶ τῇ οἰκίᾳ τῇ 'Αγάθωνος, ἀνεῳγμένην καταλαμβάνειν τὴν θύραν, καί τι ἔφη αὐτόθι γελοῖον παθεῖν. οἱ μὲν γὰρ εὐθὺς παῖδά τινα τῶν ἔνδοθεν ἀπαντήσαντα ἄγειν οὗ κατέκειντο οἱ ἄλλοι, καὶ καταλαμβάνειν ἤδη μέλλοντας δειπνεῖν· εὐθὺς δ' οὖν ὡς ἰδεῖν τὸν 'Αγάθωνα, ὦ, φάναι, 'Αριστόδημε, εἰς καλὸν ἥκεις ὅπως συνδειπνήσῃς.

18.5 Plato **Republic** §337a3-c1 Socrates reduces Thrasymachus' argument to an absurdity by claiming that he has in fact constructed his question in such a way as to prohibit his opponent from giving any of the possible answers.

καὶ ὃς ἀκούσας ἀνεκάγχασέ τε μάλα σαρδάνιον καὶ εἶπεν· ὦ Ἡράκλεις, ἔφη, αὕτη 'κείνη ἡ εἰωθυῖα εἰρωνεία Σωκράτους, καὶ ταῦτ' ἐγὼ ᾔδη τε καὶ τούτοις προύλεγον, ὅτι σὺ ἀποκρίνασθαι μὲν οὐκ ἐθελήσοις, εἰρωνεύσοιο δὲ καὶ πάντα μᾶλλον ποιήσοις ἢ

ἀποκρινοῖο, εἴ τίς τί σε ἐρωτᾷ. σοφὸς γὰρ εἶ, ἦν δ' ἐγώ, ὦ Θρασύ-
μαχε· εὖ οὖν ᾔδησθα ὅτι εἴ τινα ἔροιο ὁπόσα ἐστὶν τὰ δώδεκα καὶ
ἐρόμενος προείποις αὐτῷ" ὅπως μοι, ὦ ἄνθρωπε, μὴ ἐρεῖς ὅτι, ἔστιν
τὰ δώδεκα δὶς ἓξ μηδ' ὅτι τρὶς τέτταρα μηδ' ὅτι ἑξάκις δύο μηδ' ὅτι
τετράκις τρία· ὡς οὐκ ἀποδέξομαί σου ἐὰν τοιαῦτα φλυαρῇς"ᾧ
δῆλον, οἶμαί, σοι ἦν ὅτι οὐδεὶς ἀποκρινοῖτο τῷ οὕτως πυνθανομένῳ.
ἀλλ' εἴ σοι εἶπεν· "ὦ Θρασύμαχε, πῶς λέγεις; μὴ ἀποκρίνωμαι ὧν
προεῖπες μηδέν; πότερον, ὦ θαυμάσιε, μηδ' εἰ τούτων τι τυγχάνει ὄν,
ἀλλ' ἕτερον εἴπω τι τοῦ ἀληθοῦς; ἢ πῶς λέγεις"; τί ἂν αὐτῷ εἶπες
πρὸς ταῦτα;

18.6 Thucydides 6.28.2-29.2. This is Thucydides' version of the
story of Alcibiades and the mutilation of the herms, an event that
provoked a violent outcry from the Athenian citizens.   It took
place at the beginning of the Sicilian expedition in 415 B.C.

καὶ αὐτὰ ὑπολαμβάνοντες οἱ μάλιστα τῷ 'Αλκιβιάδῃ ἀχθόμενοι
ἐμποδὼν ὄντι σφίσι μὴ αὐτοῖς τοῦ δήμου βεβαίως προεστάναι, καὶ
νομίσαντες, εἰ αὐτὸν ἐξελάσειαν, πρῶτοι ἂν εἶναι, ἐμεγάλυνον καὶ
ἐβόων ὡς ἐπὶ δήμου καταλύσει τά τε μυστικὰ καὶ ἡ τῶν Ἑρμῶν
περικοπὴ γένοιτο καὶ οὐδὲν εἴη αὐτῶν ὅ τι οὐ μετ' ἐκείνου ἐπράχθη,
ἐπιλέγοντες τεκμήρια τὴν ἄλλην αὐτοῦ ἐς τὰ ἐπιτηδεύματα οὐ
δημοτικὴν παρανομίαν. ὁ δ' ἔν τε τῷ παρόντι πρὸς τὰ μηνύματα
ἀπελογεῖτο καὶ ἑτοῖμος ἦν πρὶν ἐκπλεῖν κρίνεσθαι, εἴ τι τούτων
εἰργασμένος ἦν (ἤδη γὰρ καὶ τὰ τῆς παρασκευῆς ἐπεπόριστο), καὶ
εἰ μὲν τούτων τι εἴργαστο, δίκην δοῦναι, εἰ δ' ἀπολυθείη, ἄρχειν.
καὶ ἐπεμαρτύρετο μὴ ἀπόντος πέρι αὐτοῦ διαβολὰς ἀποδέχεσθαι,
ἀλλ' ἤδη ἀποκτείνειν, εἰ ἀδικεῖ, καὶ ὅτι σωφρονέστερον εἴη μὴ μετὰ
τοιαύτης αἰτίας, πρὶν διαγνῶσι¹, πέμπειν αὐτὸν ἐπὶ τοσούτῳ
στρατεύματι.

[1]πρὶν διαγνῶσι· the ἄν has been omitted from the temporal clause. Such omission is common in Homer and persists in the Attic historians, especially in Thucydides, as an archaizing tendency; see **Smyth** §2444b.

18.7 Thucydides 6.34.2-8 (repeated from **13.5**).

δοκεῖ δέ μοι καὶ ἐς Καρχηδόνα ἄμεινον εἶναι πέμψαι· οὐ γὰρ ἀνέλπιστον αὐτοῖς ἀλλ' αἰεὶ διὰ φόβου εἰσὶ μή ποτε 'Αθηναῖοι αὐτοῖς ἐπὶ τὴν πόλιν ἔλθωσιν ὥστε τάχ' ἂν ἴσως νομίσαντες, εἰ τάδε προήσονται, κἂν σφεῖς ἐν πόνῳ εἶναι, ἐθελήσειαν ἡμῖν ἤτοι κρύφα γε ἢ φανερῶς ἢ ἐξ ἑνός γέ του τρόπου ἀμῦναι. δυνατοὶ δὲ εἰσὶ μάλιστα τῶν νῦν, βουληθέντες· χρυσὸν γὰρ καὶ ἄργυρον πλεῖστον κέκτηνται, ὅθεν ὅ τε πόλεμος καὶ τἆλλα εὐπορεῖ. πέμπωμεν δὲ καὶ ἐς τὴν Λακεδαίμονα καὶ ἐς Κόρινθον δεόμενοι δεῦρο κατὰ τάχος βοηθεῖν καὶ τὸν ἐκεῖ πόλεμον κινεῖν. ὃ δὲ μάλιστα ἐγώ τε νομίζω ἐπίκαιρον ὑμεῖς τε διὰ τὸ ξύνηθες ἥσυχον ἥκιστ' ἂν ὀξέως πείθοισθε, ὅμως εἰρήσεται. Σικελιῶται γὰρ εἰ ἐθέλοιμεν ξύμπαντες, εἰ δὲ μή, ὅτι πλεῖστοι μεθ' ἡμῶν, καθελκύσαντες ἅπαν τὸ ὑπάρχον ναυτικὸν μετὰ δυοῖν μηνοῖν τροφῆς ἀπαντῆσαι 'Αθηναίοις ἐς Τάραντα καὶ ἄκραν 'Ιαπυγίαν, καὶ δῆλον ποιῆσαι αὐτοῖς ὅτι οὐ περὶ τῆς Σικελίας πρότερον ἔσται ὁ ἀγὼν ἢ τοῦ ἐκείνους περαιωθῆναι τὸν 'Ιόνιον, μάλιστ' ἂν αὐτοὺς ἐκπλήξαιμεν καὶ ἐς λογισμὸν καταστήσαιμεν ὅτι ὁρμώμεθα μὲν ἐκ φιλίας χώρας φύλακες (ὑποδέχεται γὰρ ἡμᾶς Τάρας), τὸ δὲ πέλαγος αὐτοῖς πολὺ περαιοῦσθαι μετὰ πάσης τῆς παρασκευῆς, χαλεπὸν δὲ διὰ πλοῦ μῆκος ἐν τάξει μεῖναι, καὶ ἡμῖν ἂν εὐεπίθετος εἴη, βραδεῖά τε καὶ κατ' ὀλίγον προσπίπτουσα. εἰ δ' αὖ τῷ ταχυναυτοῦντι ἀθροωτέρῳ κουφίσαντες προσβάλοιεν, εἰ μὲν κώπαις χρήσαιντο, ἐπιθοίμεθ' ἂν κεκμηκόσιν, εἰ δὲ μὴ δοκοίη, ἔστι καὶ ὑποχωρῆσαι ἡμῖν ἐς Τάραντα· οἱ δὲ μετ' ὀλίγων ἐφοδίων ὡς ἐπὶ ναυμαχίᾳ περαιωθέντες ἀποροῖεν ἂν κατὰ χωρία ἐρῆμα, καὶ ἢ μένοντες πολιορκοῖντο ἂν ἢ πειρώμενοι παραπλεῖν τήν τε ἄλλην παρασκευὴν ἀπολείποιεν ἂν καὶ τὰ τῶν πόλεων οὐκ ἂν βέβαια ἔχοντες, εἰ ὑποδέξοιντο, ἀθυμοῖεν. ὥστ' ἔγωγε τούτῳ τῷ λογισμῷ ἡγοῦμαι ἀποκληομένους αὐτοὺς οὐδ' ἂν ἀπᾶραι ἀπὸ Κερκύρας, ἀλλ' ἢ διαβουλευσαμένους καὶ κατασκοπαῖς χρωμένους, ὁπόσοι τ' ἐσμὲν καὶ ἐν ᾧ χωρίῳ, ἐξωσθῆναι ἂν τῇ ὥρᾳ ἐς χειμῶνα, ἢ καταπλαγέντας τῷ ἀδοκήτῳ καταλῦσαι ἂν τὸν πλοῦν, ἄλλως τε καὶ τοῦ ἐμπειροτάτου τῶν στρατηγῶν, ὡς ἐγὼ ἀκούω, ἄκοντος ἡγουμένου καὶ ἀσμένου ἂν πρόφασιν λαβόντος, εἴ τι ἀξιόχρεων ἀφ' ἡμῶν ὀφθείη. ἀγγελλοίμεθα δ' ἂν εὖ οἶδ' ὅτι ἐπὶ τὸ πλέον· τῶν δ' ἀνθρώπων πρὸς τὰ λεγόμενα καὶ αἱ γνῶμαι ἵστανται, καὶ τοὺς προεπιχειροῦντας ἢ τοῖς γε ἐπιχειροῦσι προδηλοῦντας ὅτι ἀμυνοῦνται μᾶλλον πεφόβηνται, ἰσοκινδύνους ἡγούμενοι. ὅπερ ἂν νῦν Ἀθηναῖοι πάθοιεν. ἐπέρχονται γὰρ ἡμῖν ὡς οὐκ ἀμυνουμένοις, δικαίως κατεγνωκότες ὅτι αὐτοὺς οὐ μετὰ Λακεδαιμονίων ἐφθείρομεν·

EXERCISES:

I. Rewrite **18.4** in Direct speech; then rewrite after εἶπεν ὅτι.
II. Write the conditions of **18.3**, **18.6** and **18.7** in direct speech.
III. Write in Greek:

A. Write the following sentences as indirect statements after εἶπεν ὅτι, then after ἔφη. After εἶπεν ὅτι change into corresponding tenses of the optative whenever possible. You may also need to change the person. Many of these sentences are from previous exercises.

1. Are you afraid that you will suffer misfortunes greater than the present ones?
2. In order not to do wrong Socrates was willing to die.
3. Let them not fear telling the truth more than lying.

4. The laws should speak to Socrates and say the following things.

5. Let us consider nothing else but whether Socrates committed an unjust act; if he did, let us execute him, if not, let us release him.

6. If he could have, Demosthenes would have prevented the unification of Greece.

7. Since the doorkeeper had not yet arrived, we were unable to spend the day with Socrates.

8. When we destroy that which health improves and sickness harms, we also destroy what men call the soul, whatever it may be.

9. Whenever we visit Socrates in order to spend the day with him, we must first wait until the doorkeeper arrives.

10. If you were a wise man, Thrasymachus, you would consider committing an injustice worse than suffering an unjust act.

B Sentences:

1. He said that Thrasymachus asked Socrates to answer the question directly instead of indulging in his favorite method of argument—question and answer. Thrasymachus seemed, he said, to those present to be angry at Socrates, and after a short time he decided to leave, but the others persuaded him to stay. He was beginning to argue that justice was whatever those who had power chose to make it, when he said he had to go away. We never found out who won the debate.

2. They thought that Alcibiades was so popular with the people that if he stood trial immediately after the mutilation of the Herms, he would surely have been acquitted. Therefore, they decided to keep quiet and allow him to lead the expedition to Sicily. But secretly they proposed to recall him as soon as public sentiment had changed. Alcibiades, for his part, said that he wished to be tried immediately, and that it was foolhardy for the Athenians to send him out as the head of an expedition, if they could not trust him.

3. He told them that it would have been better to have the Athenians as allies than as enemies, but since this was no longer possible, he advised them to prepare for war. They ought already to have sent envoys to the Carthaginians and to any other Greeks who might be well disposed towards them, in order to persuade them to send support, or at least not to enter into an alliance with

the Athenians, and they should have done this before making any other preparations. But since they had not, he urged them to strengthen their navy, to increase the provisions and the number of rowers, and be prepared for an early attack. The Athenians, he said, claimed that they were not at war with them and that they would prefer peace, but he, at least, was not inclined to trust them. (This paragraph is adapted from Chapter Thirteen).

CHAPTER NINETEEN—INDIRECT QUESTIONS AND COMMANDS[1]

Indirect questions are structurally similar to indirect statements expressed after ὡς or ὅτι. "What was he doing? is a direct question; "They asked what he was doing" is indirect. They are usually introduced by an interrogative verb or phrase, though they sometimes occur after verbs of speaking. The negative (οὐ or μή) depends on the character of the direct question.

1. Indirect questions are introduced by the same range of interrogative pronouns, adjectives, adverbs, and conjunctions that introduce direct questions, e.g, τίς, ποῖος, πόσος, πότερος, πῶς, but they may also be introduced by a set of **indirect interrogatives**, also used for indefinite relatives, e.g., ὅστις, ὁποῖος, ὁπόσος, ὁπότερος, ὅπως.

(a) Both direct and indirect forms may be used in the same sentence, e.g., Xenophon, **Memorabilia** 4.4.13: οὐ γὰρ αἰσθάνομαί σου ὁποῖον νόμιμον ἢ ποῖον δίκαιον λέγεις. = "I don't understand what you mean by 'conformable to law' and 'just.' "

(b) εἰ may also introduce indirect questions (though ἐάν or ἤν never does), e.g., ἤρετο εἰ ἀφίκοιντο. = "She asked if they had arrived." When used in this way εἰ is often translated "whether."

(c) Alternate indirect questions may be introduced by any of the following: πότερον (or πότερα) . . . ἤ, εἰ. . .ἤ, εἴτε. . .εἴτε, or εἰ. . .εἴτε, ἤ. . .ἤ.

2. Indirect questions that follow a verb in **primary sequence retain the tense and mood of the direct question** (usually indicative for ordinary questions, subjunctive for deliberative questions, optative + ἄν for potential optative). In contrast, note that Latin always uses the subjunctive in this construction. When the leading verb is

---

[1] For further discussion see **Smyth** §§2663-2680, **GG** §§1505, 1607, **MT** §§ 669-68 (questions), **Smyth** §§2612, 2633 (commands).

in **secondary sequence** subordinate verbs may be changed into a corresponding tense of the **optative or the original tenses may be retained for clarity or emphasis.**

(a) When a question is potential, i.e., constructed with an indicative or optative + ἄν, the tense, mood, and the ἄν of the direct form are retained after both primary and secondary sequence, since to do otherwise would obscure the potential force of the question.

(b) Both primary and secondary sequence can occur in the same sentence, e.g., ἤρετο ὅ τι θαυμάζοι καὶ ὁπόσοι αὐτῶν τεθνᾶσεν = "He asked what surprised him and how many of them were dead."

Commands may be expressed as dependent statements in the following ways:

(a) A periphrasis with χρή or δεῖ, e.g., μένωμεν (direct) becomes ἔφη χρῆναι αὐτοὺς μένειν.

(b) A periphrasis dependent on a verb of ordering or of will or desire, e.g., ἐκέλευεν αὐτοὺς μένειν.

(c) Sometimes the command may be expressed as an infinitive. See below **19.3.**

READINGS:

19.1 Xenophon, **Cyropaedia** 3.1.4-6. The "Education of Cyrus" is a partly historical, partly philosophical, partly fictional account of the proper education for princes. This episode treats the young Cyrus's handling of an encounter with the king of the Armenians.

ὁ δὲ βασιλεὺς αὐτός (= the king of the Armenians), ὡς ᾔσθετο τὰ

γιγνόμενα, ἀπορῶν **ποῖ τράποιτο** ἐπὶ λόφον τινὰ καταφεύγει. ὁ δ᾽

αὖ Κῦρος ταῦτα ἰδὼν περιίσταται τὸν λόφον τῷ παρόντι στρατεύ-

ματι, καὶ πρὸς Χρυσάνταν πέμψας **ἐκέλευε·φυλακὴν τοῦ ὄρους**

καταλιπόντα ἥκειν. τὸ μὲν δὴ στράτευμα ἠθροίζετο τῷ Κύρῳ·

ὁ δὲ πέμψας πρὸς τὸν ᾿Αρμένιον κήρυκα ἤρετο ὧδε· εἰπέ μοι, ἔφη, ὦ
᾿Αρμένιε, **πότερα βούλει** αὐτοῦ **μένων** τῷ λιμῷ **καὶ** τῷ
δίψει μάχεσθαι ἢ εἰς τὸ ἰσόπεδον καταβὰς ἡμῖν δι-
αμάχεσθαι; ἀπεκρίνατο ὁ ᾿Αρμένιος ὅτι οὐδετέροις βούλοιτο
μάχεσθαι. πάλιν ὁ Κῦρος πέμψας ἡρώτα τί οὖν **κάθησαι**
ἐνταῦθα καὶ οὐ καταβαίνεις; ἀπορῶν, ἔφη, ὅ τι χρὴ ποιεῖν.
ἀλλ᾿ οὐδέν, ἔφη ὁ Κῦρος, **ἀπορεῖν σε δεῖ·** ἔξεστι γάρ σοι ἐπὶ
δίκην καταβαίνειν. τίς δ᾿, ἔφη, ἔσται ὁ δικάζων; δῆλον ὅτι ᾧ ὁ θεὸς
ἔδωκε καὶ ἄνευ δίκης· χρῆσθαί σοι **ὅ τι βούλοιτο.** ἐνταῦθα δὴ ὁ
᾿Αρμένιος γιγνώσκων τὴν ἀνάγκην καταβαίνει.

19.2 Plato, **Euthyphro** §§4b7-d5 (repeated from **4.1**).

γελοῖον, ὦ Σώκρατες, ὅτι οἴει τι διαφέρειν **εἴτε ἀλλότριος εἴτε**
οἰκεῖος ὁ **τεθνεώς,** ἀλλ᾿ οὐ τοῦτο μόνον δεῖν φυλάττειν, **εἴτε ἐν**
δίκῃ ἔκτεινεν ὁ **κτείνας εἴτε μή,** καὶ εἰ μὲν ἐν δίκῃ, ἐᾶν, εἰ
δὲ μή, ἐπεξιέναι, ἐάνπερ ὁ κτείνας συνέστιός σοι καὶ ὁμοτράπεζος ᾖ·
ἴσον γὰρ τὸ μίασμα γίγνεται ἐὰν συνῇς τῷ τοιούτῳ συνειδὼς καὶ
μὴ ἀφοσιοῖς σεαυτόν τε καὶ ἐκεῖνον τῇ δίκῃ ἐπεξιών. ἐπεὶ ὅ γε
ἀποθανὼν πελάτης τις ἦν ἐμός, καὶ ὡς ἐγεωργοῦμεν ἐν τῇ Νάξῳ,
ἐθήτευεν ἐκεῖ παρ᾿ ἡμῖν. παροινήσας οὖν καὶ ὀργισθεὶς τῶν
οἰκετῶν τινι τῶν ἡμετέρων ἀποσφάττει αὐτόν. ὁ οὖν πατὴρ
συνδήσας τοὺς πόδας καὶ τὰς χεῖρας αὐτοῦ, καταβαλὼν εἰς τάφρον
τινά, πέμπει δεῦρο ἄνδρα πευσόμενον τοῦ ἐξηγητοῦ **ὅ τι χρείη**
ποιεῖν. ἐν δὲ τούτῳ τῷ χρόνῳ τοῦ δεδεμένου ὠλιγώρει τε καὶ
ἠμέλει ὡς ἀνδροφόνου καὶ οὐδὲν ὂν πρᾶγμα εἰ καὶ ἀποθάνοι, ὅπερ
οὖν καὶ ἔπαθεν· ὑπὸ γὰρ λιμοῦ καὶ ῥίγους καὶ τῶν δεσμῶν
ἀποθνήσκει πρὶν τὸν ἄγγελον παρὰ τοῦ ἐξηγητοῦ ἀφικέσθαι.

19.3 Thucydides 1.25.1-2. One of the causes of the Peloponnesian war was a dispute over Epidamnus. Thucydides is here giving the background of the story. The democrats in Epidamnus were seeking protection first from Corcyra, who refused help, then from the Corinthians.

γνόντες δὲ οἱ Ἐπιδάμνιοι οὐδεμίαν σφίσιν ἀπὸ Κερκύρας τιμωρίαν

οὖσαν ἐν ἀπόρῳ εἴχοντο θέσθαι τὸ παρόν, καὶ πέμψαντες ἐς Δελφοὺς

τὸν θεὸν ἐπήροντο εἰ **παραδοῖεν** Κορινθίοις τὴν πόλιν ὡς

οἰκισταῖς καὶ τιμωρίαν τινὰ πειρῷντ᾽ ἀπ᾽ αὐτῶν

ποιεῖσθαι. ὁ δ᾽ αὐτοῖς ἀνεῖλε **παραδοῦναι καὶ ἡγεμόνας**

ποιεῖσθαι. ἐλθόντες δὲ οἱ Ἐπιδάμνιοι ἐς τὴν Κόρινθον κατὰ τὸ

μαντεῖον παρέδοσαν τὴν ἀποικίαν, τόν τε οἰκιστὴν ἀποδεικνύντες

σφῶν ἐκ Κορίνθου ὄντα καὶ τὸ χρηστήριον δηλοῦντες, ἐδέοντό τε μὴ

σφᾶς περιορᾶν φθειρομένους, ἀλλ᾽ ἐπαμῦναι.

19.4 Demosthenes, **On the False Embassy** §§121-122. The Athenians have elected a set of ambassadors to send to Philip that includes Aeschines and Demosthenes; Demosthenes, however, declared he will not leave the city at that particular time, so the remaining ambassadors met to decide whom to leave behind to watch him.

ἐπειδὴ γὰρ ἀπεστέλλετ᾽αὖθις αὖ τὸ τρίτον τοὺς πρέσβεις ὡς τὸν

Φίλιππον, ἐπὶ ταῖς καλαῖς καὶ μεγάλαις ἐλπίσι ταύταις αἷς οὗτος

ὑπέσχετο, ἐχειροτονήσατε καὶ τοῦτον κἀμὲ καὶ τῶν ἄλλων τοὺς

πλείστους τοὺς αὐτούς. ἐγὼ μὲν δὴ παρελθὼν ἐξωμοσάμην εὐθέως,

καὶ θορυβούντων τινῶν καὶ **κελευόντων βαδίζειν**, οὐκ ἂν ἔφην

ἀπελθεῖν· οὗτος (= Aeschines) δ᾽ ἐκεχειροτόνητο. ἐπειδὴ δ᾽ ἀνέστη

μετὰ ταῦθ᾽ ἡ ἐκκλησία, συνελθόντες ἐβουλεύονθ᾽ **οὗτοι τίν᾽**

αὐτοῦ καταλείψουσιν.

EXERCISES:

I. Rewrite 19.1 in direct speech.
II. Write in Greek:

A Sentences:

Write the following questions after ἐρωτᾷ then after ἤρετο. Change to corresponding tenses of the optative whenever possible. These sentences are from previous exercises.

1. Where are we to go? What friends are we to seek?
2. How should we escape if you are concerned for our reputation?
3. Must we suffer these things?
4. Didn't you say that no one must ever commit injustice?
5. Is it possible that he is telling the truth when he says he did not receive the money?
6. Didn't he pay attention to the praises of his teacher?
7. Who will honor the wicked more than the just?
8. Where did he happen to exercise?
9. Will you answer whatever question I put to you?
10. Did you speak for us or against us?

Write the following commands after a verb of ordering or wishing in the past tense or with a form of χρή. These sentences are from previous exercises.

1. Examine the matter, my friends, in the way that seems best to you.
2. Do not obey every man who tells you such things.
3. Let all men honor the city's gods and let them keep their oaths.
4. Do not allow sycophants to harm Socrates.
5. Order one of the slaves to bring Socrates to us.
6. Don't keep worrying about throwing away all your money.
7. Let them order Socrates to come in.
8. Let them recline next to Socrates and let us recline next to Agathon.
9. Let him not deceive his friends or his relations.
10. Obey your parents and respect your friends.

B Sentences (these have been adapted from paragraphs in Chapters Six and Seven).

1. He asked how a man who refused to follow the guidance of someone who understood how to exercise the body, but instead listened to the opinions of the many could not come to harm. Such a man, he said, must surely run the risk of serious injury. We had no answer to give him. Well then, he asked, why have you not exercised and eaten properly? Have you not been instructed wisely? Again we fell silent.

2. We have always sacrificed to the gods of the city and held to its laws, considering that the one was a mark of piety, the other of good sense. Further, we believe that men should not ignore religious matters or disobey the laws of their city. He asked us why we thought this. Did we, he asked, imagine that we ran the risk of offending the gods?

3. Lysias asked him whether he was one of those in the council chamber who spoke against those urging the killing of honorable citizens. He denied that he was, but admitted that he had arrested his brother Polemarchus. Lysias asked him whether he thought Polemarchus guilty of a crime or not. He said that he did not think that he was guilty of anything. Why then, asked Lysias, did you arrest him? He claimed he was afraid of the Thirty. When asked what he actually said in the council chamber, he replied that he could not answer, for whether he lied or told the truth they would not believe him.

CHAPTER TWENTY—CAUSAL CLAUSES[1]

1. Subordinate clauses that offer an explanation for an event or circumstance may be introduced by a variety of conjunctions:

(a) ἐπεί, ἐπειδή, and less commonly, ὅτε, ὁπότε (= since, seeing that). These are analogous to temporal clauses and have been discussed in Chapter Seventeen.

(b) ὅτι, διότι, διόπερ, ὡς (= because). These are analogous to constructions that follow verbs of speaking.

(c) ὡς (= on the grounds that) is also used with a circumstantial participle, see Chapter Four 3 (b).

2. Causal clauses denoting a **fact** take the indicative after **both primary and secondary sequence**. The indicative is retained even in indirect statement. Those denoting an **alleged or reported fact** (that is, a statement for which the author wishes to assume no responsibility) will take the **optative in secondary sequence**.

Example: Xenophon, **Sym.** §4.6: οἶσθα ἐπαινέσαντα αὐτὸν (sc. Homer) τὸν ᾿Αγαμέμνονα, ὡς βασιλεὺς . . . εἴη ἀγαθός. "You know that he praised Agamemnon because he was **(allegedly)** a good king."

3. Occasionally a causal clause introduced by ἐπεί may have a concessive force

Example: Plato, **Sym.** §187a1-4: μουσικὴ δὲ καὶ παντὶ κατάδηλος τῷ καὶ σμικρὸν προσέχοντι τὸν νοῦν ὅτι κατὰ ταὐτὰ ἔχει τούτοις, ὥσπερ ἴσως καὶ ᾿Ηράκλειτος βούλεται λέγειν, ἐπεὶ τοῖς γε ῥήμασιν οὐ καλῶς λέγει. "It is clear to anyone who gives it the slightest attention that music is in this same

---

[1] For further discussion see **Smyth** §§2240-2248, **GG** §§1463-1465, **MT** §§712-719.

situation, as perhaps Heraclitus also was intending to say, **though** in his actual wording he does not express it very well."

4. Verbs denoting an emotion (e.g., ἄγαμαι, ἄχθομαι, αἰσχύνομαι, ἀγανακτέω, θαυμάζω) are often followed by a clause introduced by ὅτι or ὡς to explain the reason for the emotion. They may also be followed by an if-clause.

READINGS:

20.1 Demosthenes, **Against Timocrates** §§152-153 (repeated from **6.3**).

ἡ γὰρ πόλις ἡμῶν, ὦ ἄνδρες δικασταί, νόμοις καὶ ψηφίσμασιν διοικεῖται. εἰ δή τις τὰ ψήφῳ κεκριμένα νόμῳ καινῷ λύσει, τί πέρας ἔσται; ἢ πῶς τοῦτον δίκαιόν ἐστι νόμον προσαγορεύειν, ἀλλ' οὐκ ἀνομίαν; ἢ πῶς οὐ τῆς μεγίστης ὀργῆς ὁ τοιοῦτος νομοθέτης ἄξιός ἐστιν; ἐγὼ μὲν γὰρ τῶν ἐσχάτων νομίζω, **οὐχ ὅτι** τοῦτον μόνον τὸν νόμον ἔθηκεν, **ἀλλ' ὅτι** καὶ τοῖς ἄλλοις ὁδὸν δείκνυσι καὶ περὶ δικαστηρίων καταλύσεως καὶ περὶ τῶν φευγόντων καθόδου καὶ περὶ τῶν ἄλλων τῶν δεινοτάτων. τί γὰρ κωλύει, ὦ ἄνδρες δικασταί, εἰ οὗτος χαίρων ἀπαλλάξει ὁ τοιοῦτον νόμον τιθείς, ἕτερον φανῆναι ἄλλο τι τῶν τῆς πόλεως ἰσχυροτάτων καταλύοντα νόμῳ καινῷ; ἐγὼ μὲν γὰρ οἶμαι οὐδέν.

20.2 Thucydides 1.86.1-5 (repeated from **8.2**).

τοὺς μὲν λόγους τοὺς πολλοὺς τῶν Ἀθηναίων οὐ γιγνώσκω· ἐπαινέσαντες γὰρ πολλὰ ἑαυτοὺς οὐδαμοῦ ἀντεῖπον ὡς οὐκ ἀδικοῦσι τοὺς ἡμετέρους ξυμμάχους καὶ τὴν Πελοπόννησον· καίτοι εἰ πρὸς τοὺς Μήδους ἐγένοντο ἀγαθοὶ τότε, πρὸς δ' ἡμᾶς κακοὶ νῦν, διπλασίας ζημίας ἄξιοί εἰσιν, **ὅτι ἀντ' ἀγαθῶν κακοὶ γεγένηνται**.

20.3 Plato, **Apology** §38c1-d1 (repeated from **1.3**).

οὐ πολλοῦ γ' ἕνεκα χρόνου, ὦ ἄνδρες 'Αθηναῖοι, ὄνομα ἕξετε καὶ
αἰτίαν ὑπὸ τῶν βουλομένων τὴν πόλιν λοιδορεῖν **ὡς Σωκράτη**
ἀπεκτόνατε, ἄνδρα σοφόνῷφήσουσι γὰρ δὴ σοφὸν εἶναι, εἰ καὶ μή
εἰμι, οἱ βουλόμενοι ὑμῖν ὀνειδίζεινῷεἰ γοῦν περιεμείνατε ὀλίγον
χρόνον, ἀπὸ τοῦ αὐτομάτου ἂν ὑμῖν τοῦτο ἐγένετο· ὁρᾶτε γὰρ δὴ τὴν
ἡλικίαν ὅτι πόρρω ἤδη ἐστὶ τοῦ βίου θανάτου δὲ ἐγγύς. λέγω δὲ
τοῦτο οὐ πρὸς πάντας ὑμᾶς, ἀλλὰ πρὸς τοὺς ἐμοῦ καταψηφισαμένους
θάνατον.

20.4 Demosthenes, **On the False Embassy** §§4-5. Demosthenes is
providing the jurors with what he claims are the appropriate
criteria for selecting ambassadors and subsequently evaluating
their actions.

ὡς δή μοι δοκεῖτ' ἂν ὅμως ἐκ τούτων καὶ γνῶναι τὰ δίκαια καὶ
δικάσαι νυνί, τοῦθ' ὑμῖν λέξω· εἰ σκέψαισθε παρ' ὑμῖν αὐτοῖς, ὦ
ἄνδρες δικασταί, καὶ λογίσαισθε τίνων προσήκει λόγον παρὰ
πρεσβευτοῦ λαβεῖν. πρῶτον μὲν τοίνυν ὧν ἀπήγγειλε, δεύτερον δ'
ὧν ἔπεισε, τρίτον δ' ὧν προσετάξατ' αὐτῷ, μετὰ ταῦτα τῶν
χρόνων, ἐφ' ἅπασι δὲ τούτοις, εἰ ἀδωροδοκήτως ἢ μὴ πάντα ταῦτα
πέπρακται. τί δήποτε τούτων; **ὅτι ἐκ μὲν τῶν ἀπαγγελιῶν**
τὸ βουλεύσασθαι περὶ τῶν πραγμάτων ὑμῖν ἐστίν· ἂν
μὲν οὖν ὦσιν ἀληθεῖς, τὰ δέοντ' ἔγνωτε, ἂν δὲ μὴ τοιαῦται, τἀ-
ναντία. τὰς δὲ συμβουλίας πιστοτέρας ὑπολαμβάνετ' εἶναι τὰς
τῶν πρέσβεων· ὡς γὰρ εἰδότων περὶ ὧν ἐπέμφθησαν ἀκούετε· οὐδὲν
οὖν ἐξελέγχεσθαι δίκαιός ἐστιν ὁ πρεσβευτὴς φαῦλον οὐδ' ἀσύμφορον
ὑμῖν συμβεβουλευκώς.

20.5 Plato, Sym. §§189d7-190b5 (with an omission). This is from the speech of Aristophanes where he is describing the original human beings—round creatures with four arms and legs—who, because of their impudence, were cut in half by the gods to form the creatures we are today.

πρῶτον μὲν γὰρ τρία ἦν τὰ γένη τὰ τῶν ἀνθρώπων, οὐχ ὥσπερ νῦν δύο, ἄρρεν καὶ θῆλυ, ἀλλὰ καὶ τρίτον προσῆν κοινὸν ὂν ἀμφοτέρων τούτων, οὗ νῦν ὄνομα λοιπόν, αὐτὸ δὲ ἠφάνισται· ἀνδρόγυνον γὰρ ἓν τότε μὲν ἦν καὶ εἶδος καὶ ὄνομα ἐξ ἀμφοτέρων κοινὸν τοῦ τε ἄρρενος καὶ θήλεος, νῦν δὲ οὐκ ἔστιν ἀλλ' ἢ ἐν ὀνείδει ὄνομα κείμενον. ἔπειτα ὅλον ἦν ἑκάστου τοῦ ἀνθρώπου τὸ εἶδος στρογγύλον, νῶτον καὶ πλευρὰς κύκλῳ ἔχον, χεῖρας δὲ τέτταρας εἶχε, καὶ σκέλη τὰ ἴσα ταῖς χερσίν, καὶ πρόσωπα δύ' ἐπ' αὐχένι κυκλοτερεῖ, ὅμοια πάντῃ. . . .ἦν δὲ διὰ ταῦτα τρία τὰ γένη καὶ τοιαῦτα, **ὅτι τὸ μὲν ἄρρεν ἦν τοῦ ἡλίου τὴν ἀρχὴν ἔκγονον, τὸ δὲ θῆλυ τῆς γῆς, τὸ δὲ ἀμφοτέρων μετέχον τῆς σελήνης, ὅτι καὶ ἡ σελήνη ἀμφοτέρων μετέχει·** περιφερῆ δὲ δὴ ἦν καὶ αὐτὰ καὶ ἡ πορεία αὐτῶν διὰ τὸ τοῖς γονεῦσιν ὅμοια εἶναι.

EXERCISES:

I. Write in Greek:

A Sentences:

1. Did he send us away because he was angry with us?
2. He was praising us because we agreed with him.
3. She sent for the doctor because he was near to death.
4. Why did they do that? Because it seemed best for all of us.
5. Since you refuse to vote in accordance with the laws, you will not be able to prevent such wicked behavior.
6. Do you think that the Athenians will be reviled because they killed Socrates?
7. Are they not ready to obey you because you are just?

8. We did not consider whom to send on the embassy because our time for discussion had run out.

9. I said that they could not have done this. Why? Because they are incapable of insulting you.

10. She decided that we were the most trustworthy on the grounds that we had not voted to condemn Socrates.

11. Since the sun is their parent, they are round in shape.

12. I do not believe what Aristophanes says about human nature, because he only wishes to make us laugh.

13. Aristophanes claims that human beings were originally three in kind because (allegedly) they were descended from the sun, the earth, and the moon.

14. Why does Aristophanes call his third type of human "androgynous"? Because it has the characteristics of both the male and the female.

15. Why do you believe that Aristophanes claims that humankind was originally round with four hands and feet? Because Plato says so.

B Sentences:

1. Why did he refuse to tell you, gentlemen of the jury, about the crimes that this man has committed? Because he hoped to receive money from him in exchange for silence. However, you should all be aware that his silence, if left unpunished, will destroy the laws. Why is that? Because it prevents you from fulfilling your sacred oaths to judge fairly and to mete out justice to the guilty.

2. Because I know him to be a criminal, because I hope to demonstrate to you, gentlemen, his monstrous crimes, I have undertaken this prosecution. But since I have never been either a prosecutor or a defendant on any charge whatsoever and I am inexperienced in speaking, I ask that you listen to the facts in the case, but ignore my failings as a speaker, so that justice may be done.

3. Why did the Athenians choose to execute Socrates, seeing as he was of such an age that he was likely to die within a short time? Because they feared his continuing to converse with young men of good family, even for a short period. But why should they fear this? Since Socrates believes that men must understand what was

good or what was just before they could in reality be good or be just, many parents feared that their sons were being persuaded by Socrates to question their authority and social conventions.

APPENDIX A—DECLENSION OF NAMES IN ATTIC

1. First declension masculine names in -ης or -ας are declined like πολίτης. A number of names in -ης, however, show a fusion of first and third declension forms. Names in -κράτης, -μένης, -γένης and -φάνης are declined in accordance with the following pattern:

Nominative	Σωκράτης
Genitive	Σωκράτους
Dative	Σωκράτει
Accusative	Σωκράτη
Vocative	Σώκρατες

But note that names in -κλῆς are declined as follows in Attic:

Ἡρακλῆς
Ἡρακλέους
Ἡρακλεῖ
Ἡρακλέα
Ἡράκλεις

2. Names in long -α are declined as follows: Most Roman names in -α are declined in Greek in this way:

Ἀννίβας
Ἀννίβου (or Ἀννίβα, the so-called Doric genitive)
Ἀννίβᾳ
Ἀννίβαν
Ἀννίβα

Note that contracts like Βορρᾶς or Ἑρμῆς follow this pattern but have a circumflex in all cases.

3. Names whose nominative end in -ις are accented like δύναμις; whose nominative end in -εύς, are accented like βασιλεύς.

4. Names in -ων are declined like ἡγεμών, though the accent is usually recessive: Note the way in which Apollo is declined:

Ἀπόλλων
Ἀπόλλωνος

'Απόλλωνι
'Απόλλωνα (but sometimes 'Απόλλω, as if contracted)
"Απολλον

5. Note the declension of women's names like Λητώ, 'Αργώ, Σαπφώ
(but in Aeolic the accent is recessive, so Σάπφω or Ψάπφω).

Λητώ
Λητοῦς
Λητοῖ
Λητῶ
Λητοῖ

INDEX A: ENGLISH-GREEK VOCABULARY

This index is intended to be an aid in translating from English into Greek, but it should not be used as a substitute for consulting the standard Greek lexicon, nor as a substitute for reading the passages in each chapter and familiarizing yourself with their vocabulary. Words are entered by one form only: nouns by nominative singular, adjectives by nominative singular masculine, verbs by first person singular of first principal part in common use, by the third person, if impersonal. Attic spellings are used throughout.

Although, it contains most words, not every word that occurs in the exercises will be found below, intentionally, to encourage you to build vocabulary by reading. If you cannot find a word, consider an English synonym or a periphrasis. For example, there is no entry for "conversation," although there is for the verb "converse." And while the expression "unanimous" is not entered, the phrase μιᾷ γνώμῃ occurs in the readings for the chapter in which you are asked to write "unanimous." All names used in the exercises may be found in the readings; for the declension of Attic names, see Appendix.

abide ἐμμένω
abundance εὐπορία
abuse λοιδορέω
accept ἀποδέχομαι
accomplish διαπράττω,
  ἐργάζομαι,
according to κατά (+ acc.)
account λογισμός
account book γραμματεῖον
accusation ἔγκλημα
accuse αἰτιάομαι, ἐγκαλέω,
  κατηγορέω
accuser (in court) κατήγορος
acquit ἀποψηφίζομαι
act piously εὐσεβέω
activity πρᾶξις
add προστίθημι, ἐπιλέγω (in
  speaking)
address προσαγορεύω
  address the assembly δημηγορέω
admit ὁμολογέω, προσίημι

adulterer μοιχός
advertise ἐπαγγέλλω
advice συμβουλία
advise συμβουλεύω
after μετά (+ acc.)
again αὖ, αὖθις, πάλιν
against πρός, ἐπί (+ acc.), κατά
  (+ gen.)
age αἰών, ἡλικία
agree ὁμολογέω, συμφωνέω
aid βοηθέω, ὠφελέω
all πᾶς
alliance συμμαχία
allow ἀφίημι, ἐάω, προσίημι
ally σύμμαχος
already ἤδη
always ἀεί
ambassador πρεσβευτής,
  πρέσβεις (in plural)
ambition φιλοτιμία
ancestor πρόγονος

ancestral πάτριος
ancient ἀρχαῖος
anger ὀργή (n); ὀργίζω (v)
animal θήρ, θηρίον
announce ἀγγέλλω, ἐπαγγέλλω
annoying δυσχερής
another ἄλλος, ἕτερος (of two)
answer ἀποκρίνομαι
appear φαίνομαι, ἀναφαίνομαι
approve δοκιμάζω
argument λόγος
army στρατιά
around ἀμφί, περί
arrange τάττω, συντάττω
arrangement τάξις
arrive ἀφικνέομαι
as καθότι, ὡς, ὥσπερ
as much (many) as ὁπόσος
ask a question ἐρωτάω
ask for αἰτέω, δέομαι
assemble ἀθροίζω, ἐκκλησιάζω
assembly ἐκκλησία, σύλλογος
assist συμβάλλω
assisting βοηθός
associate with συγγίγνομαι,
    σύνειμι (sum)
association συνουσία
at home οἴκοι
at least γε, γοῦν
attack ἐπιβολή (n); ἐπιτίθημι,
    προσβάλλω (v)
authority ἐξουσία
available πρόχειρος
avenge τιμωρέω
away from ἀπό (+ gen.)

bad κακός, πονηρός
bar μοχλός
battle μάχη
be εἰμί
  be a defendant φεύγω
  be a laborer θητεύω
  be a slave δουλεύω
  be able δύναμαι
  be absent ἀπογίγνομαι
  be accustomed ἔθω (εἴωθα)
  be afraid δείδω, φοβέομαι
  be angry ὀργίζομαι
  be annoyed ἄχθομαι
  be anxious ἀγωνιάω
  be at a loss ἀπορέω

be at home ἐπιδημέω
be born γίγνομαι
be captured ἁλίσκομαι
be clean καθαρεύω
be concerned σπουδάζω
be convicted ἁλίσκομαι
be discouraged ἀθυμέω
be disobedient ἀπειθέω
be disposed διάκειμαι
be eloquent δεινὸς λέγω
be fitting πρέπω
be healthy ὑγιαίνω
be ignorant ἀγνοέω
be in charge of προΐστημι
be inside ἔνειμι
be jealous of ζηλοτυπέω,
    φθονέω
be of concern to μέλω
be poor πένομαι
be possible ἔξεστι
be present πάρειμι (sum)
be proper προσήκω
be puzzled ἀπορέω
be sick νοσέω
be silent σιγάω
be vexed ἄχθομαι
be weak ἀσθενέω
bear φέρω
bear fruit καρπόω
bear up ἀνέχω
beautiful καλός
beauty κάλλος
because of ἕνεκα (+ gen.)
become γίγνομαι
before πρό (+ gen.), πρότερον,
    πρίν See Chapter Seventeen
beget γεννάω
begin ἄρχω
beginning ἀρχή
begrudge φθονέω
behave drunkenly παροινέω
behind ὄπισθεν
believe νομίζω
belong to πρόσειμι
benefit εὖ ποιέω, εὐεργετέω,
    ὠφελέω
besiege πολιορκέω
betray προδίδωμι
better ἀμείνων, βελτίων
    (comparatives of ἀγαθός)
beyond ὑπέρ (+ acc.)

bid παρακαλέω
bind δέω
bird ὄρνεον, ὄρνις
blame ψόγος
blessed μακάριος
blow πληγή
boat πλοῖον
body σῶμα
bold θρασύς
boldness θράσος, τόλμα
bond δεσμός
both ἀμφότερος
box λάρναξ
boy friend παιδικά (pl.)
breaker of a treaty παράσπονδος
breathe ἐμπνέω
bring κομίζω, προσφέρω, φέρω
  bring back from exile κατάγω
  bring back to life ἀναβιώσκομαι
  bring to ἐπιφέρω
  bring to one's side προσάγομαι
  bring together συμφέρω
  bring up τρέφω
brother ἀδελφός
burden ἐμποδίζω
burial ταφή
burn καίω
bury θάπτω
business ἐπιτήδευμα
by διά (+ acc. or gen.), ὑπό (+ gen.)

call καλέω
  call to witness ἐπιμαρτύρομαι
calm ἥσυχος
campaign στρατεία, στράτευμα
carefully ἐπιμελῶς
carry φέρω
  carry away ἀπαίρω, ἀποφέρω
  carry out (in burial) ἐκφέρω
cease ἀποκάμνω, παύομαι See
  Chapter Four, 3(c) n.1
challenge προκαλέω
chance τύχη
change μετατίθημι
  change one's mind μετανοέω
charge αἰτία
chatter ἐκλαλέω
check κωλύω, παύω See Chapter
  Four, 3(c) n.1
  hold in check ἀνέχω
child βρέφος παιδίον, παῖς
choice αἵρεσις

choose αἱρέομαι, ἀπολέγω,
  προαιρέομαι
choral leader χορηγός
citizen ἀστός, πολίτης
city, city-state πόλις
claim ἀξίωσις
clear δῆλος
clever δεινός
close κλείω
coeval ἡλικιώτης
collectively συλλήβδην
colony ἀποικία
come ἔρχομαι, ἥκω
  come to aid ἐπαμύνω
  come upon ἐντυγχάνω,
    ἐπέρχομαι
command (an army) ἄρχω, ἡγέομαι
command (= order) ἐντολή (n);
  προστάττω, παρακαλέω (v)
commander ταξίαρχος
commit ἐπιτρέπω
  commit adultery with μοιχεύω
  commit sacrilege ἀσεβέω
common κοινός
compel ἀναγκάζω
conceal κρύπτω, ἐπικρύπτω
concede συγχωρέω
confusion ἀπορία
consider ἐνθυμέομαι, ἡγέομαι
conspicuous φανερός
constitution πολιτεία
constrain βιάζω, βιάω
consume δαπανάω
contempt καταφρόνημα,
  καταφρόνησις
contentedly ἀγαπητῶς
contest ἀγών
continue διατελέω
continuous συνεχής
contradict ἀντιλέγω
contrive μηχανάομαι
control διοικέω
convention νόμος
converse διαλέγομαι
corrupt φθείρω, διαφθείρω
couch κλίνη
council βουλή
council chamber βουλευτήριον
count λογίζομαι
country χώρα
courage θάρσος

courageous ἀνδρεῖος
court δικαστήριον
court case δίκη
cowardly δειλός , κακός .
craftsman δημιουργός
cross over διαβαίνω
crowd ὅμιλος
crown ἀναδέω, στέφω
cruel πονηρός
cry out ἀνευφημέω, βοάω
custom ἔθος
customary συνήθης
cut τέμνω
  cut through διακόπτω

danger κίνδυνος
dare θαρρέω, τολμάω
dawn ἕως
day ἡμέρα
death θάνατος, τελευτή
deceit ἀπάτη
decide κρίνω
decision δόγμα
decree ψήφισμα
dedicate ἀνατίθημι
deed ἔργον
deep βαθύς
defeat νικάω (v)
defend ἀμύνω, ἀπολογέομαι (in court)
deity δαίμων
delegate σύνεδρος (n.)
deliberate βουλεύω, δια-βουλεύομαι
demand ἐξαιτέομαι
democracy δημοκρατία
democratic δημοκρατικός
demonstrate δείκνυμι
denounce ἀντιλέγω
deposit κατατίθημι
deprive στερέω, ἀποστερέω
depth βάθος
describe διηγέομαι
despise καταφρονέω, ὀλιγωρέω
destroy διαφθείρω, διόλλυμι, καθαιρέω, καταλύω
die ἀποθνῄσκω, τελευτάω
differ διαφέρω
difficult ἄπορος, χαλεπός
dine δειπνέω, συνδειπνέω (dine with)

disappear ἀφανίζομαι
disbelieve ἀπιστέω
discover εὑρίσκω, καταλαμβάνω
disgraceful αἰσχρός, ἀναιδής, πονηρός
dishonor ἀτιμάζω
dismiss προίεμαι
dispose διατίθημι, διάκειμαι (be disposed)
disregard παροράω
dissolution λύσις, κατάλυσις
dissolve καταλύω
dissuade ἀπαγορεύω
distinguish διαγιγνώσκω
distinguished διαπρεπής, εὔδοξος
disturb ταράττω
ditch τάφρος
divide διαλαμβάνω
divine δαιμόνιος, θεῖος
do δράω, ποιέω, πράττω
do wrong ἀδικέω, ἐξαμαρτάνω
door θύρα
door-keeper θυρωρός
doubt ἀπιστέω
dread ὀρρωδέω
drink ποτόν (n); πίνω (v)
drinking companion συμπότης
drive out ἐκπλήσσω, ἐξελαύνω
drug φάρμακον
dwell οἰκέω

each ἕκαστος, ἑκάτερος (each of two)
each time ἑκάστοτε
eager πρόθυμος
early πρῴ
earth γῆ
easy ῥᾴδιος
eat ἐσθίω, ἀπεσθίω (eat off, gnaw off)
educate παιδεύω
elect αἱρέομαι, χειροτονέω
embassy θεωρία
empty κενός
encourage παρακελεύω
encouragement παρακέλευσις
endure ὑπομένω
enemy ἐχθρός, πολέμιος
enough ἱκανός
entertain ἑστιάω
entreaty ἀντιβόλησις, δέησις
entrust ἐπιτρέπω

envoy πρεσβευτής, πρέσβεις (in
  plural), θεωρός (to an oracle)
equip κατασκευάζω
escape notice λανθάνω
especially μάλιστα
establish καθίστημι
estrange ἀλλοτριόω
eternity αἰών
evening ἑσπέρα
ever ποτέ, πώποτε
evidence τεκμήριον
exact punishment δίκας λαμβάνω
  παρά, τιμωρέομαι
examine ἐξετάζω
excellence ἀρετή
except πλήν
exercise μελέτη (n), γυμνάζομαι
  (v)
exile φυγή
exist ὑπάρχω
exit ἔξοδος
expect προσδοκάω
expedition στόλος, στρατεία
expenditure ἀνάλωσις, δαπάνη
experienced ἔμπειρος
expert (in Plato) ἐπιστάτης (n);
  ἐπαΐω (v, be expert)
extremely σφόδρα

fall πίπτω
  fall in ἐμπίπτω
  fall out ἐκπίπτω
  fall short ἐλλείπω
falsehood ψεῦδος
family οἶκος
farm γεωργέω
farmer γεωργός
farther πόρρω
farthest ἔσχατος
fast ὀξύς
fate μοῖρα
father πατήρ
fear φόβος (n); δείδω, φοβέομαι
  (v)
fearlessly ἀδεῶς
fee μισθός
female θῆλυς
few ὀλίγος
find εὑρίσκω
finish ἀπεργάζομαι
fire πῦρ
firm βέβαιος

first πρῶτος
flee ἀποδιδράσκω, φεύγω,
  ἀποφεύγω
follow ἀκολουθέω; διώκω
food τροφή
foolish ἀνόητος, ἀξύνετος,
  ἄφρων
foolishness ἄνοια
foot πούς
for (conj.) γάρ
force βία, ῥώμη
force out ἐξωθέω
forcible βίαιος
foreign ἀλλότριος, βάρβαρος,
  ξένος
foresight προμήθεια
forget ἐπιλανθάνομαι
form εἶδος
four τέτταρες
  four hundred τετρακόσιοι
  four thousand τετρακισχίλιοι
  four times τετράκις
freedom ἐλευθερία
friend φίλος
friendly εὐμενής
friendship φιλία
from ἀπό, παρά (+ gen.)
  from dawn ἕωθεν
  from within ἔνδοθεν
  from without ἔξωθεν
fruit καρπός
funeral procession ἐκφορά
funny γελοῖος
furnish πορίζομαι

gain κέρδος
gate πύλη
gather ἀθροίζω, συλλέγω
gaze at θεάομαι
general στρατηγός
generosity ἀφθονία
gentle πρᾶος
geometry γεωμετρία
gift δῶρον
give δίδωμι
give attention to προσέχω
give back ἀποδίδωμι
give birth τίκτω
glad ἄσμενος
gladly ἀγαπητῶς
gnaw off ἀπεσθίω

go βαδίζω, εἶμι, ἔρχομαι
  go around περίειμι
  go away ἀπέρχομαι, οἴχομαι
  go before προέρχομαι
  go in εἰσέρχομαι
  go out ἐκβαίνω, ἐξέρχομαι
  go through διέρχομαι
  go to προσέρχομαι
god, goddess θεός
going to μέλλω
gold χρυσός
golden χρυσοῦς
good ἀγαθός, χρηστός
  good deed εὐεργεσία
  good will εὔνοια
great μέγας (comparative, μείζων,
  superlative, μέγιστος)
grow weary ἀποκάμνω
guard φύλαξ (n); φυλάττω (v)
guilt αἰτία

hand χείρ
  hand over διαδίδωμι,
    παραδίδωμι
happen γίγνομαι, τυγχάνω,
  συμβαίνει (it happens)
harm βλάβη (n); βλάπτω (v)
harsh πικρός
hate μισέω
hatred ἔχθρα
have ἔχω
  have a care for προμηθέομαι
  have difficulty χαλεπαίνω
  have no concern for ἀμελέω
  have self-control σωφρονέω
having the same name ὁμωνυμία
head κεφαλή
health ὑγίεια
healthy ὑγιεινός
hear ἀκούω, πυνθάνομαι
help ὠφελία (n); βοηθέω, ὠφελέω
  (v)
  help in turn ἀντιβοηθέω
hence ἐνθένδε
herald κῆρυξ
here ἐνταῦθα
hesitate ἀποκάμνω, ὀκνέω
high ὑψηλός
holy ἱερός
homeland πατρίς
homeward οἴκαδε

honor τιμή (n); τιμάω (v)
hope ἐλπίς
hoplite ὁπλίτης
horse ἵππος
horsemanship ἱππική
house οἰκία
how πῶς, ὅπως
how much, how many πόσος,
  ὁπόσος
human being ἄνθρωπος
hunger λιμός

if εἰ, ἐάν See Chapter Fourteen
ignorance ἀμαθία
ill-judged ἀγνώμων
immediately αὐτίκα, εὐθύς
immortal ἀθάνατος
important ἄξιος
  consider important περὶ
    πολλοῦ ποιεῖσθαι
impress τύπτω
improve oneself γίγνομαι ἀμείνων
  in ἐν (+ dat.)
  in control of oneself σώφρων
  in one's way ἐμποδών
  in order that ἵνα, ὅπως See
    Chapter Nine
inclination ὁρμή
incorruptible ἀδωροδόκητος
increase αὐξάνω
incur a charge of ὀφλισκάνω
incursion ὁρμή, προσβολή
indeed γε, δή, δῆτα, τοι, καίτοι
  (and indeed)
indictment γραφή
infantry ὁ πεζός, τὰ πεζά
information μήνυμα
initiate μυέω
injustice ἀδικία
innocent ἀναίτιος
inquire ἐπερωτάω
inside ἔνδον
insignificant φαῦλος
instead of ἀντί (+ gen.)
insult ὄνειδος, ὕβρις, ὕβρισμα
  (n);
  ὀνειδίζω, ὑβρίζω (v)
intelligence διάνοια
intend μέλλω
intent upon σπουδάζω
interpreter ἐξηγητής
interrupt ὑπολαμβάνω

invent εὑρίσκω
invisible ἀφανής
inward εἴσω

journey πορεία
judge δικάζω
judgment κρίσις
juryman δικαστής
just δίκαιος (adj); ἄρτι (adv)
justice δικαιοσύνη

keep quiet ἡσυχίαν ἄγω
kill ἀπόλλυμι, κτείνω, ἀποκτείνω
kind-hearted φιλάνθρωπος
king βασιλεύς
kingdom βασιλεία
know γιγνώσκω, ἐπίσταμαι, οἶδα
knowledge ἐπιστήμη

lack ἀπορία
  lack of self-control ἀκρασία,
    ἀκράτεια
lament θρηνέω, ὀλοφύρομαι
land γῆ
last ὕστατος
later ὕστερος
laugh γελάω
launch καθέλκω
law νόμος
lawlessness ἀνομία
lawmaker νομοθέτης
lead ἄγω
  lead a chorus χορηγέω
  lead away ἀπάγω
  lead forth προάγω
  lead in εἰσάγω
learn μανθάνω, πυνθάνομαι
learned πολυμαθής
learning μάθημα
least ἥκιστος
leave λείπω, ἀπολείπω,
    καταλείπω
  leave behind ἐπιλείπω
legendary μυθώδης
leisure σχολή
length μῆκος
less ἥττων(comparative of κακός,
    μικρός)
lesson ἄκουσμα
let go προίεμαι
letter γράμμα
lie ψεύδομαι

life βίος
lighten κουφίζω
like ὅμοιος (also accented ὁμοῖος)
likely εἰκός
listen to ἀκροάομαι
live ζάω
lofty ὑψηλός
lonely ἐρῆμος
long μακρός
look at βλέπω, ἀποβλέπω
lose ἀποβάλλω, ἀπόλλυμι
love ἔρως, φιλία (n); ἀγαπάω,
    ἐράω,
  στέργω, φιλέω (v)
lover ἐραστής
lover of learning φιλομαθής

madness μανία
make ποιέω, πράττω
  make an attack ὁρμάω
  make clear δηλόω
  make money χρηματίζομαι
  make noise θορυβέω
  make plain προδηλόω
  make promises κατεπαγγέλλομαι
  make war πολεμέω
male ἄρρην
man ἀνήρ, ἄνθρωπος
manage διοικέω
manliness ἀνδρεία, ἀρρενωπία
manner τρόπος
many πολλοί, τοσοῦτοι (so many)
market place ἀγορά
marvelous θαυμάσιος,
    θαυμαστός
mean φαῦλος
meet ἀπαντάω, ἐντυγχάνω,
    συνέρχομαι
meeting ἀπάντησις
memory μνήμη
mention ὑπομιμνήσκω
messenger ἄγγελος
military command στρατηγία
mind νοῦς, φρόνημα
miserable ἄθλιος
misfortune ἀτύχημα, συμφορά
mislead παράγω
mistreat λωβάομαι
moderate μέτριος
money ἀργύριον, χρήματα

month μείς , μηνός (gen.)
more μᾶλλον
mortal θνητός
mother μήτηρ
motive πρόφασις
mount ἀναβαίνω
move κινέω
much πολύς
multitude πλῆθος
must See Chapter Eight
mutilation περικοπή
mystery θαῦμα
mysteries τὰ μυστικά

name ὄνομα
narrate διεξέρχομαι, διηγέομαι
narrow στενός
native ἐγχώριος
nature φύσις
naval ναυτικός
near ἐγγύς, πλησίον
nearly σχεδόν, μόνον οὐ
necessity ἀνάγκη See Chapter
  Eight
need χρεία (n); δέομαι, χράομαι
  (v) See Chapter Eight
neglect ἀμελέω, ὀλιγωρέω,
  περιοράω
negligence ἀμέλεια, ἀμελετησία
neighbor γείτων
neither. . .nor οὔτε. . .οὔτε, μήτε.
  . .μήτε
never οὐδέποτε, μηδέποτε
nevertheless ὅμως
new καινός, νεός
next day ἡ ὑστεραία
night νύξ
no longer οὐκέτι, μηκέτι
no one οὐδείς, μηδείς
noble γενναῖος
noise θόρυβος
nonsense φλυαρία
nose ῥίς
not οὐ, μή
  not even οὐδέ, μηδέ
  not only οὐ μόνον, μὴ μόνον
  not yet οὔπω, μήπω
nothing οὐδέν, μηδέν
now νῦν, ἤδη (already)
number ἀριθμός

oath ὅρκος

obey ὑπακούω
occasion καιρός
occur προσπίπτω, συμβαίνω
off ἀπό (+ gen.)
offer ἐπέχω
offspring ἔκγονος
often πολλάκις
old παλαιός
older πρεσβύτερος
oligarchy ὀλιγαρχία
omit παραλείπω
on ἐπί (+ gen. or dat.)
  on behalf of ὑπέρ (+ gen.)
  on condition that ἐφ' ᾧτε
one εἷς, τις
  one another ἀλλήλων
  one by one καθ' ἕκαστον
only μόνον
open ἀνοίγνυμι
opinion γνώμη
oppose ἀνθίσταμαι, ἐναντιόομαι
opposite ἐναντίον
or, either. . .or ἤ, ἤ. . .ἤ
oracle χρησμός
order ἐντολή (n); κελεύω,
  παραγγέλλω (v)
other ἄλλος
outrage ὕβρις (n); ὑβρίζω (v)
outside ἔξω
overturn ἀπαλάσσω, λύω,
  καταλύωώ
own ἴδιος, οἰκεῖος

pain λύπη
painful λυπηρός
pardon συγγνώμη
parent γονεύς
part μερίς
party συμπόσιον
pass παρέρχομαι, διαβαίνω
  (pass over)
pass (a law) τίθημι
passage πάροδος
pay heed to προσέχω τὸν νοῦν
  pay no heed to ὑπεροράω
peace εἰρήνη
penalty δίκη
people δῆμος
perceive αἰσθάνομαι, συνίημι
perhaps ἴσως, τάχ' ἄν
peril κίνδυνος

perish ἀποθνήσκω, ἀπόλλυμι
permit ἔξεστι (impersonal)
persuade πείθω
philosophy φιλοσοφία
  discuss philosophy φιλοσοφέω
physical trainer παιδοτρίβης
physician ἰατρός
place τόπος, χωρίον
plain δῆλος, φανερός
plan βουλεύω
play παίζω
plead a case συναγορεύω
please ἀρέσκω
plot ἐπιβουλή (n); ἐπιβουλεύω (v)
pollution μίασμα
poor person πένης
possession κτῆμα
possible δυνατός
  it is possible ἔξεστι
power δύναμις
powerful δυνατός, κύριος
practice μελέτη (n); ἐπιτηδεύω,
  μελετάω (v)
praise ἔπαινος (n); ἐπαινέω (v)
pray εὔχομαι
pregnant ἔγκυος
preparation παρασκευή
prepare ἑτοιμάζω, παρασκευάζω
presence παρουσία
press πιέζω
pretend προσποιέομαι
  pretend ignorance εἰρωνεύομαι
pretense πρόφασις
prevent κωλύω
previous προτεραῖος
priest ἱερεύς
prison δεσμωτήριον
private ἴδιος
proclaim προαγορεύω
procreation παιδοποιία
profit ὠφελία (n); ὀνίνημι,
  ὠφελέω (v)
promise ὑπόσχεσις
proper ἐπιεικής, ἐπιτήδειος
property οὐσία
propose συμβουλεύω
prosecute διώκω, ἐπεξέρχομαι
prosper εὐπορέω
protect ἐπαμύνω, σώζω, φυλάττω
provide παρέχω
provoke παροξύνω

public δημόσιος, δημοσίᾳ (at
  public expense)
public informer συκοφάντης
pursue διώκω
put τίθημι

quick ταχύς
quiet ἡσυχία
quite πάνυ

race γένος
raise ἀνίστημι
rather μᾶλλον
ratify κυρόω
readiness προθυμία
ready ἑτοῖμος
rear τρέφω
rebuke μέμφομαι
receive δέχομαι, προσδέχομαι,
  ὑποδέχομαι
recline κατακλίνω
reconcile διαλλάττω
reconciliation διαλλαγή
record γράφω
recover ἀναλαμβάνω
redress τιμωρία
refuse ἀπαρνέομαι, οὐκ ἐθέλω,
  οὔ φημι
refute ἐξελέγχω
rejoice χαίρω
release λύω, ἀπολύω
remaining λοιπός
remedy φάρμακον
remember μιμνήσκω
remind ἀναμιμνήσκω,
  ὑπομιμνήσκω (remind of)
reminder ὑπόμνησις
removal ἀναίρεσις
remove ἀφίστημι, ὑφαιρέω
repel ἀπωθέω
repent μεταμέλει (impersonal)
report ἀπαγγελία (n); ἀπαγγέλλω
  (v)
reproach ὄνειδος (n); ὀνειδίζω (v)
reputation δόξα
responsible αἴτιος
return κάθοδος
reveal ἀποφαίνω
revenge τιμωρία
rich πλούσιος
right moment καιρός
risk κινδυνεύω

rite τελετή
road ὁδός
robber λῃστής
room οἴκημα
rower ἐρέτης
rule ἀρχή (n); ἄρχω (v)

sacrifice θυσία (n); θύω (v)
sacrilege ἀσέβημα
safety σωτηρία
sail πλέω
  sail away ἀποπλέω, ἐκπλέω
  sail fast ταχυναυτέω
  sail past παραπλέω
same ἴσος, ὅμοιος (also accented
  ὁμοῖος)
sandal ὑπόδημα
save σῴζω
say λέγω, φάσκω, φημί, See
  Chapter Eighteen
scarcely μόγις
scoundrel μιαρός
sea θάλαττα, πέλαγος
  sea battle ναυμαχία
search ἐρευνάω
seasonable ἐπίκαιρος
second δεύτερος
secretly λάθρᾳ
secure βέβαιος
security κατεγγύη
see ὁράω
seek μετέρχομαι
seem δοκέω
seize ἁρπάζω, καταλαμβάνω,
  συλλαμβάνω
self αὐτός
sell πιπράσκω
send πέμπω
  send away ἀποπέμπω
  send for μεταπέμπω
  send out ἐκπέμπω
sense αἰσθάνομαι
senseless ἀγνώμων, ἀνόητος,
  ἄφρων
sensible φρόνιμος
separate ἀποχωρίζω
set τίθημι
  set forth προτίθημι
  set free ἀπαλλάττω
  set in order κοσμέω
  set near παρίστημι

set out ἐκτίθημι
set right κατορθόω
set sail ἀνάγομαι
settle κατοικέω, μετοικέω
shame αἰσχύνω
shameful αἰσχρός
shameless ἀναιδής
share κοινωνέω, μεταδίδωμι,
  μετέχω
ship ναῦς
show δείκνυμι, ἀποδείκνυμι,
  ἐπιδείκνυμι, φαίνω
shut out ἀποκλείω
sickly νοσώδης
sickness νόσος
sight ὄψις
sign σημεῖον, σῆμα
silver ἄργυρος
similar ὅμοιος (also accented
  ὁμοῖος)
since ἐπεί, ἐπειδή See Chapter
  Seventeen
sit καθίζομαι, παρακάθημαι
  (sit beside)
sixty ἑξήκοντα
size μέγεθος
skill τέχνη
skilled τεχνικός
slander διαβολή
slaughter ἀποσφάττω
slave δοῦλος, παῖς
slavery δουλεία
sleep ὕπνος
small μικρός
so large τηλικοῦτος, τηλικόσδε
so that ὥστε See Chapter Ten
soldier στρατιώτης
somehow πως
sometimes ἐνίοτε
somewhere που
son υἱός
sophist σοφιστής
sophisticated ἀστικός
soul ψυχή
speak λέγω, προσλέγω
  speak against ἀντιλέγω
  speak in the assembly
    δημηγορέω
speaker's platform βῆμα
spectacle θέα
speculation σκέψις

speed τάχος
spend ἀναλίσκω, δαπανάω
  spend time διατρίβω
spread στόρνυμι
stage σκηνή
stand ἵστημι, ἐφίσταμαι (stand
  by)
stay μένω
stir up ἐπαίρω
stop κωλύω, παύω See Chapter
  Four, 3(c) n.1
strange ἄτοπος
strength ἰσχύς, σθένος .
stretch out ἀποτείνω
strike τύπος (n); καταπλήττω,
  κρούω (v)
strong δυνατός, εὔρωστος,
  ἰσχυρός
struggle ἀγών
student μαθητής ·
subject σκέμμα
such τοιοῦτος (in quality),
  τοσοῦτος (in quantity)
suddenly ἐξαίφνης
suffer πάσχω, πονέω, ὑπέχω
suitable ἐπιεικής, ἐπιτήδειος
summon καλέω
supplication ἱκετεία
supplies ἐφόδια (pl.)
support βοηθέω
  support Philip Φιλιππίζω
suspect ὑποπτεύω
swear ὄμνυμι
sweet ἡδύς

take αἱρέω, λαμβάνω,
  ἀπολαμβάνω
  take away ἀναιρέω
  take care ἐπιμελέομαι
  take into account ὑπολογίζομαι
  take up ὑπολαμβάνω
talk λαλέω
taxiarch ταξίαρχος
teach διδάσκω
teaching διδαχή
ten thousand μυρίος
terrible δεινός
test ἐξετάζω
than ἤ, μᾶλλον. . .ἤ (rather. .
  .than)
thanks χάρις
then εἶτα, ἔπειτα, τότε

there ἐκεῖ, ἐνταῦθα
therefore διόπερ, οὖν, πρὸς
  ταῦτα
thing πρᾶγμα, χρῆμα
think δοκέω, οἴομαι (οἶμαι),
  φρονέω
  think fit ἀξιόω
thither ἐκεῖσε
thought φρόνησις
thousand χίλιος
threaten ἀπειλέω, ἐπηρεάζω
three τρεῖς
  third τρίτος
  thirty τριάκοντα
  three hundred τριακόσιοι
  three years τριετής
  thrice τρίς
through διά (+ acc.)
throw βάλλω, ῥίπτω
  throw away ἀποβάλλω
  throw down καταβάλλω
  throw in ἐμβάλλω
  throw out ἐκβάλλω
tie up συνδέω
time χρόνος
together with ἅμα
too λίαν
tool ὄργανον
towards εἰς, πρός (+ accusative)
town ἄστυ
trader ἔμπορος
trainer παιδοτρίβης
transfer μετάγω
transgression of the law
  παρανομία
travel πορεύομαι
treat badly προπηλακίζω
treaty σύμβασις
trial ἀγών
tribe φυλή
truce σπονδαί (pl.)
true ἀληθής
trustworthy εὐπίθετος, πιστός
truth ἀλήθεια
try ἐπιχειρέω, πειράομαι
twelve δώδεκα
two δύο
  twice δίς
  two hundred διακόσιοι
  two thousand δισχίλιος

understand ἐπαΐω, συνίημι
unexpected ἀπροσδόκητος,
  ἀνέλπιστος
unhappy δύσκολος, κακοδαίμων
unjust ἄδικος
unprepared ἀπαράσκευος
unshoe ὑπολύω
until μέχρι See Chapter Seventeen
unwilling ἄκων
unworthy ἀνάξιος
up ἄνω
upon ἐπί (+ gen. and dat.)
urge ἐπείγω
use χρεία (n); χράομαι (v)
  use up καταναλίσκω
useful ἐπιτήδειος, χρήσιμος

very λίαν, μάλα, σφόδρα; or use
  superlative
victory monument τρόπαιον
view σκέπτομαι, σκοπέω
villainy κακουργία, πανουργία
violence ἀσέλγεια
violent ἀσελγής
virtue ἀρετή
visit φοιτάω
voice φωνή
vote ψηφίζω
  vote against καταχειροτονέω,
  καταψηφίζομαι
voting pebble ψῆφος
voyage πλοῦς
vulgar πάνδημος, φαῦλος

wagon ἅμαξα
wait μένω, περιμένω
  wait for ἀναμένω
  wait in ambush ἐλλοχάω
wall τεῖχος
war πόλεμος
watch carefully διαφυλάττω
water ὕδωρ
weapon ὅπλον
weep δακρύω, ὀδύρομαι
welcome ἀσπάζομαι
well εὖ
well-arranged εὔθετος
what? τί
when ἐπεί, ἐπειδή, ὁπότε See
  Chapter Seventeen
whence ὅθεν
where ποῦ, ὅπου

whether πότερον
whither ὅποι
who? τίς
whole ὅλος
wicked πονηρός
wife γυνή
willing αὐτόματος, ἑκών (adj);
  ἐθέλω (v)
win νικάω
winter χειμών
wisdom σοφία
wise σοφός
wish βούλομαι, ἐθέλω
with μετά (+ genitive)
withdraw ἀποσπάω
without ἄνευ
withstand ἀντέχω
witness μάρτυς
woman γυνή
wonder ἄγαμαι, θαυμάζω
word λόγος
work ἐργασία, ἔργον
workshop ἐργαστήριον
worry φροντίζω
worse ἥττων (comparative of
  κακός, μικρός)
worthy ἄξιος
wretched μοχθηρός, σχέτλιος
write γράφω
  write down ἀπογράφω
writing tablet γραμματεῖον
wrong ἀδικέω
wrongdoing πονήρευμα

year ἔτος
yes See Chapter Six
yet ἔτι
young man μειράκιον, νεανίας

INDEX B—GREEK-ENGLISH VOCABULARY

ἁβρός delicate, graceful
ἀγαθός good, brave
ἄγαμαι wonder at
ἀγαπάω love, feel affection for
ἀγαπητῶς contentedly, scarcely
ἀγγέλλω announce
ἄγγελος messenger
ἀγνοέω not know, be ignorant
ἀγνώμων ill-judged, senseless
ἀγορά marketplace
ἄγροικος rustic
ἄγω lead
ἀγών contest, struggle, trial
ἀγωνιάω be distressed, be anxious
ἀγωνιστής combatant, master
ἀδελφός brother
ἀδεῶς fearlessly
ἀδικέω wrong
ἀδικία injustice
ἄδικος unjust
ἀδόκητος unexpected
ἀδωροδόκητος incorruptible
ἀεί (also αἰεί) always
ἀθάνατος immortal
ἀθλητής athlete
ἄθλιος miserable
ἀθροίζω gather
ἀθρόος gathered, crowded
  together
ἀθυμέω be discouraged
αἴξ goat
αἵρεσις choice
αἱρέω take, choose (middle)
αἰσθάνομαι sense, perceive
αἰσχίων (comparative of αἰσχρός)
αἰσχρός shameful, ill-formed
αἰσχύνω dishonor
αἰτέω ask for
αἰτία charge, responsibility
αἰτιάομαι accuse
αἴτιος responsible for
αἰών age, eternity
ἀκληρωτί without casting lots
ἀκολουθέω follow
ἄκουσμα lesson
ἀκούω hear, listen

ἄκρα cape
ἀκρασία lack of self-control
ἀκροάομαι listen to
ἄκων unwilling
ἀλήθεια truth
ἀληθής true
ἁλίσκομαι be captured, be
  convicted
ἀλλήλων one another
ἄλλος other
ἄλλοσε to another place
ἀλλότριος another's, foreign
ἀλλοτριόω estrange
ἅμα together with
ἀμαθία ignorance
ἅμαξα wagon
ἀμείνων (comparative of ἀγαθός)
ἀμελετησία want of practice
ἀμελέω be unconcerned, neglect
ἀμύνω defend
ἀμφί around
ἀμφίθυρος with double doors
ἀμφότερος both
ἀναβαίνω mount
ἀναβιώσκομαι bring back to life
ἀναγκάζω compel
ἀνάγκη necessity
ἀνάγομαι set sail
ἀναδέω crown
ἀναιδής shameless
ἀναίρεσις removal
ἀναιρέω take away
ἀναισχυντία shamelessness
ἀναλίσκω spend
ἀνάλωσις expenditure
ἀναμένω wait for
ἀναμιμνήσκω remind
ἀνάξιος unworthy
ἀναφαίνομαι appear
ἀναφέρω bring up
ἀναχάσκω gape, yawn
ἀνδρεία manliness
ἀνδρόγυνος hermaphrodite
ἀνδροφόνος man-slaying,
  homicide
ἀνέλπιστος unexpected

ἄνευ without
ἀνευφημέω cry out
ἀνέχω bear up
ἀνήρ man
ἀνθίσταμαι oppose
ἀνθρώπινος human
ἄνθρωπος human being, man
ἀνίστημι raise
ἀνόητος foolish
ἄνοια foolishness
ἀνοίγνυμι open
ἀνομία lawlessness
ἀντέχω withstand
ἀντί against, instead of
ἀντιβοηθέω help in turn
ἀντιβόλησις entreaty
ἀντιλέγω contradict, speak
  against
ἀντιπέρας on the other side
ἀντιστασιώτης of the opposite
  party
ἄνω up, above
ἄξιος worthy
ἀξιόχρεως worthwhile
ἀξιόω think fit, deem worthy
ἀξίωσις claim
ἀξύνετος foolish
ἀπαγγελία report
ἀπαγγέλλω report
ἀπαγορεύω dissuade, give up
ἀπάγω lead away
ἀπαίρω carry away
ἀπαλλάττω set free
ἀπαντάω meet
ἀπάντησις meeting
ἄπας all
ἀπάτη deceit
ἀπειθέω be disobedient
ἀπελαύνω march away, drive off
ἀπεργάζομαι finish, complete
ἀπερείδω fix on, settle upon
ἀπέρχομαι go away
ἀπεσθίω eat up, gnaw off
ἀπέχω keep away
ἀπιστέω disbelieve
ἀπό off, away from
ἀποβάλλω throw away
ἀποβλέπω look at
ἀπογίγνομαι be absent
ἀπογράφω write down
ἀποδείκνυμι show

ἀποδέχομαι accept, appoint
ἀποδιδράσκω flee, run off
ἀποδίδωμι give back
ἀποθνῄσκω die
ἀποικία colony
ἀποκάμνω grow weary, hesitate
ἀποκλείω shut out
ἀποκρίνομαι answer
ἀποκτείνω kill
ἀπολαμβάνω take
ἀπολέγω choose, refuse
ἀπολείπω leave
ἀπόλλυμι kill, destroy
ἀπολογέομαι defend oneself
ἀπολύω release
ἀποπέμπω send away
ἀποπλέω sail away
ἀπορέω be puzzled, be at a loss
ἀπορία confusion
ἄπορος difficult
ἀποσπάω withdraw
ἀποστέλλω send away
ἀποστερέω rob, deprive
ἀποσφάττω slaughter
ἀποτείνω stretch out
ἀποφαίνω reveal
ἀποφέρω carry away
ἀποφεύγω flee
ἀποχωρίζω separate
ἀποψηφίζομαι acquit
ἀπωθέω repel, drive back, spurn
ἄρα then
ἆρα See Chapter Six
ἀργύριον money
ἄργυρος silver
ἀρέσκω please
ἀρετή excellence, virtue
ἀριθμός number
ἄριστος best
ἁρπάζω seize
ἀρρενωπία manliness
ἄρρην male
ἄρτι just
ἀρχαῖος ancient
ἀρχή rule, beginning
ἄρχω rule, begin
ἀσεβέω commit sacrilege
ἀσέβημα sacrilege
ἀσέλγεια violence
ἀσελγής violent
ἀσθενέω be weak

ᾆσμα song
ᾆσμενος glad
ἀσπάζομαι welcome
ἀσπίς shield
ἀστικός sophisticated
ἀστός citizen
ἀστρονομία astronomy
ἀσύμφορος prejudicial
ἀτιμάζω dishonor
ἄτοπος strange
ἀτύχημα misfortune
αὖ again
αὐθημερόν immediately
αὖθις again
αὐξάνω increase
αὐτίκα immediately
αὐτόθι on the spot
αὐτόματος willing
αὐτός self, he, she, it
αὐχήν neck, throat
ἀφανής invisible
ἀφανίζομαι disappear
ἀφθονία generosity
ἀφίημι allow
ἀφικνέομαι arrive
ἀφίστημι remove
ἀφοσιόω acquit, purify
ἄφρων foolish
ἄχθομαι be annoyed

βαδίζω go, walk
βάθος depth
βαθύς deep
βακτηρία staff
βάρβαρος foreign, non-Greek
βασιλεία kingdom
βασιλεύς king
βδελυρία bad behavior
βέβαιος firm, secure
βελτίων better
βῆμα tribunal, speaker's platform
βία force
βιάζω constrain
βίαιος forcible
βιάω constrain
βίος life
βιωτός worth living
βλάβη harm
βλάπτω harm
βλέπω look
βοάω cry, shout

βοηθέω help
βοηθός assisting
βουκόλος cowherd
βουλευτήριον council chamber
βουλεύω plan, deliberate
βουλή council
βούλομαι wish
βραδύς slow
βρέφος child

γάρ for
γε indeed, at least
γείτων neighbor
γελάω laugh
γελοῖος funny, laughable
γενναῖος noble
γεννάω beget
γένος kind, race
γεωμετρία geometry
γεωργέω farm
γῆ earth, land
γίγνομαι become, be born
γιγνώσκω know
γνώμη opinion
γονεύς parent
γοῦν at least
γράμμα letter
γραμματεῖον tablet, account book
γραφή indictment
γράφω write
γυμνάζομαι exercise
γυνή woman, wife

δαιμόνιος divine
δαίμων deity
δακρύω weep
δάμαλις heifer
δαπανάω consume, use, spend
δέησις entreaty
δεῖ is necessary
δείδω fear
δείκνυμι show
δεινός terrible, clever
δειπνέω dine
δεσμός bond
δεσμωτήριον prison
δεῦρο thither
δεύτερος second
δέχομαι receive
δέω bind
δέω, δέομαι need, ask for

δή indeed
δῆλος clear
δηλόω make clear
δημηγορέω speak in the assembly
δημιουργός craftsman,
    practitioner
δημοκρατία democracy
δημοκρατικός democratic
δῆμος people
δημόσιος public
δήποτε at last, at some time
δήπου doubtless, surely
δῆτα indeed
διά through, by
διαβαίνω pass over
διαβολή slander
διαβουλεύομαι deliberate
διαγιγνώσκω decide, determine
διαδίδωμι hand over
διάκειμαι be disposed
διακόπτω cut through
διακόσιοι two hundred
διαλαμβάνω divide
διαλέγομαι converse
διαλλαγή reconciliation
διαλλάττω reconcile
διαμηχανάομαι contrive
διάνοια intelligence
διαπεράω cross
διαπράττω accomplish
διαπρεπής distinguished
διατίθημι dispose
διατρίβω spend time
διαφέρω differ
διαφθείρω corrupt, destroy
διαφυλάττω watch carefully
διδάσκω teach
διδαχή teaching
δίδωμι give
διεξέρχομαι relate
διέρχομαι go through
διηγέομαι describe, narrate
δικάζω judge
δίκαιος just
δικαιοσύνη justice
δικαστήριον court
δικαστής juryman
δίκη justice, court case, penalty
διοικέω manage
διόλλυμι destroy
διόπερ therefore

διπλοῦς double
δίς twice
δισχίλιος two thousand
διττός double
δίψος thirst
διώκω pursue, prosecute
δόγμα decision
δοκέω think, seem
δοκιμάζω approve
δόξα reputation
δοξόσοφος claiming wisdom
δουλεία slavery
δουλεύω be a slave
δοῦλος slave
δράω do
δύναμαι be able
δύναμις power
δυνατός powerful, capable
δύο two
δύσκολος irrascible
δυσχερής annoying, difficult
δώδεκα twelve
δωρεά gift

ἐάν if See Chapter Fourteen
ἐάω allow
ἐγγύς near
ἔγκλημα accusation
ἔγκυος pregnant
ἐγχώριος of the country
ἔδομαι (future of ἐσθίω) eat
ἐθέλω wish
ἐθίζω accustom
ἔθος custom
ἔθω be accustomed
εἰ if See Chapter Fourteen
εἶδος form
εἰκός likely
εἰμί be
εἶμι go
εἶπον (used as aorist of λέγω)
    said
εἰρήνη peace
εἰρωνεία pretence of ignorance
εἰρωνεύομαι pretend ignorance
εἰς to
εἰσάγω lead in
εἴσειμι enter, go in
εἰσέρχομαι enter, go in
εἴσω inward
εἶτα then

εἴωθα be accustomed (ἔθω)
ἑκάστοτε each time
ἐκβαίνω go out
ἐκβάλλω throw out
ἔκγονος offspring, descendant
ἐκεῖ there
ἐκεῖσε thither
ἐκκλησία assembly
ἐκκλησιάζω assemble
ἐκλαλέω chatter, talk
ἐκπλέω sail away
ἐκπλήττω startle
ἐκπέμπω send out
ἐκπίπτω fall out
ἐκποδών out of the way
ἐκτίθημι set out
ἐκτρέφω rear
ἐκφορά carrying out (of a corpse)
ἑκών willing
ἐλευθερία freedom
ἐλλείπω leave out, fall short
ἐλλοχάω wait in ambush
ἐλπίς hope
ἐμβάλλω throw in
ἐμμένω abide
ἔμπειρος experienced
ἐμπίπτω fall in
ἐμπλέκω involve
ἐμπνέω breathe
ἐμποδίζω burden
ἐμποδών in the way
ἔμπορος trader
ἐν in, among
ἐναντίον opposite
ἐναντιόομαι oppose
ἐνδείκνυμι show
ἔνδοθεν from within
ἔνδον inside
ἔνειμι be inside
ἕνεκα because of
ἐνθένδε hence, hereafter
ἐνθυμέομαι consider
ἐνίοτε sometimes
ἐνταῦθα here, there
ἐντολή order, command
ἐντυγχάνω come upon
ἐξαιτέω demand
ἐξαίφνης suddenly
ἑξάκις six times
ἐξαμαρτάνω do wrong
ἐξανίστημι cause to get up

ἔξεστι is possible
ἐξελαύνω drive out
ἐξελέγχω refute
ἐξέρχομαι go out
ἐξετάζω examine, test
ἐξηγητής interpreter
ἑξήκοντα sixty
ἔξοδος exit
ἐξόμνυμι deny upon oath
ἐξουσία authority
ἔξω outside
ἔξωθεν from without
ἐξωθέω force out
ἑορτή festival
ἐπαγγέλλω announce, proclaim
ἐπαινέω praise
ἔπαινος praise
ἐπαίρω stir up
ἐπαΐω understand
ἐπαμύνω aid, protect
ἐπεί, ἐπειδή since, when
See Chapter Seventeen
ἐπείγω urge, hasten
ἔπειμι remain
ἔπειτα then
ἐπεξέρχομαι prosecute
ἐπέρχομαι come upon
ἐπερωτάω inquire
ἐπέχω stay, stop
ἐπηρεάζω threaten abusively
ἐπί on, upon
ἐπιβολή assault, enterprise
ἐπιβουλεύω plot
ἐπιβουλή plot, plan
ἐπιδείκνυμι show
ἐπιδημέω be at home
ἐπίκαιρος seasonable
ἐπικρύπτω conceal
ἐπιλέγω add
ἐπιλείπω leave behind, run out
ἐπιμαρτύρομαι call to witness
ἐπιμελέομαι take care of
ἐπιμελῶς carefully
ἐπίσταμαι know
ἐπιστάτης expert
ἐπιστήμη knowledge
ἐπιτήδειος useful
ἐπιτήδευμα business
ἐπιτηδεύω practice
ἐπιτίθημι add
ἐπιτρέπω turn to, entrust

ἐπιτυγχάνω meet with
ἐπιφέρω bring to
ἐπιχειρέω try
ἐπιψηλαφάω seek by touching
ἕπομαι follow
ἐπονείδιστος disgraceful
ἑπταετής seven years old
ἐραστής lover
ἐράω love
ἐργάζομαι accomplish, do
ἐργασία work
ἐργαστήριον workshop
ἔργον deed
ἐρευνάω search
ἐρέω (used as future of λέγω) say
ἐρῆμος lonely
ἔρχομαι come, go
ἐρωτάω ask
ἐσθίω eat
ἑσπέρα evening
ἑστιάω entertain
ἔσχατος farthest
ἑτέρωθι on the other side
ἔτι still, yet
ἑτοιμάζω prepare
ἑτοῖμος ready (also accented
   ἕτοιμος)
ἔτος year
εὖ well
εὐδόκιμος glorious
εὐεργεσία good deed
εὔθετος well-arranged
εὐθύς straight, immediately
εὐμενής friendly, kindly
εὔνοια goodwill
εὐνοϊκός kindly, well-disposed
εὐπίθετος trustworthy
εὐπορέω prosper
εὐπορία abundance
εὐπρεπής comely
εὑρίσκω find, invent
εὔρωστος strong
εὐσεβέω act piously
εὔχομαι pray
ἐφήδομαι exult over
ἐφίσταμαι stand by
ἐφόδια supplies (pl.)
ἔχθρα hatred, enmity
ἐχθρός enemy
ἔχω have
ἕως dawn (Attic for ἠώς)

ἕως until See Chapter Seventeen
ἔωθεν from dawn

ζάω live
ζηλοτυπέω be jealous of

ἤ or, than
ἡγέομαι believe, lead
ἤδη already
ἡδύς sweet, pleasant
ἥκιστα least of all
ἥκω come
ἡλικία age
ἡλικιώτης coeval
ἥλιος sun
ἡμέρα day
ἡσυχία quiet
ἥσυχος calm
ἥττων (comparative of κακός)

θάλαττα sea
θάνατος death
θάπτω bury
θαρρέω be brave, dare
θάρρος courage
θαυμάζω wonder
θαυμάσιος marvelous
θαυμαστός marvelous
θέα spectacle
θεάομαι gaze at
θεῖος divine (adj.); uncle (n.)
θεός god, goddess
θεωρία embassy
θεωρός envoy to an oracle
θῆλυς female
θηριωδῶς savagely
θητεύω be a serf
θνητός mortal
θορυβέω make a noise
θόρυβος noise
θράσος boldness
θρασύς bold
θρηνέω lament
θροῦς noise, report
θύρα door
θυρωρός door-keeper
θυσία sacrifice
θύω sacrifice

ἰατρός physician
ἴδιος one's own, private

ἱερεύς priest
ἱερός holy
ἱκανός enough
ἱκετεία supplication
ἵνα See Chapter Nine
ἱππική horsemanship
ἵππος horse
ἰσοκίνδυνος fairly equal risk (adj.)
ἰσόπεδος level, even with
ἴσος same, equal
ἵστημι stand
ἰσχυρός strong
ἰσχύς strength

καθαιρέω destroy
καθαρεύω be clean, be pure
καθέλκω launch
καθίζομαι sit
καθίημι let down, send down
καθίστημι establish
κάθοδος return
καθότι as
καινός new
καιρός right moment
καίτοι and indeed, and yet
καίω burn
κακός bad, cowardly
καλέω call
κάλλος beauty
καλοκἀγαθία attribute of a gentleman
καλός beautiful
καρπός fruit
καρπόω bear fruit
κατά according to
καταβαίνω descend
καταβάλλω throw down
καταδύω go down, cause to sink
κατάκειμαι lie down, recline
κατακλίνω recline
καταλαμβάνω seize, find
καταλείπω leave
κατάλυσις dissolution
καταλύω dissolve, destroy
καταναλίσκω use up
καταπλήττω strike
καταπροδίδωμι betray
κατασκευάζω equip
κατασκοπή spying
κατατίθημι deposit

καταφεύγω flee for refuge
καταχειροτονέω vote against
καταψηφίζομαι vote against
κατεγγύη security
κατεπαγγέλλομαι make promises
κατέφαγον (aorist of κατεσθίω) ate up
κατηγορέω accuse
κατήγορος accuser
κατοικέω settle
κατορθόω set right
κελεύω order
κενός empty
κεραμευτικός of a potter
κέρδος gain
κεφαλή head
κῆρυξ herald
κινδυνεύω risk
κίνδυνος danger
κινέω move
κλείω close
κλίνη couch
κοιμάω put to sleep
κοινός common
κοινωνέω share
κόλαξ parasite
κορδακισμός indecent dancing
κοσμέω set in order
κουφίζω lighten, raise
κρείττων (comparative of ἀγαθός, κρατύς)
κρίνω decide
κρίσις judgment
κρούω strike
κρύπτω conceal
κρύφα secretly
κτείνω kill
κτῆμα possession
κυβεία dice playing
κυβευτικός skilled at dice playing
κύκλος circle
κυκλοτερής circular
κυπαρίσσινος made of cypress
κύριος powerful
κυρόω ratify
κτάομαι get, acquire
κωλύω prevent
κώπη oar

λάθρᾳ secretly
λαλέω talk

λαμβάνω take
λανθάνω escape notice
λάρναξ box
λέγω say
λείπω leave
λήθη forgetfulness
ληστής robber, pirate
λίαν very, too
λιμός hunger
λογίζομαι count
λογισμός account
λόγος word, speech, argument
λοιδορέω abuse
λοιπός remaining
λόφος crest of hill, ridge
λύπη pain
λυπηρός painful
λύσις dissolution
λύχνος lamp
λύω release, dissolve
λωβάομαι mistreat

μάθημα learning
μαθητής student
μακάριος blessed
μακρός long
μάλα very
μάλιστα especially
μᾶλλον more, rather
μανθάνω learn
μανία madness
μανικός possessed
μαντεῖον oracle
μάρτυς witness
μέγας great, large
μέγεθος size
μέγιστος (superlative of μεγάς)
μέθη drunkenness
μεθύω be drunk
μείζων (comparative of μεγάς)
μειράκιον young man
μείς (μήν) month
μελέτη practice
μέλλω going to, intend to
μέλω be of concern to
μέμφομαι rebuke
μέντοι however
μένω wait
μερίς part
μέρος portion, share
μεσολαβέω seize, take down

μετά with (+ gen.), after (+ acc.)
μετάγω transfer
μεταδίδωμι share
μεταμέλει (impersonal) repent
μετανοέω change one's mind
μεταπέμπω send for
μετατίθημι change
μετέρχομαι seek
μετέχω share in
μετοικέω settle
μέτριος moderate
μέχρι until, as long as
    See Chapter Seventeen
μηδαμῶς in no way
μηδέ and not, nor (conj); not even
    (adv)
μηδείς no one
μῆκος length
μῆλον apple
μήνυμα information
μήποτε never
μήτε neither, nor
μήτηρ mother
μιαίνω defile, stain
μιαρός polluted (adj), scoundrel
    (noun)
μίασμα pollution
μικρός small
μιμνήσκω remember
μῖμος actor, mime
μισέω hate
μισθός fee
μῖσος hatred
μνήμη memory
μόγις scarcely
μοῖρα fate, lot
μοιχεύω commit adultery with
μοιχός adulterer
μόνος one, only
μοχθηρός wretched
μοχλός bar
μυθώδης legendary
μυρίος ten thousand
μῶν surely not?

ναί yes, indeed
ναύαρχος admiral
ναυμαχία sea battle
ναῦς ship
ναυτικόν fleet
ναυτικός naval
νεαλής fresh

νεός new
νεώριον dockyard
νικάω win
νομίζω believe
νομοθετέω enact laws
νομοθέτης lawmaker
νόμος law, custom
νοσώδης sickly
νοῦς mind
νῦν now
νύξ night
νῶτον back

ξένος foreign
ξυ- See below συ-

ὁδός road
ὀδύρομαι weep
ὅθεν whence
οἶδα know
οἴκαδε homeward
οἰκεῖος one's own
οἰκέω dwell
οἴκημα room
οἰκία house
οἰκιστής founder
οἴκοι at home
οἴομαι (οἶμαι) think, suppose
οἴχομαι go away
ὀκνέω hesitate
ὀλιγαρχία oligarchy
ὀλίγος few
ὀλιγωρέω neglect
ὅλος whole
ὀλοφύρομαι lament
ὅμιλος crowd
ὄμνυμι swear
ὅμοιος same, like
ὁμολογέω agree
ὁμοτράπεζος sharing a table with
ὁμωνυμία having the same name
ὅμως nevertheless
ὀνειδίζω reproach, insult
ὄνειδος reproach, insult
ὀνίνημι profit
ὄνομα name
ὀνομάζω name
ὀνομαστός named
ὀξύς fast
ὄπισθεν behind
ὁπλίτης hoplite

ὅπλον weapon
ὅποι whither
ὁπόσος as many as, as much as
ὁπότε when
ὅπου where
ὅπως how, in order that
ὁράω see
ὄργανον implement, tool
ὀργή anger
ὀργίζομαι be angry
ὀργίζω anger
ὄρθρος dawn
ὅρκος oath
ὁρμάω make an attack
ὁρμή inclination
ὄρνεον bird
ὄροβος bitter vetch
ὄρος mountain
ὀρρωδέω dread
ὀρχέομαι dance
ὀστέον bone
οὐκέτι no longer
οὔκουν not...therefore, certainly not
οὐκοῦν therefore
οὐσία property
ὀφλισκάνω incur a charge of
ὄψις sight

παιδεύω educate
παιδικά (pl.) boy friend
παιδίον child
παιδοποιία procreation
παιδοτρίβης physical trainer
παίζω play
παῖς child, slave
παλαιός old
πάλιν again
πάνδημος vulgar, common
πανοίκιος with the whole house
πάνυ quite
παρά from, beside
παραγγέλλω order
παράγω mislead
παραδίδωμι hand over, betray
παρακάθημαι sit beside
παρακαλέω call in, summon
παρακέλευσις encouragement
παρακελεύω urge, order
παραλαμβάνω capture, overcome
παραλείπω omit, pass over

παραμένω stay
παρανομία transgression of the law
παραπλέω sail past
παρασκευάζω prepare
παρασκευή preparation
παράσπονδος breaker of a treaty
πάρειμι (sum) be present
πάρειμι (ibo) pass by, pass on
πάρεργος (with χράομαι) treat as an accessory
παρέρχομαι pass by, pass on
παρέχω provide
παρίσταμαι come to terms
πάροδος passage
παροινέω be violently drunk
παροξύνω provoke
παροράω disregard
παρουσία presence
παρωθέω reject, push aside
πᾶς all
πάσχω suffer
πατήρ father
πάτριος ancestral
πατρίς homeland
παύω stop
πεδίον plain
πεζά, τά, ὁ πεζός infantry
πείθω persuade
πειράομαι try
πέλαγος sea
πελάτης client, dependent
πέλεκυς axe
πέμπω send
πένης poor person
πένομαι be poor
περαιόομαι cross over
περί around, about
περιγίγνομαι be superior
περίδειπνον funeral feast
περίειμι go around
περιίστημι surround
περικοπή mutilation
περιλαμβάνω enthrall
περιμένω wait
περιοράω neglect
περιφερής circular, revolving
περιχέω pour around, surround
πεττεία draughts (a board game)
πεττευτικός skilled at draughts
πιέζω press

πικρός harsh
πίνω drink
πιπράσκω sell
πίπτω fall
πιστός trustworthy
πλευρά side (pl.)
πλέω sail
πληγή blow
πλῆθος multitude, number
πλήν except
πλησίον near
πλοῖον boat
πλοῦς voyage
πλούσιος rich
ποι to somewhere (indefinite)
ποιέω do, make
ποιητής maker, inventor
πολεμέω make war
πολεμικός fit for war
πολέμιος enemy
πόλεμος war
πολιορκέω besiege
πόλις city, city-state
πολιτεία constitution
πολίτης citizen
πολλάκις often
πολυμαθής learned
πονέω suffer, work hard
πονήρευμα wrongdoing
πονηρός base, worthless
πόνος hard work, toil
πορεία journey, course
πορεύομαι travel
πορίζω furnish
πόρρω farther
πόσος how much? how many?
ποτέ ever
ποτέον (from πίνω)
πότερον whether
ποτόν drink
που somewhere (indefinite)
ποῦ where?
πούς foot
πρᾶγμα thing, affair
πρᾶξις activity
πρᾶος gentle
πράττω do, make
πρέπω be fitting
πρέσβεις ambassadors
πρεσβευτής ambassador
πρεσβύτερος older

πρίν before See Chapter Seventeen
πρό before, in front of
προαγορεύω proclaim
προάγω lead forth
προαιρέομαι choose
προαισθάνομαι perceive beforehand
προάστειος suburban
προβάλλω accuse
πρόγονος ancestor
προδηλόω make plain
πρόειμι go before
προεπιχειρέω be first to attack
προέρχομαι go before
προήκω be first (+ dative)
προθυμία readiness
πρόθυμος eager
πρόθυρον front door
προίεμαι let go, dismiss
προΐστημι be in charge of
προκαλέω challenge
προκαταλαμβάνω seize beforehand
προλέγω say beforehand
προμηθέομαι have a care for
προπετής impulsive
προπηλακίζω treat badly
πρός to, towards
προσάγομαι bring to one's side
προσαγορεύω address
προσαπαγγέλλω announce besides
προσβάλλω attack
προσβλέπω look at
προσδοκάω expect
προσδέχομαι receive
πρόσειμι go to
προσέρχομαι go to
προσέχω pay attention to
προσήκω be proper
πρόσθεν before
προσίημι admit, allow
προσλαμβάνω add
προσλέγω speak to
προσόμοιος similar
προσπίπτω occur
προστάττω command
πρόσφατος fresh
πρόσωπον face, countenance
προτεραῖος previous
πρότερον beforehand
προτίθημι set forth

πρότριτα for a period of three days
πρόφασις motive, pretense
πρόχειρος available
πρύμνα stern
πρῴ early
πρῶτος first
πτοίησις excitement
πύλη gate
πυνθάνομαι hear, learn
πῦρ fire
πώποτε ever yet
πως somehow
πῶς how?

ῥᾳδίος easy
ῥίπτω throw
ῥίς nose
ῥώμη force

σαρδάνιος scornful
σατραπεία satrapy
σατράπης satrap
σαφής plain, clear
σελήνη moon
σῆμα sign
σημεῖον sign
σθένος strength
σιγάω be silent
σκάφος hull
σκέλος leg
σκέμμα subject for speculation
σκέπτομαι view, examine
σκέψις speculation
σκηνή stage
σκίμπους pallet
σκοπέω view, examine
σκυτοτομέω be a shoemaker
σοφία wisdom
σοφός wise
σπονδαί (pl.) truce
σποράς scattered
σπουδάζω intent upon
στενός narrow
στέργω love
στερέω deprive
στέφω crown
στόλος expedition
στόρνυμι spread, soothe
στρατεία campaign
στράτευμα campaign

στρατηγία command
στρατηγός general
στρατιά army
στρατιώτης soldier
στρογγύλος spherical
συγγενής kin, kinsman
συγγίγνομαι associate
συγγνώμη pardon
συγγνώμων disposed to pardon
συγκατάκειμαι lie with
συγχωρέω agree, concede
συκοφάντης public informer
συλλαμβάνω seize
συλλέγω gather
συλλήβδην collectively
σύλλογος assembly
συμβαίνω occur
συμβάλλω assist
σύμβασις treaty
συμβουλεύω advise
συμβουλία advice
συμμαχία alliance
σύμμαχος ally
σύμπας all, whole
συμπλέκω entwine
συμπότης drinking companion
συμπράττω join in doing
συμφέρω bring together
συμφορά misfortune, mishap
συμφωνέω agree
σύν with (rare in prose)
συναγορεύω plead a case
συνάγω gather together
συνδειπνέω dine with
συνδέω tie up
σύνεδρος delegate
σύνειμι (sum) associate with
σύνειμι (ibo) meet
συνεισβάλλω enter together
συνέστιος sharing a hearth
συνεχής continuous
συνήθης customary
συνίημι perceive, understand
συνουσία association
σύνοιδα be conscious of
συντάττω arrange
συχνός many, much
σφόδρα extremely
σχέτλιος wretched
σχολή leisure
σῴζω preserve, save

σῶμα body
σωτηρία safety
σωφρονέω have self-control
σώφρων in control of oneself

ταινία ribbon
τάλαντον talent
τᾶν sir (term of address)
ταξίαρχος taxiarch
τάξις order, contingent of men
ταράττω disturb
ταριχεύω pickle
τάττω arrange
ταφή burial
τάφρος ditch
τάχος speed
ταχυναυτέω sail fast
ταχύς quick :
τεθνεώς (per. part. of
  ἀποθνήσκω) τεῖχος wall
τεκμήριον evidence
τελετή rite
τελευτάω die
τελευτή death
τεμάκιον slice
τέμνω cut
τετράκις four times
τετρακισχίλιοι four thousand
τετρακόσιοι four hundred
τέτταρες four
τέχνη skill
τεχνικός skilled
τέως while
τηλικόσδε so large
τηλικοῦτος so large
τί what?
τίθημι put, place
τίκτω give birth
τιμάω honor
τιμή honor
τιμωρέω avenge
τιμωρία revenge
τίς who?
τμῆμα slice
τοι indeed
τοίνυν therefore
τόλμα boldness
τολμάω dare
τόπος place
τότε then
τρέφω rear

τριάκοντα thirty
τριακόσιοι three hundred
τριετής three years
τρίς thrice
τρίτος third
τρόπαιον victory monument
τρόπος habit, manner
τροφή food
τυγχάνω happen
τύπος impression
τύπτω strike
τύχη chance

ὑβρίζω outrage
ὕβρις outrage
ὑγιεινός healthy
ὕδωρ water
υἱός son
ὑπακούω obey
ὑπάρχω exist
ὑπέρ above, beyond
ὑπεροράω pay no heed to
ὑπέχω suffer
ὑπισχνέομαι undertake, promise
ὕπνος sleep
ὑπό under, by
ὑποδέχομαι receive
ὑπολαμβάνω interrupt, take up
ὑπολείπω leave
ὑπολογίζομαι take into account
ὑπολύω unshoe
ὑπομένω endure
ὑπομιμνήσκω remind of
ὑπόμνησις reminder
ὑποπτεύω suspect
ὑπόσχεσις promise
ὑπουργέω serve
ὕστατος last
ὑστεραῖος next
ὕστερος after, later, next
ὑφαιρέω remove
ὑψηλός high, lofty

φαίνω show, appear (mid/pass)
φανερός conspicuous
φάρμακον drug
φάσκω say
φαῦλος mean, insignificant
φέρω carry ·
φεύγω flee
φημί say

φθείρω corrupt
φθονέω begrudge
φιλάνθρωπος kind-hearted
φιλεραστία devotion to a lover
φιλέω love
φιληκοΐα fondness for listening
φιλία love, friendship
Φιλιππίζω support Philip
φιλομαθής lover of learning
φίλος dear, friend
φιλοτιμία ambition, love of honor
φλυαρία nonsense
φλύαρος foolish
φοβέομαι be afraid
φόβος fear
φοιτάω visit
φρονέω think
φρόνημα mind
φρόνησις thought
φρόνιμος sensible
φροντίζω worry
φυγή exile
φύλαξ guard
φυλάττω guard
φυλή tribe
φύσις nature
φωνή voice

χαίρω rejoice
χαλεπαίνω have difficulty
χαλεπός difficult
χάρις gratitude
χειμών winter
χείρ hand
χειροτονέω elect
χίλιος thousand
χορηγέω lead a chorus
χορηγία office of choral leader
χορηγός choral leader
χράομαι need, use
χρεία need, use
χρή one must
χρῆμα thing, belonging, money (pl)
χρηματίζομαι make money
χρήσιμος useful
χρησμός oracle
χρηστήριον oracle
χρηστός good, worthy
χρόνος time
χρυσίον gold piece, made of gold
χρυσός gold

χώρα country
χωρίον place

ψεύδομαι lie
ψεῦδος falsehood
ψηφίζω vote
ψήφισμα decree
ψῆφος voting pebble
ψόγος blame

ψυχή soul

ὤνιος for sale, be bought
ὡς ασ
ὥσπερ as
ὥστε so that See Chapter Twelve
ὠφελέω do good, be of help
ὠφελία help, profit

INDEX C: LIST OF PASSAGES FROM GREEK AUTHORS